IMAGES
of America

INDEPENDENCE

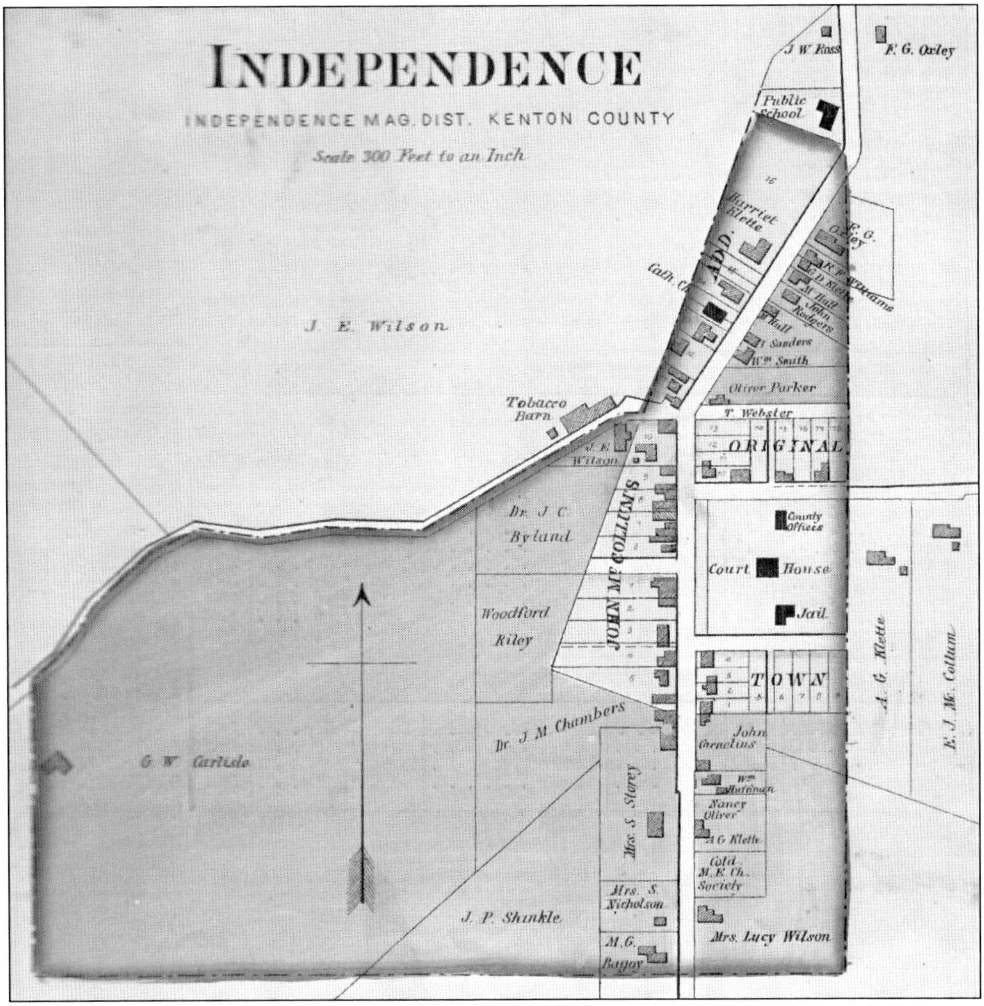

This map of Independence, from page 43 of *An Atlas of Boone, Kenton and Campbell Counties, Kentucky 1883*, shows the original town with the five-acre courthouse square donation; John McCollum's Addition, totaling 21.475 acres; and the 1869 expansion to the west and south. All of the buildings are shown, along with some names of residents, as they existed in 1883. The town boundaries are outlined in bold. (Gailen and Debra Kerr Bridges.)

On the Cover: St. Cecilia Church's Labor Day Festival, begun in 1919, is the longest running and biggest event in Independence. In 1963, a publicity shot was taken, supposedly showing the different modes of transportation people used to attend the festival. Having arranged for the car and sulky, a baseball team practicing behind the church was also drafted to participate. Posing in front of the still-existing rectory on the left and the church (demolished in 2008 for additional church parking) on the right are Jimmy Scherder in the sulky, Tonka the pony, and Alberta Scherder stealing the cover. Marty Nie is in the car advertising Nie's Pharmacy, and the baseball manager, Al Meese, is driving his 1962 Chevrolet pickup. From left to right on the truck are assistant pastor Fr. William Bush, who shed his priestly attire for this photograph, Paul Eckerle, Bryson "Skip" Fisk, coach Max Hughes, Jim Osbourn, Chris "Kit" Carson slightly behind, and Tom Wainscott. Some baseball gloves are visible on the top of the truck. (Photograph by diocese photographer Ray Hadorn; courtesy of Mary Lou Schoborg Kaub.)

IMAGES
of America

INDEPENDENCE

Gailen and Debra Bridges

ARCADIA
PUBLISHING

ISBN 978-0-7385-8232-0

Published by Arcadia Publishing
Charleston, South Carolina

Printed in the United States of America

Library of Congress Control Number: 2010940121

For all general information, please contact Arcadia Publishing:
Telephone 843-853-2070
Fax 843-853-0044
E-mail sales@arcadiapublishing.com
For customer service and orders:
Toll-Free 1-888-313-2665

Visit us on the Internet at www.arcadiapublishing.com

Dedicated to Ashley, Amber, Gailen III, Abigail, Damian, Alina, Addison, and the wonderful people of Independence, past and present.

Contents

ACKNOWLEDGMENTS

We enjoyed visiting our old and new friends and neighbors as they helped us put together this labor of love. Thank you for sitting for hours around your kitchen table as you let us see, search, sort, scan, and share your treasured family history. We looked through albums, scrapbooks, piles, and tubs of thousands of photographs that you brought from your drawers, basements, walls, attics, and barns so that the reader could have the most historic and interesting images possible. Our thanks to our contributors of threads that wove this historical tapestry: Betty Veith Adams; Kimberly M. Back; Peggy Powers Baum; Dorothy Breeden; Gailen and Debra Kerr Bridges; Glenna Lancaster Bridges; Wendel Bridges; Rodney "Biz" Cain; Cincinnati Bell; the City of Independence and its helpful personnel, including the police department; Barbara Giles Gabbard; Bob and Thelma Gibson; Marrilyn Mershon Hamilton; Brenda Schoborg Hopkins; Independence Fire District; M.W. Jackson; Mary Lou Schoborg Kaub; Kenton County Extension Service; Kenton County Public Library; Doris Wicklund King; Karen Fisk Koch; Janet Glass Kreidler; Mark Lillard; J.B. Losey; Al Meese; Eunice Mershon; Virginia Pruett Moffett; Cheryl Osterbrook Peebles; Elizabeth Russell; Marion Schadler; Jerry Schneider; Aleda Smallwood; Jean Wilson Smith; Senator Katie Kratz Stine; Inez Straw; Miley Sue Bird Van Horn; Randall Wagner; Virginia Coleman Watson; Greg White; and Betty Northcutt Williams. The contributors' names can be found at the end of the captions of the images they furnished.

Special thanks are due to: those who actually took these photographs and entrusted them to their family who shared them with us; Jessie England, who photographed Independence in the 1950s and 1960s, practically anticipating a book of this nature, and passed those photographs to her daughter, Eunice Mershon; and Dorothy Schneider, whose collection of clippings and articles was an invaluable research resource.

These 225 moments, frozen in time and spread over approximately 120 years, cannot pretend to be a comprehensive history; they can only hope to convey the essence and spirit of Independence in these representative images. It is our hope these images will pass on our history, showcase the attributes of this great city, and bring back memories of people and days gone by.

Thanks to God for blessing the people of Independence with such a proud history and bright future, and may He continue to do so.

INTRODUCTION

Independence is the story of hardworking, ordinary people who farmed and worshipped together, supported, married, and buried one another, and traded among themselves and their family businesses, and in these seemingly everyday routines, the extraordinary community known as Independence was born.

What is now Kenton County was part of Campbell County until January 29, 1840, when the Kentucky legislature passed an act establishing all of Campbell County west of the Licking River as Kenton County, effective April 30, 1840. The county was named for pioneer Simon Kenton, who had died in 1836. The philosophy of the time was that a county seat should allow anyone on horseback to leave home, transact their business, and return home the same day. The best way to assure this was obviously to center the county seat within the county. Thus, the act also provided "that the seat of justice thereof be, and the same is hereby, established at the most eligible point, as near the centre of said county as the face of the country will admit."

The exact center of the county was determined and suitable ground found at one of the highest elevations in the county on which to build the courthouse in the new county seat (the exact center was determined to be 750 feet to the south in a deep ravine). No town as such was near the site, but a post office had been established in the vicinity on November 20, 1837, called Crewitts Creek, and by some accounts, Everetts Creek. On December 26, it was changed to Crews Creek, and on July 6, 1838, it was named Bagby for a local family. The new county seat and post office were renamed "Independence" on October 7, 1840, to celebrate Kenton County's independence from Campbell County.

Local farmer John McCollum donated five acres of meadow of the 100 acres he owned to the new county to build the new courthouse on May 28, 1840. The deed transferring the property was signed on February 15, 1841, and recorded in Deed Book 1, page 300. It recites the donation and that further consideration was the "advantage of having the seat of Justice for said County located upon or near the tract of land on which he resides." The courthouse was already under construction, as the deed references the "northwest corner of the courthouse lately erected on said ground." McCullum Road is named for him but misspells his name. He was born around 1793, married Mary Stephens, and died of cholera in 1849, leaving eight children.

On February 24, 1842, the city was incorporated by an act of the Kentucky legislature, encompassing the five-acre donation and another 16.475 acres to the north and west known as John McCollum's Addition. Acreage to the west and south was added on March 4, 1869, where the boundaries remained at least until 1883. An 1883 map of the city showing the buildings, boundaries, and some names of residents is included on the inside cover. Independence's formation was highly unusual for that time, as it began as a planned community based on political considerations, whereas almost all other towns began around some commercial center, usually involving water access.

Construction of the first courthouse began in late summer 1840, and it was reported as being recently occupied in February 1842. It was Greek Revival in style with a bell tower and was situated where the current courthouse stands. Within the same block to the south was a separate jail and to the north a county office building. The 1850 census records note 33 dwellings and 32 families in the town.

Almost immediately, Covington's residents, located in the north part of the county on the Ohio River and comprising half of the county's population, complained about traveling 12 miles south over rugged terrain to transact business. In 1851 and 1858, the legislature acted to move some court business to Covington, and in 1860, a dual courthouse system was enacted, resulting in another courthouse being built thereafter in Covington. In 1867 and 1905, voters decided to keep Independence as the county seat. Campbell County is the only other county in Kentucky with such a two-courthouse system (Newport and Alexandria).

In *Kentucky. A History of the State* (1887), W.H. Perrin stated about Independence in the entry for Kenton County,

> It is a small place . . . and no longer of any great importance. Nearly all the county business is transacted now at Covington, and the courts are mostly held there also, while it may be said of the old capital:
>
> A place for idle eyes and ears
> A cobwebbed nook of dreams
> Left by the stream whose waves are years
> The stranded village seems.

Census records of the population tell the story of why this sleepy farming community with a few small businesses received little respect from the rest of the rapidly growing county until the late 20th century:

1850	182	1940	253
1860	189	1950	285
1870	134	1960	309
1880	165	1970	1,715
1890	census records destroyed	1980	7,998
1900	193	1990	10,444
1910	153	2000	14,982
1920	153	2010	24,752
1930	260		

Note the city had fewer people after 70 years (1850–1920) and grew by only 103 people in a century (1850–1950). Lack of usable transportation hampered growth. There were no water routes nearby because of the high elevation and no rail until 1869. Even then, the closest depot was a mile and a half of rough terrain away, where Independence Station Road (hence the name) crosses the tracks. A stagecoach line referred to as "the bus" required two hours for the 12-mile journey from Covington, including climbing Independence Hill.

However, on court days and when political meetings were held, farmers would come to town to sell their products and catch up on the news, the businesses would cater to the visitors, and the town was bustling with activity. As the county seat, Independence would host political conventions at which many local politicians received their nominations for higher office. The adoption of a primary system in the 1890s ended this tradition.

In a *Kentucky Post* article on February 26, 1937, Ivanora Hume recounted her memories of Independence in the late 1800s, stating about the first courthouse,

> It was used for a private school, church, Sunday school, dancing school, plays, concerts, funerals, church suppers, dances, teachers institute, and circulation library.
>
> On Fourth of July the men had roman candle fights. They chose leaders, lined up on each side of the street and fired at each other. The lines didn't hold very long, most of the contestants being soon put to flight. On election night, throwing each others hats in the

bonfire was the game of the evening. These were men, not boys, I am talking about, some of them middle-aged. It seems that men had time to play in those days.

It really was a very peaceful village, the old jail building being seldom occupied. Only once in my school days I remember a man being kept there for a while. We school children took a peep at him once in a while, he seemed to like to see us.

By 1904, the first courthouse had fallen into disrepair and was no longer large enough for court business and meetings. There was concern over the lack of a fireproof room to preserve the land records. Officials debated the options of a new building just for the clerk, building a new courthouse, or just transferring all offices to Covington. A grand jury report stating that the courthouse was outdated spurred the decision to build a new courthouse in February 1911. Razing of the old courthouse began on July 5, 1911.

The winning construction bid for the new courthouse from Northcutt Brothers of Covington was $29,500. By September 1912, at a final cost of $35,000, the classical Beaux-Arts design fronting a Roman portico was completed. At the dedication on October 21, Lt. Gov. Edward McDermott was the special guest speaker, along with several other county officials. A feast of burgoo fed the estimated crowd of 5,000. The new Independence School, also just recently completed, had its dedication the same day to take advantage of the large crowd in town, making it possibly the greatest day in Independence history. The courthouse remains in everyday use, its portico proudly proclaiming "KENTON COVNTY COVRT HOVSE" (the Roman Vs confounding many) over the stately trees and lawn. This grand lady is without question the iconic face of Independence.

The development of roads and increase in automobiles began to weave the entire county together. Electricity became available in 1937 and city water lines in 1961. New cities began forming in Kenton County to avoid annexation by Covington with its higher taxes. By 1960, Independence was at a crossroads. City officials decided they had no future without growing by annexation. Board of Trustees chairman Goebel Armstrong explained their thinking in the May 1961 issue of *The Cincinnati Telephone Bulletin*: "There is only one thing we can do to survive as a corporate entity with any meaning. We must grow, too, with the new communities springing up around us or be a city without a future. We plan to do this by annexing areas around us so that we will have room to grow." He recounted a recent annexation to the north that added 450 people (1960 population 309), and a proposed southern annexation to add another 700. After discussing future plans for water and eventually sewer lines, he added, "We have let a nice town lay static, now we propose to get it out of its lethargy." Howard Stephens, former police judge and trustee, agreed, "Independence is on the verge of large expansion and greater economic gains. We goofed before but we do not propose to let it slip by us this time. If we don't expand, we will be surrounded by many municipalities."

These rural visionaries followed through with their plan with a determination never before seen in the history of Northern Kentucky. Their philosophy was that the best way to stop other cities from annexing unincorporated land was to make sure they got there first. From the 1960s to the 1980s, the city expanded from the west side of the county against the Boone County line almost to the east line of the Licking River, encompassing the middle third of the county and becoming the largest city in Northern Kentucky geographically. In the early 1960s, areas along Madison Pike were annexed, followed by the Cherokee area in 1968. The years 1973 and 1974 saw the city expand north to Richardson Road and south to Bristow Road. The Villages of Beechgrove and east of Taylor Mill Road were added in 1978 and 1979. In 1981, the city annexed west to the Boone County line, including part of the industrial park. The City of Ridgeview Heights voted to join Independence effective January 1, 1984. The passage of a state law in 1980 giving residents a vote on being annexed effectively ended the Kenton County annexation battles. Since then, the city has grown mostly by subdivision developers agreeing to annexation in return for access to water and sewer lines.

Fires took a heavy toll in the early days of the city. Mrs. Hume (quoted previously) stated that of 50 buildings in the city in 1883, only 12 remained in 1937, most having been destroyed by fire at various times. From 1905 to 1919, at least five major fires destroyed buildings downtown, the last one in March 1919, when St. Cecilia Church and a neighboring house burned. The church then moved south to its present location.

In December 1936, a group formed to start a fire department. On March 20, 1937, James Davis died in a fire at his home on Independence Station Road. His son, Harley, died later of burns suffered trying to rescue his father. The community rallied after this tragedy, and the Independence & Community Fire Department became a reality. A new 1936 International pumper was purchased in August 1937. The first formal business meeting was December 5, 1937, at which Ira Lower was named chief. A system of five cisterns was dug around town to supply water for the pumper. The firehouse was constructed next door to the courthouse to the south in 1939, with additions in 1949, 1967, and 1985. At first a pledge system funded the department, but from the 1940s until the last one in 1996, the July Firemen's Picnic was the primary fundraiser, until taxing authority was acquired. Station No. 2 was built on Cox Road in 1974 and Station No. 3 on Richardson Road in 1976. In 1991, the city was annexed into the Independence Fire District, which is a separate body from the city. A new Station No. 1 was constructed further south on Madison Pike in 1999.

Manning of law enforcement in Independence was sporadic, generally with part-time officers or none at all until the 1960s. Even when the city had a full-time officer, 40 hours a week only afforded part-time protection. One officer has died in the line of duty. Col. Nicholas Hopperton, 35, became Independence town marshal in early 1902. In the late afternoon of November 8, 1902, he received word of an unruly man who had been drinking. He found the man outside a tavern, took the man's shotgun away, and told him to leave town. He followed the man to the town limit and gave him back the shotgun. The man then shot Hopperton twice, killing him. Hopperton was able to hit the man with three shots, and though not expected to live, the man did survive. Colonel Hopperton was entered into the Northern Kentucky Police Memorial in Covington on May 10, 1999.

In 1867, Eleonore von Richthofen, a widow, and her children emigrated from Germany and settled on a 200-acre farm on Cody Road. The family was active in the Independence Presbyterian Church. Six family members are buried in Independence Cemetery. They had a very famous nephew and cousin back in Germany, Capt. Manfred von Richthofen. He is better known as the World War I flying ace "the Red Baron," credited with 80 personal aerial victories before being shot down and killed on April 21, 1918.

Today, Independence's secret is out as a desirable and fast-growing residential city that still maintains its small-town feel. It has all the amenities today's families desire. Newly built and remodeled schools, numerous parks and the largest golf course in the county, a growing retail center at Madison Pike and Route 536, newly built or widened roads, particularly the new Route 17, and attractive newer housing on relatively large lots guarantee Independence a bright future. Managing growth is the main problem of city officials now, in stark contrast to most of city history. Because of its large area, it appears to only be a matter of time before Independence reaches a population of 40,000 to 60,000 and becomes Northern Kentucky's largest city (it is currently third). As that unfolds, perhaps the ultimate irony will occur as the pressure of the last 170 years reverses and there are calls to move more county and court business to Independence.

One

Early Days

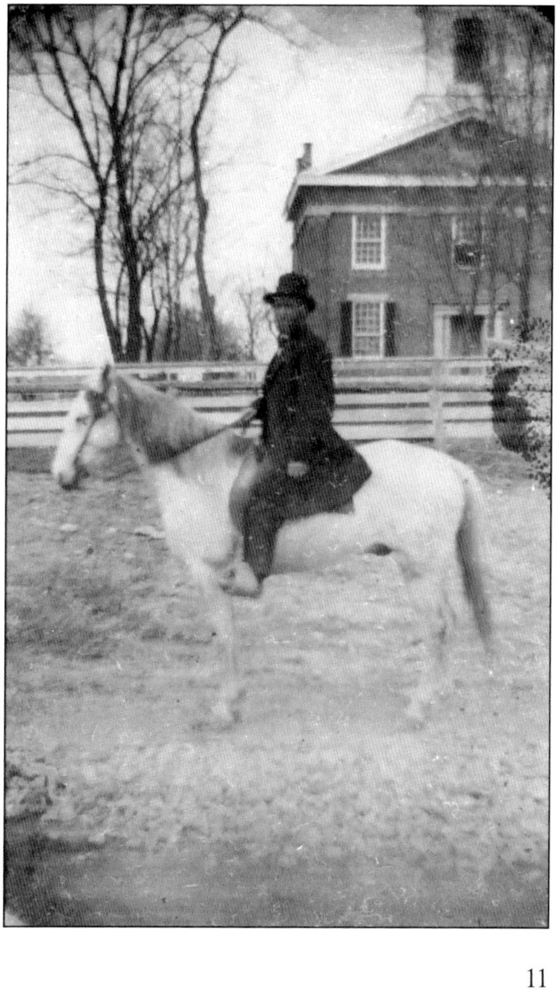

Dr. John Monroe Chambers poses before the oldest known image of the first courthouse in the 1870s. The first courthouse was a Greek Revival with a bell tower, and this is the only image showing the north (left) side at all. The clerk's building, present in 1883, is not present to the left. Dr. Chambers (1833–1928) was born in Indiana and moved to Independence in 1859. He lived in the southwest part of town and had a 340-acre farm in the county. He represented the county in the Kentucky legislature in 1865–1866 and 1879–1880. This previously unknown historic tintype image was discovered during the authors' research. (Jerry Schneider.)

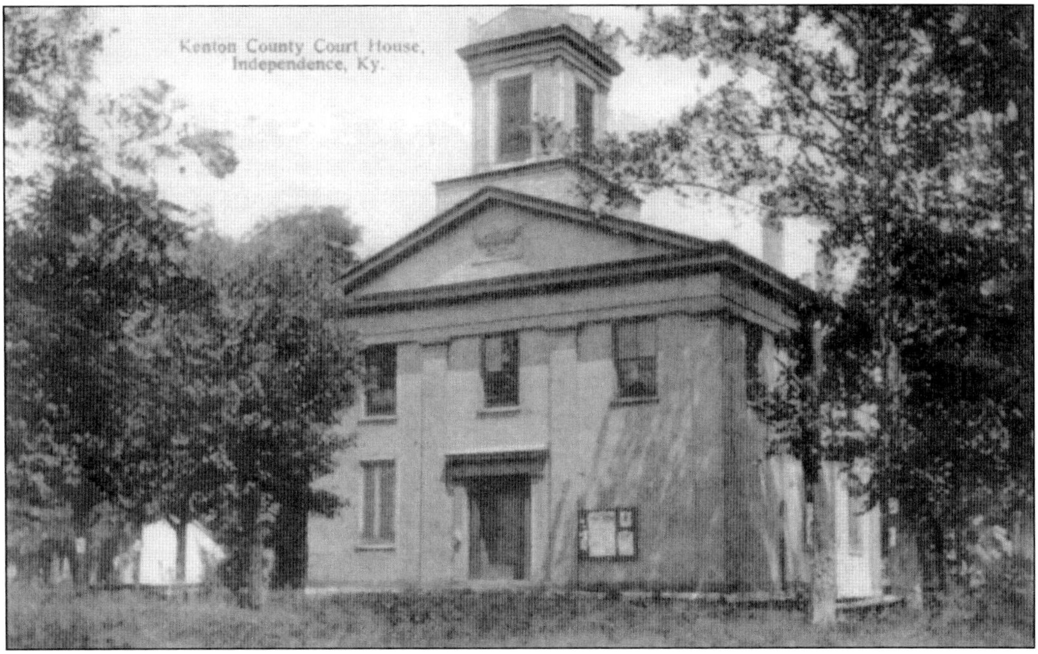

This 1890s photograph circulated as a postcard and was published in newspapers of the day. The first courthouse was constructed in 1840 or 1841 and was razed in 1911 for construction of the new courthouse. The separate clerk's office is visible to the left. The courthouse was used for a variety of community uses in addition to court and county business. The windows have been replaced between this image and the previous one. (Gailen and Debra Kerr Bridges.)

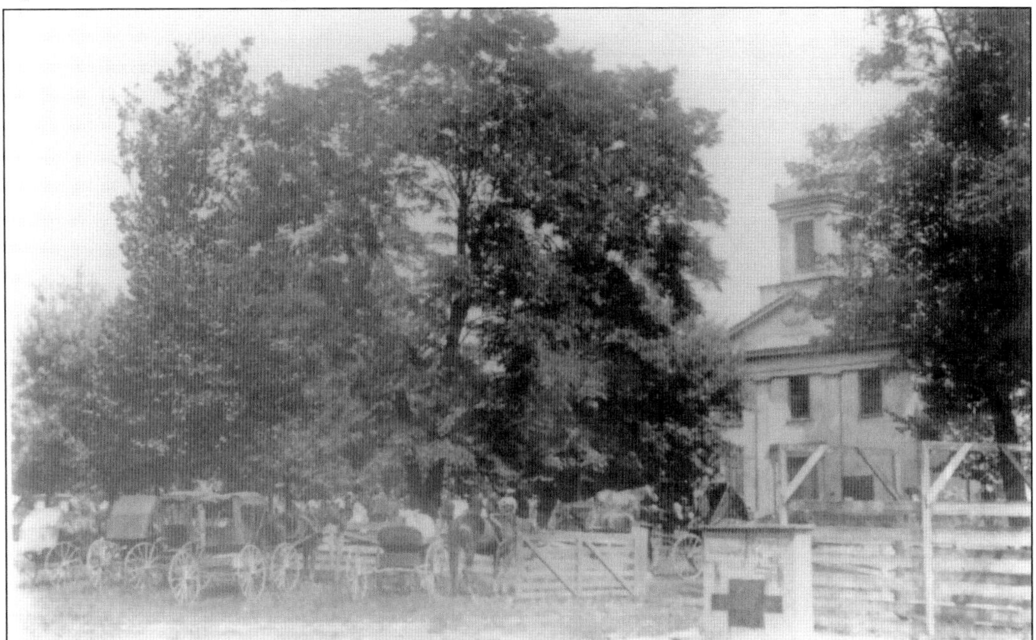

Court days were busy times in the county seat. Samuel H. Folmer took this picture using a Graflex camera some time between 1900 and 1911. This image has been used in articles on city history because it is such an interesting unposed slice-of-life photograph. (Kenton County Public Library.)

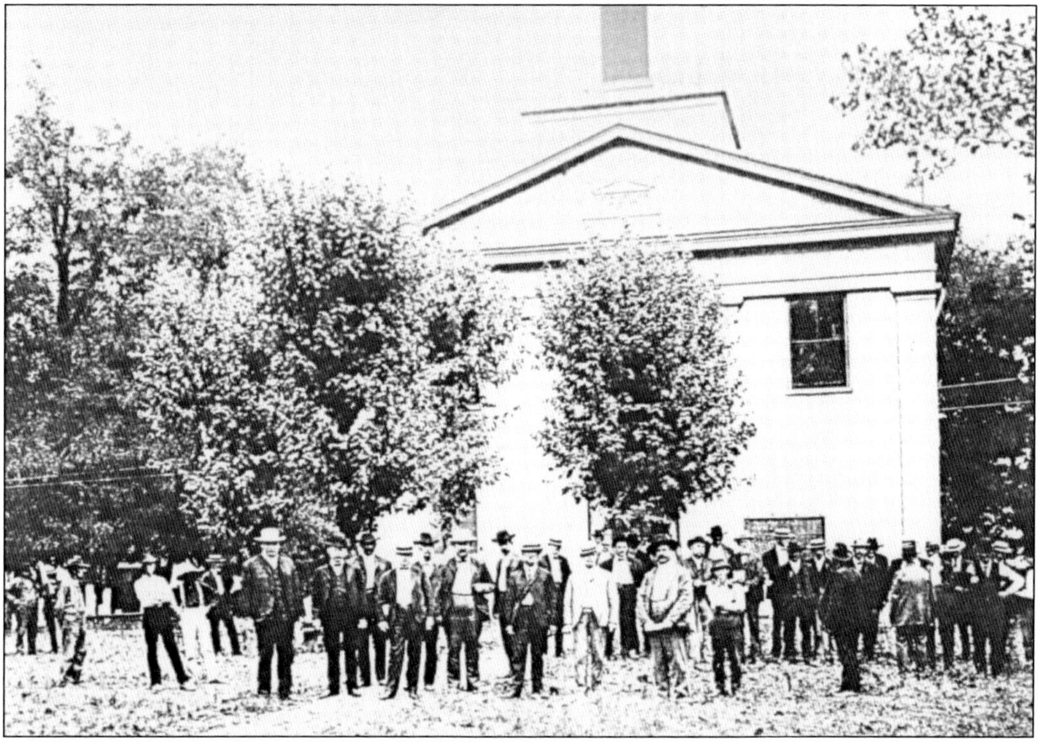

An undated image (probably taken around 1900) of the first courthouse shows bustling activity. These four images comprise all known, full exterior views of the first courthouse. (Eunice Mershon.)

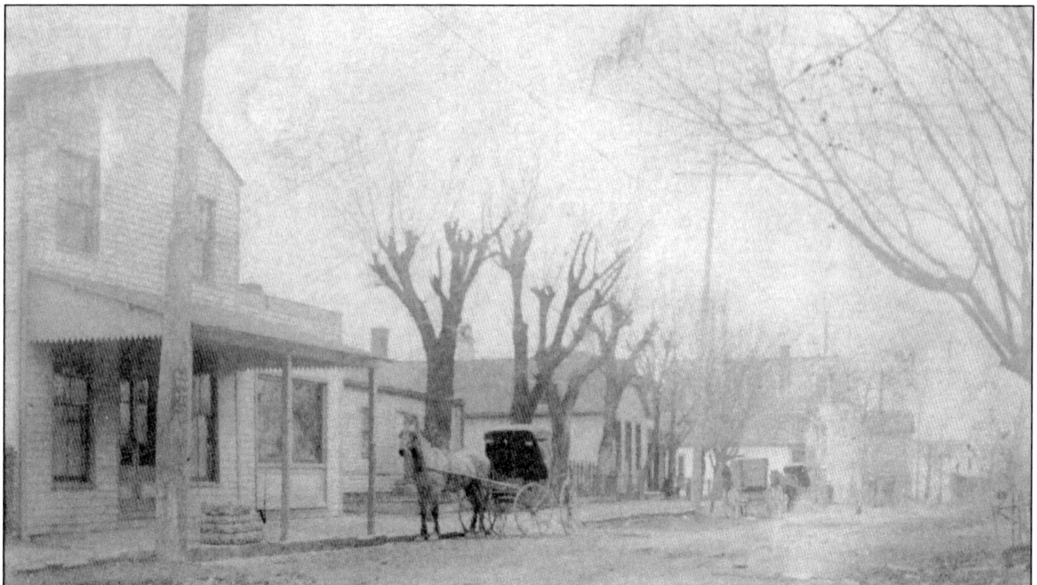

This is a very early street scene of unpaved Main Street (now Madison Pike) looking north around 1905. Carrie Schoborg's store is on the left. Note the telephone pole. Independence Telephone Company of Kenton County began service in 1903 with Dr. John Chambers as president. (Al Meese.)

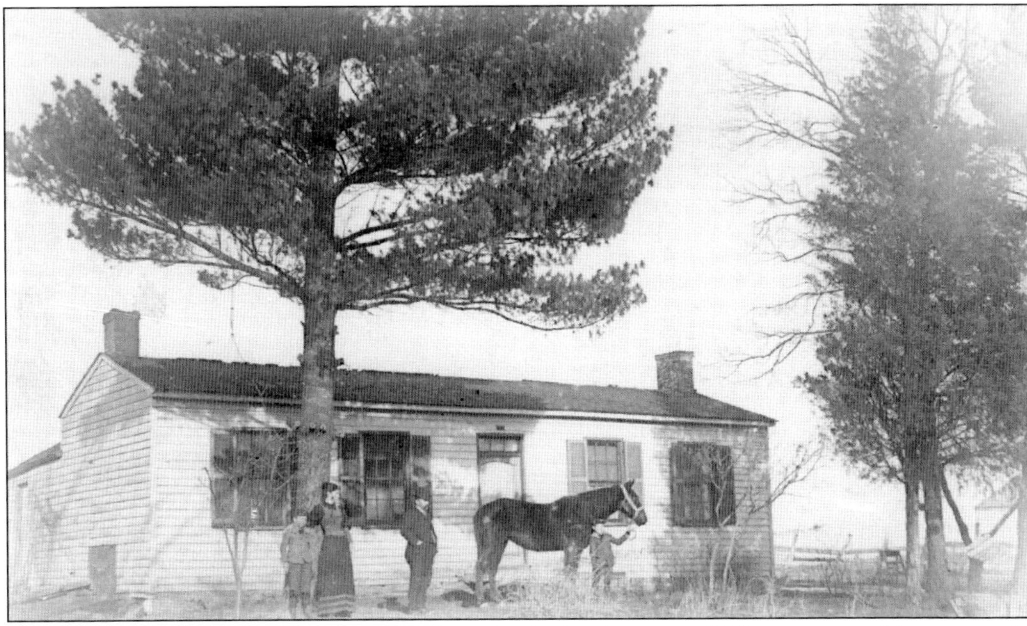

Elijah J. McCollum, son of John McCollum, built this home in 1883, the second home on the south side of McCullum Road (the road name is a misspelling of McCollum) from the courthouse, pictured in the 1890s. One room had rare wallpaper with scenes from *The Lady of the Lake*. The home has been demolished. (Jerry Schneider.)

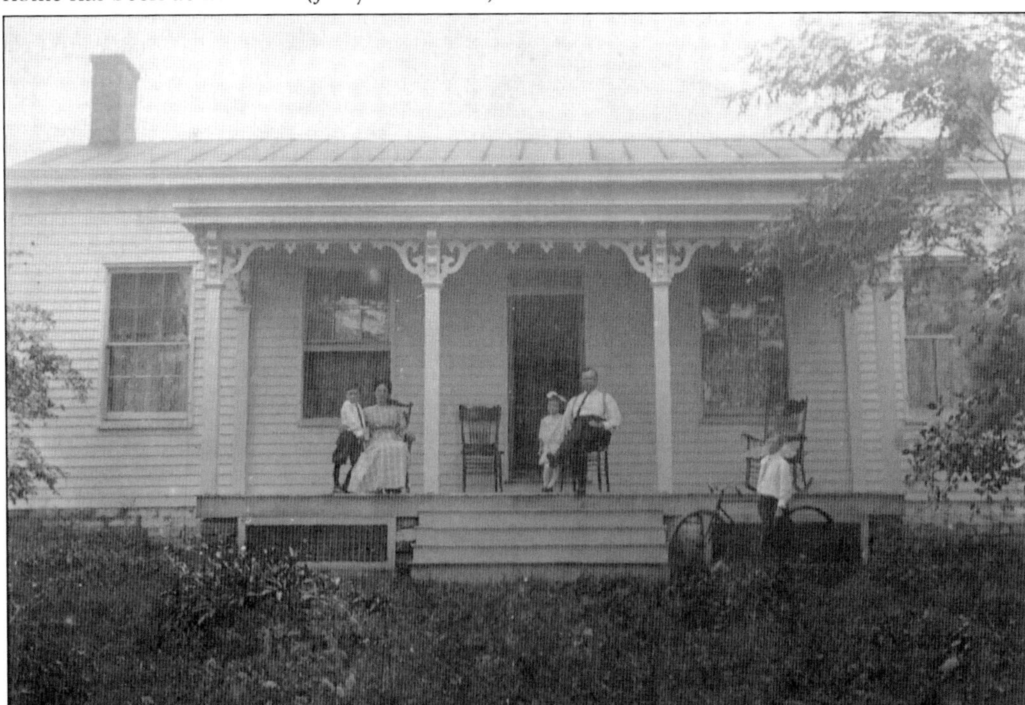

The same home, then owned by the Mills family, is shown around 1912 with an added porch. Parents and children, from left to right, are Grafton, mother Nellie, Margie, father E.O., and Clifford. (Peggy Powers Baum.)

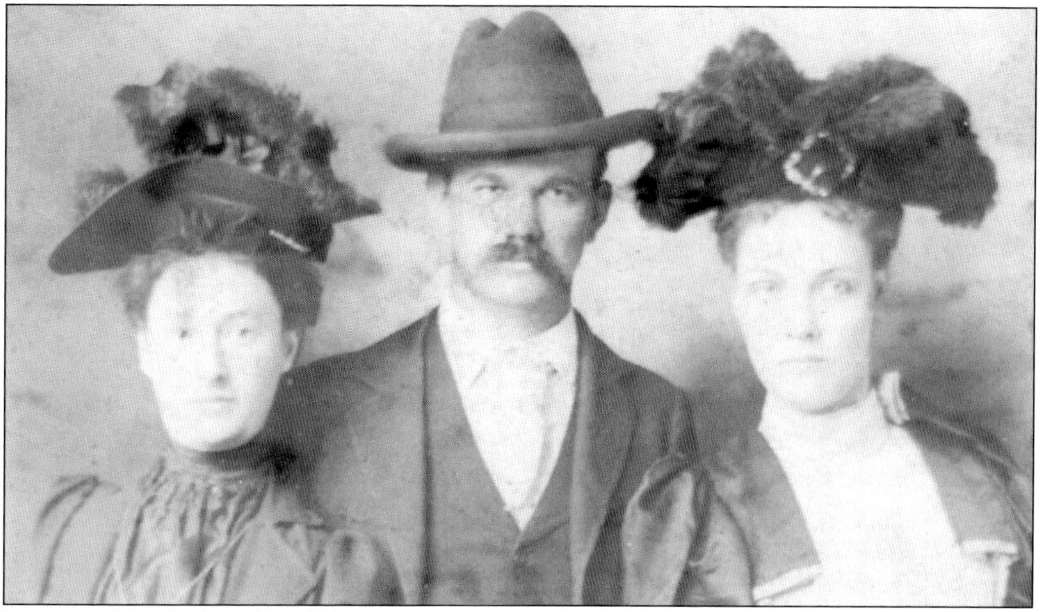

Here is a closer look at, from left to right, Nellie Sweeney Mills, her husband, E.O., and her cousin Mary Slater around 1900. E.O. Mills was a civil engineer and served one year as Kenton County School superintendent. Style and fashion were certainly not strangers to Independence. (Peggy Powers Baum.)

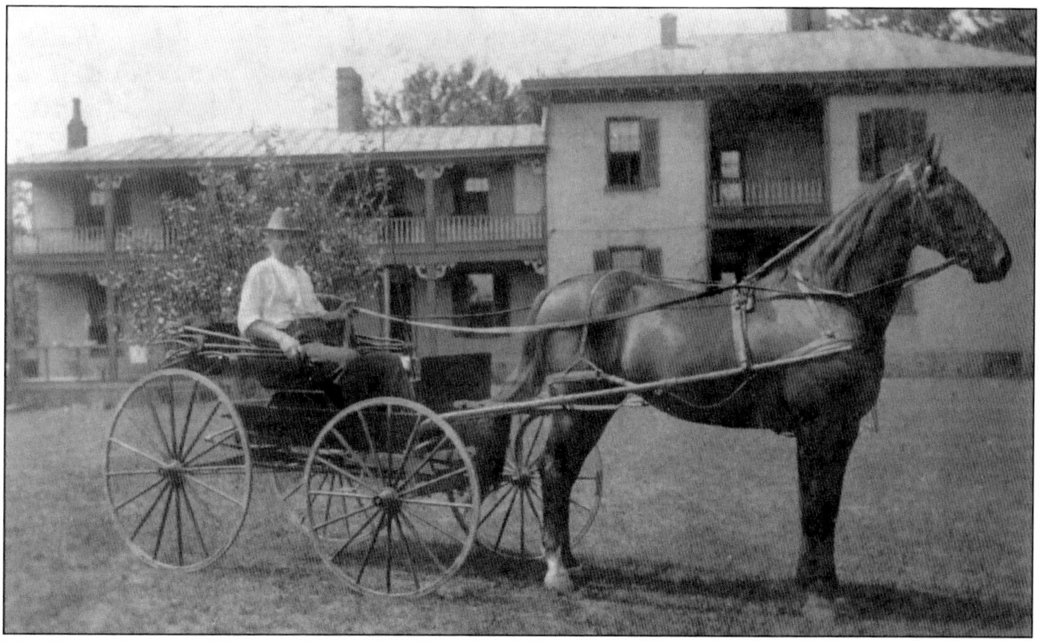

Mr. Young from Moffett Road visits his friends at the Oxley home in 1910. The New Orleans–style brick and frame home sports second-floor balconies and was built in the 1840s by the Oxley family. They came from Louisiana and operated a barrel factory in Cincinnati. This was their weekend and summer home. The family owned it until the early 1900s, and by the 1930s, it was divided into apartments. This home at 5234 Madison Pike is the oldest surviving building in downtown Independence. (Marion Schadler.)

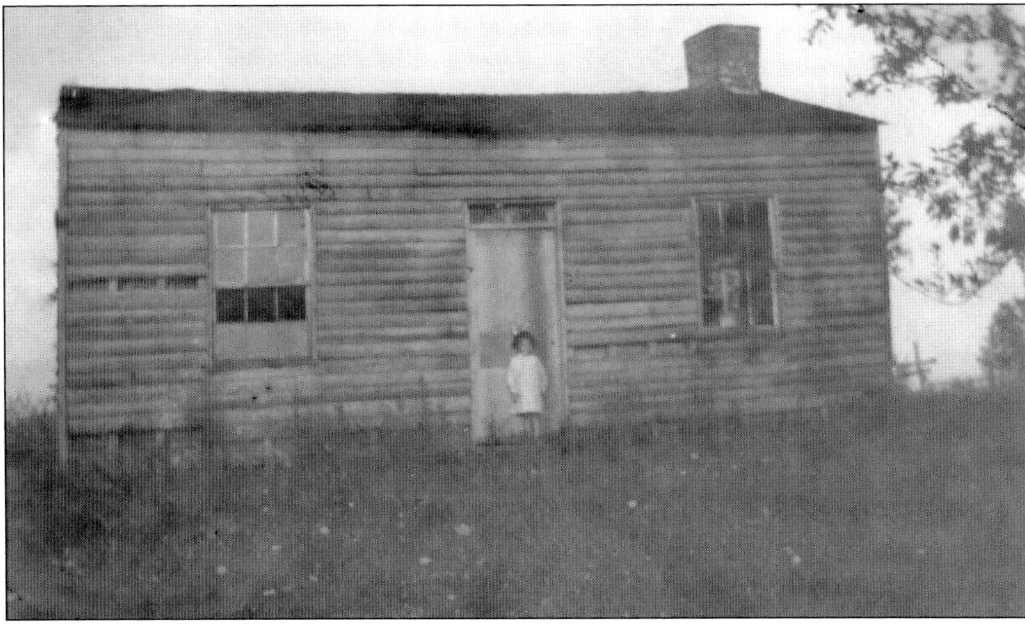

This home and farm at 10669 Taylor Mill Road was owned by the Coleman family in the late 1800s and early 1900s. This home was replaced by a new home by 1896, so this image is from the early 1890s. (Virginia Coleman Watson.)

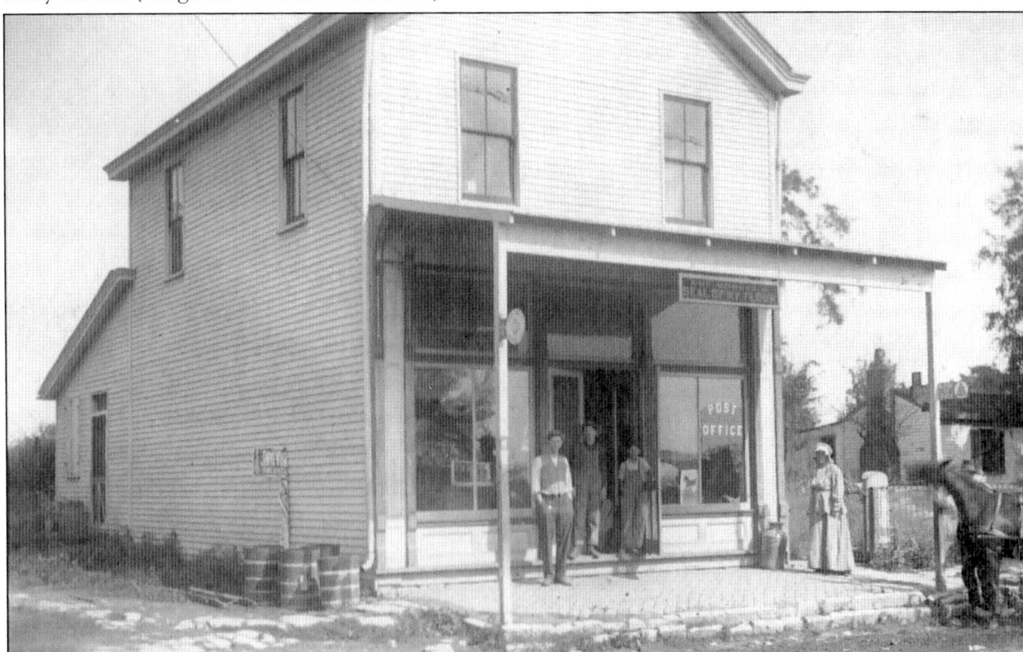

This 1900s photograph shows a store that has since been razed at approximately 5251 Madison Pike. It was the W.H. Schoborg grocery in 1920 and Bagby's after that. The right window says "Post Office," and the sign hanging from the awning says "Buy Dorsel's Seal of Ky. Flour." The lady on the right is in full period dress, including bonnet, with a cistern pump behind her. (Karen Fisk Koch.)

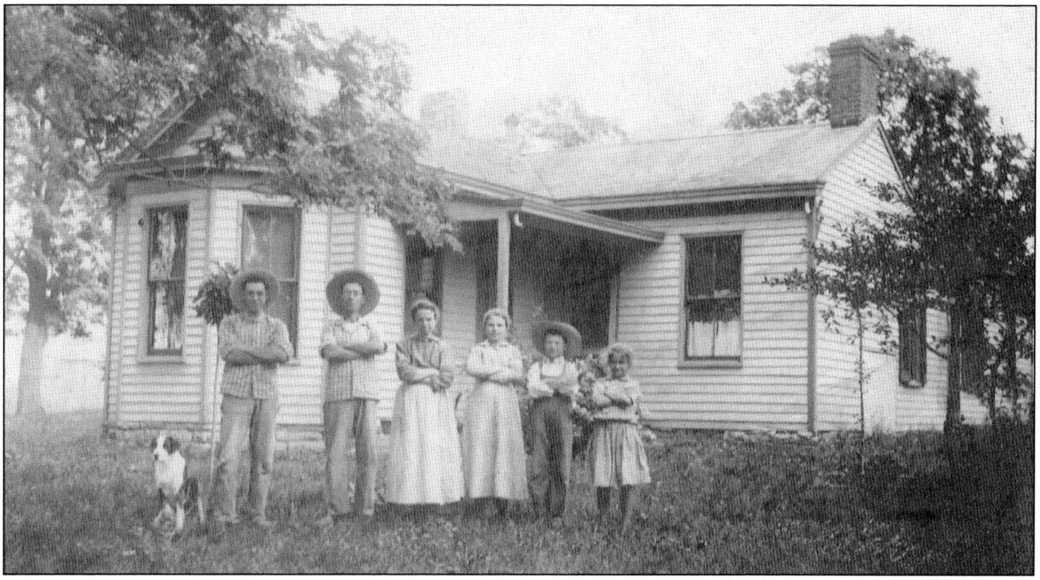

The Stephens family poses in front of their farmhouse on the east side of Madison Pike, now Liberty Orchard subdivision, in the summer of 1914. They are, from left to right, unidentified; Charles Abram "Peanut Charlie" Stephens; his wife, Mary Katherine; and their children, Mary Esther, Lester Tilford, and Katie Mae. The identical poses, the men's matching hats, and Lester's bib overalls are charming. (Bob and Thelma Gibson.)

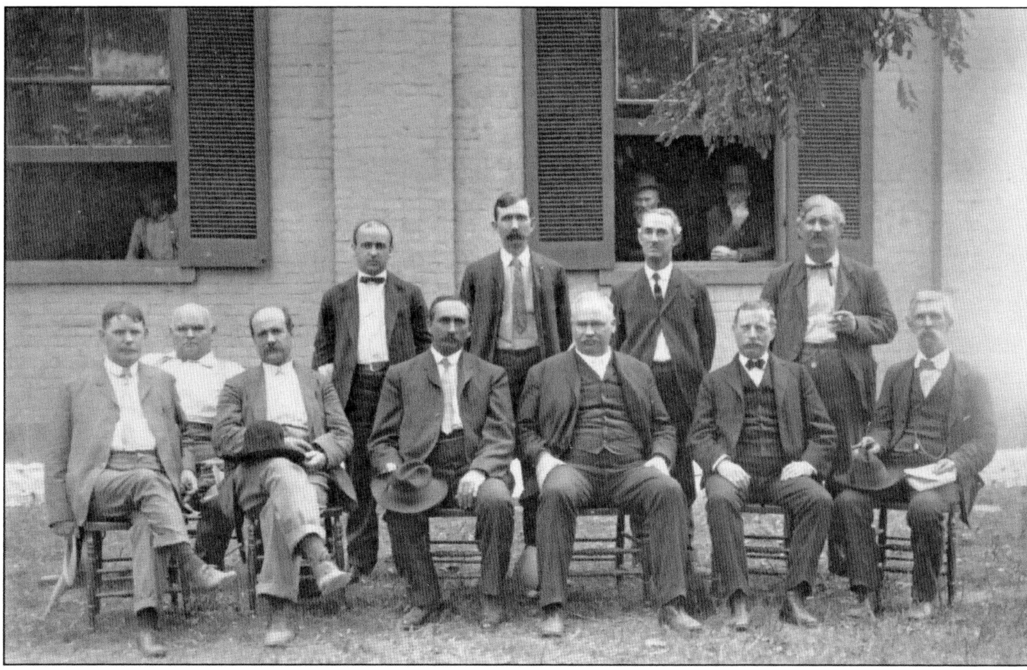

The Kenton Fiscal Court is seated in a rare close view of the old courthouse in 1908. It is not the front of the building. The court is, from left to right, (first row) Tom Dunn, George Stephens, E.L. Mann, H.P. Stephens, Charles Durain, and ? Shearer; (second row) Frank Stith, Judge Frank Tracy, clerk W.T. Loomis, William Martin, and Dr. Tilford T. Metcalf. Both men on the right of their rows are holding cigars. (Kenton County Public Library.)

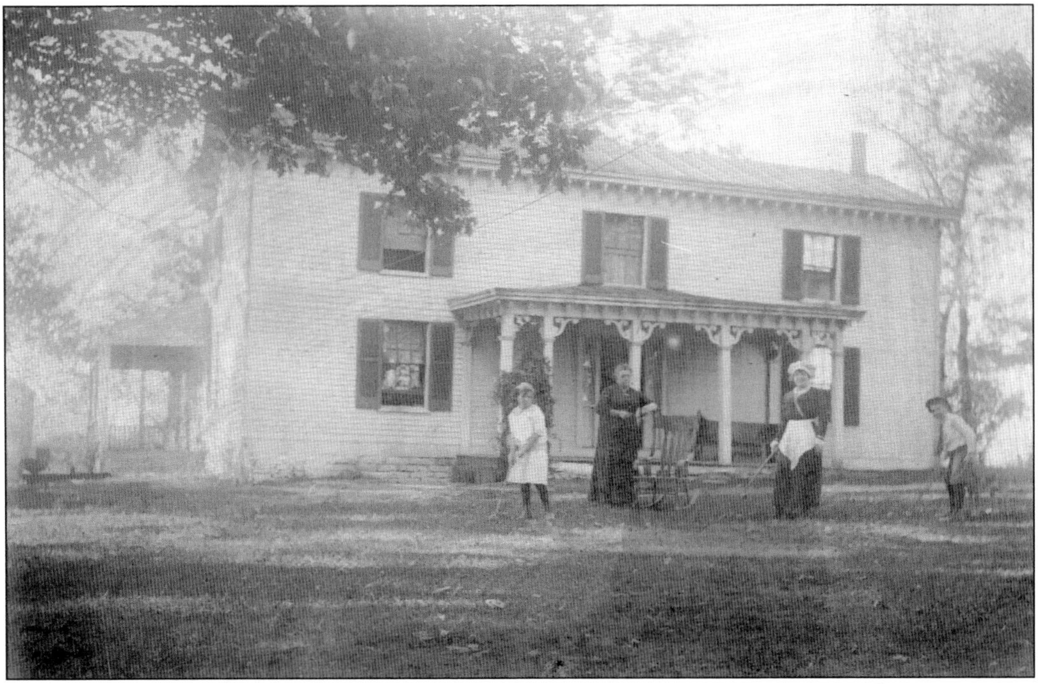

Croquet was a popular pastime for the Cain family in 1915. John C. Cain is on the right. He is the father of Rodney "Biz" Cain. This house at 1818 Independence Road is still used as a home. (Rodney "Biz" Cain.)

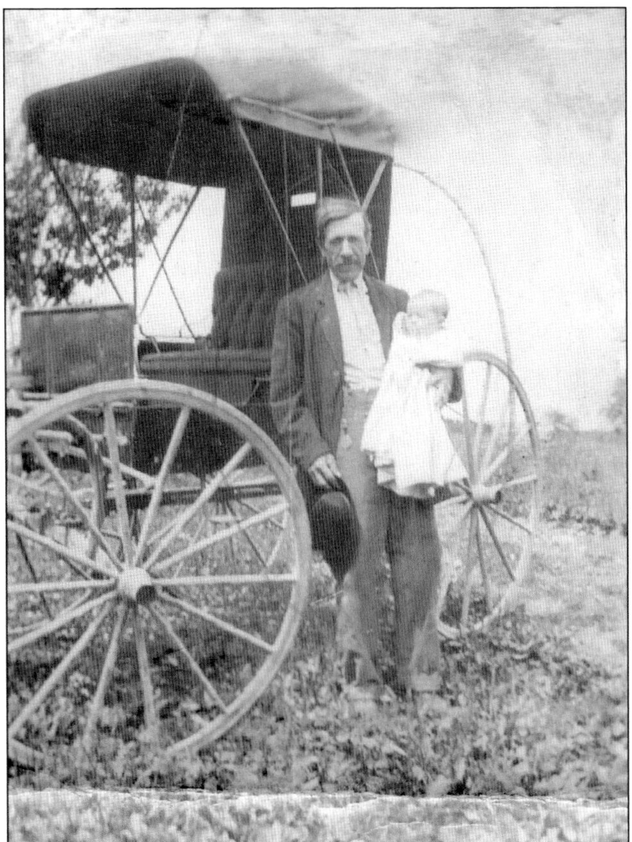

Scott Cain, father of John C. (above), holds his daughter beside his handsome buggy around 1910. He lived from February 20, 1862, to May 24, 1937. (Rodney "Biz" Cain.)

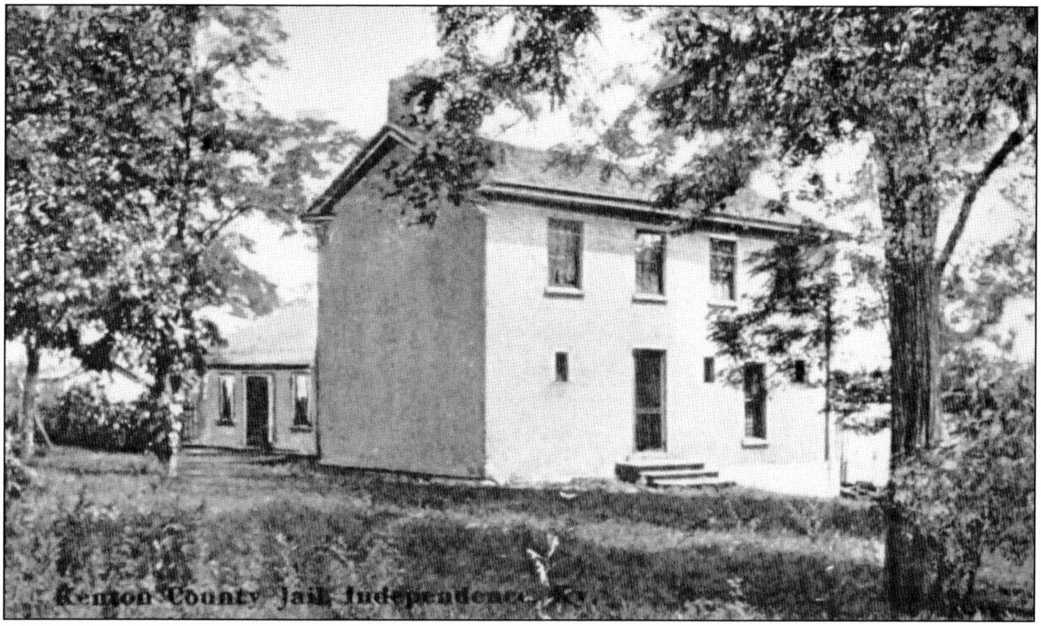

The Kenton County jail was located on the courthouse square, south of the courthouse. It was L-shaped. This postcard view is from around 1900. The first Independence & Community Fire Department firehouse was constructed on this site in 1939. (Gailen and Debra Kerr Bridges.)

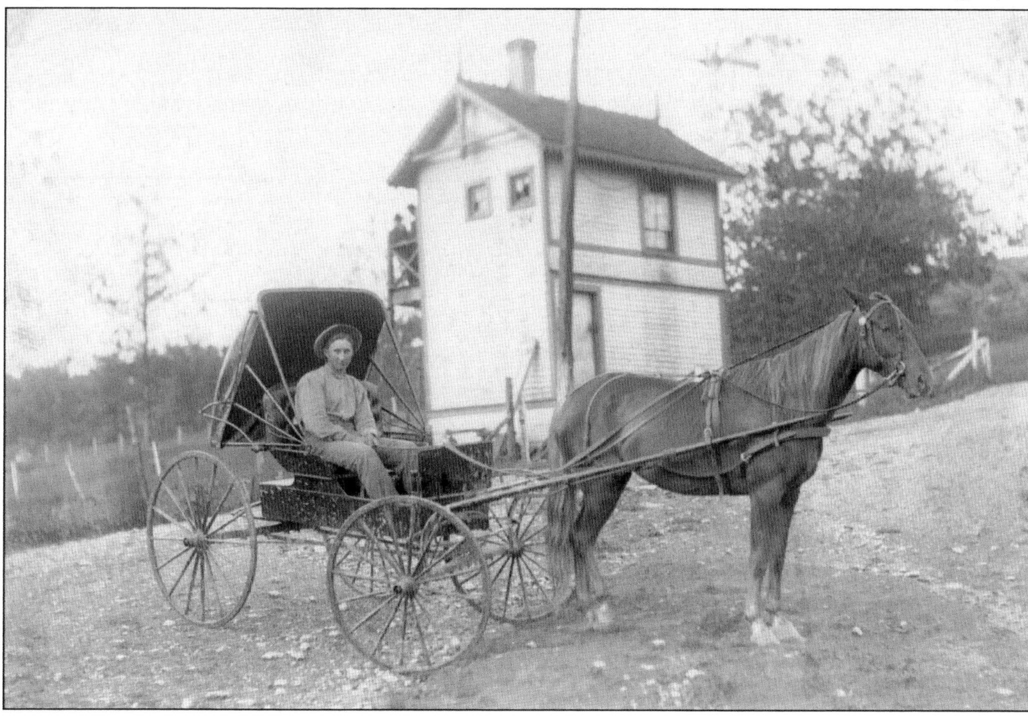

Foster Armstrong (1889–1958) visits his brother-in-law James T. Stone (not pictured), who operated this telegraph at the Independence railroad station on the aptly named Independence Station Road in 1909. Armstrong built the Blue Star Tavern and was a Kenton County School Board member. (Betty Veith Adams.)

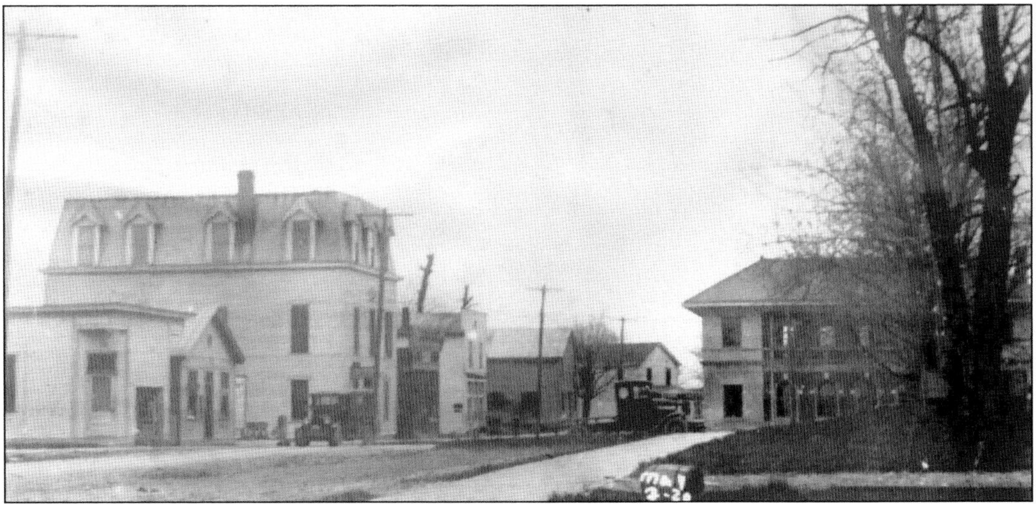

W.H. Folmer took this photograph on May 3, 1920, looking north on Madison Pike. The first building on the left had a second story added later for a theater. The third building is the Odd Fellows hall with its mansard roof. It is the only three-story building ever built in downtown. Next is the hardware store, which started out as the bank before it moved into its then new building across the street. Next is the W.A. Northcutt grocery; the Wilson warehouse, torn down shortly after 1920; and the W.H. Schoborg grocery, also the post office. (Kenton County Public Library.)

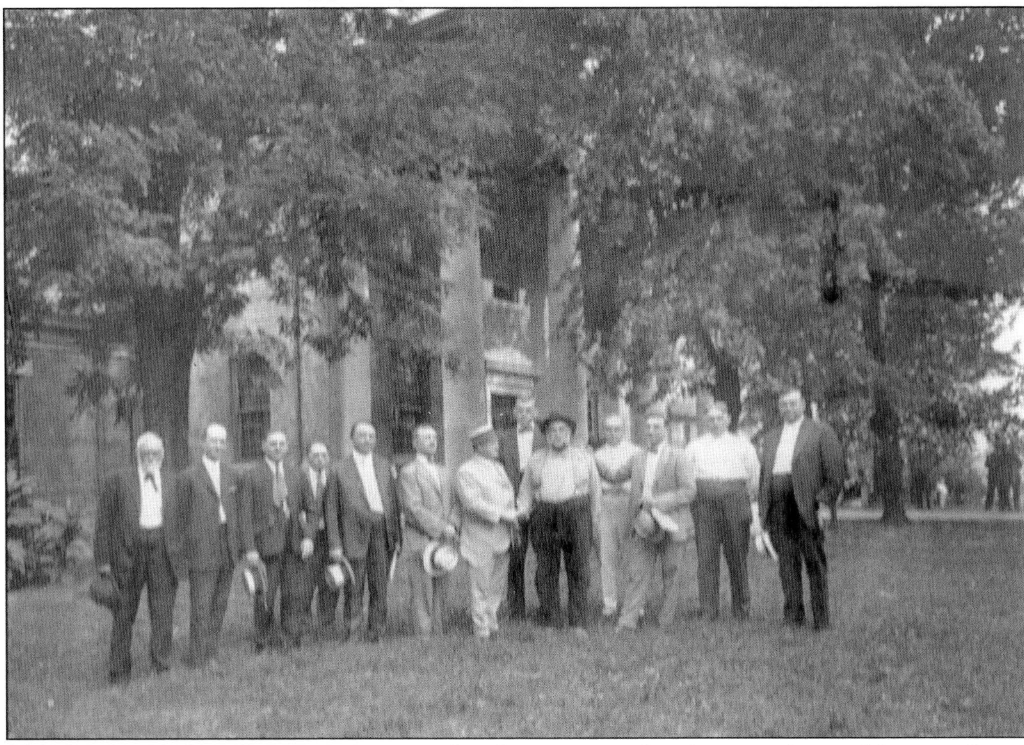

The Kenton County Commissioners stand with prominent local men in front of the courthouse around 1919. From left to right are John M. Mills, Byron Stephens, Goebel Armstrong, four unidentified men, John Clifford Mills (tall man in back), Bob Durr, unidentified, Judge John Reed, Newman Armstrong, and Edward Orson Mills. (Peggy Powers Baum.)

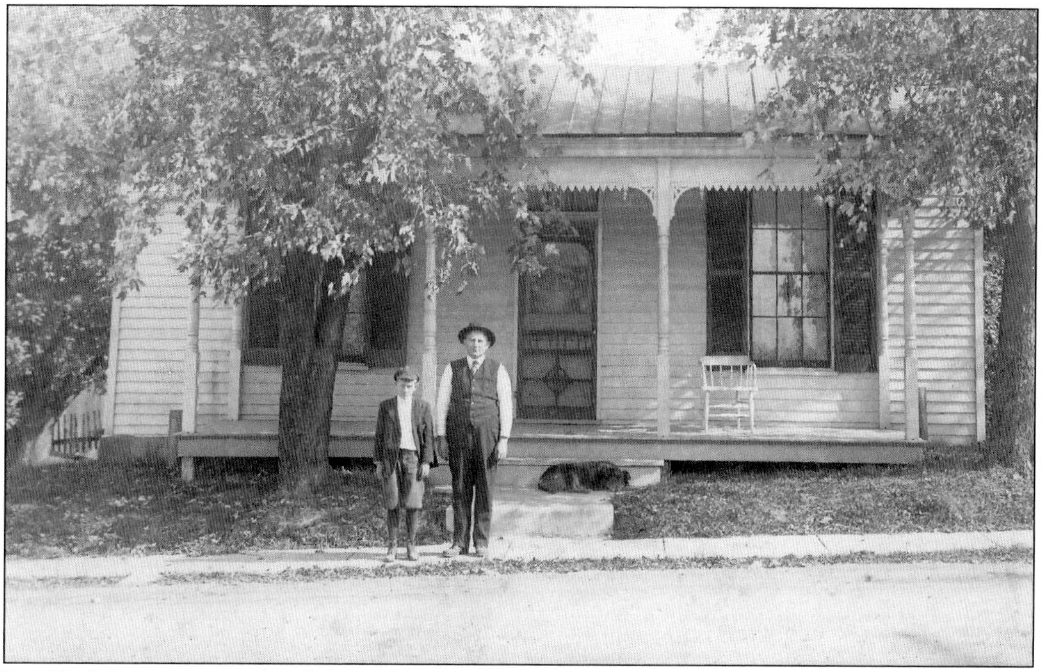

Bradford Armstrong, in his fashionable knickers, and his father, Newman, stand in front of their home (still existing) at 5306 Madison Pike around 1910. (J.B. Losey.)

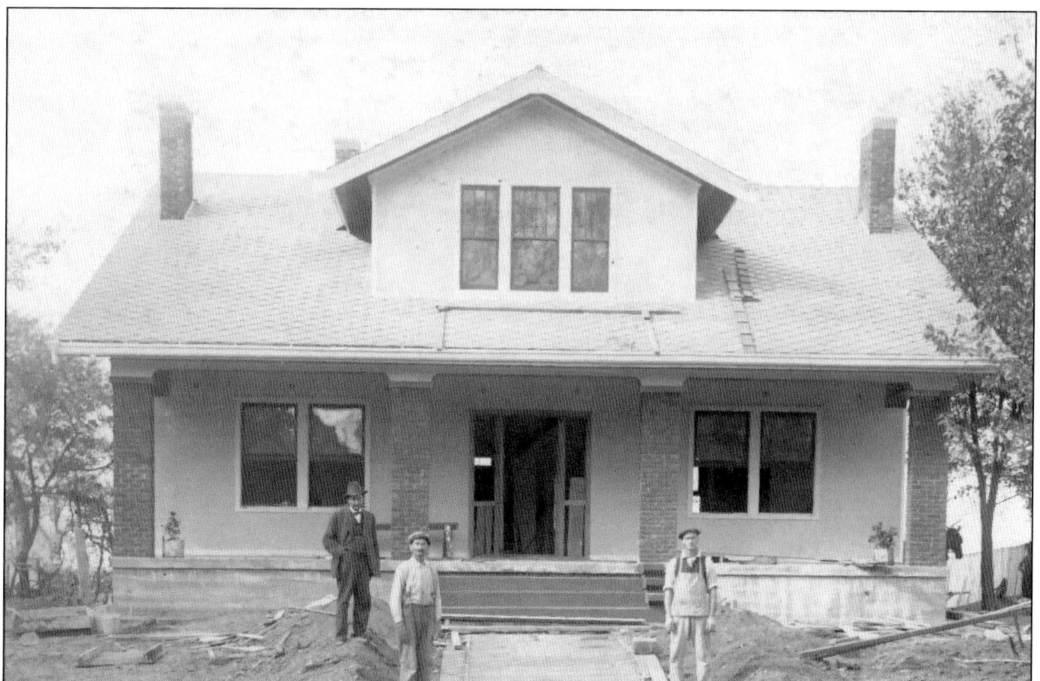

William and Kenneth Galloway built the E.O. Mills home at 47 McCullum Road around 1910. The home remains today. Note the horse to the right of the house. (Jerry Schneider.)

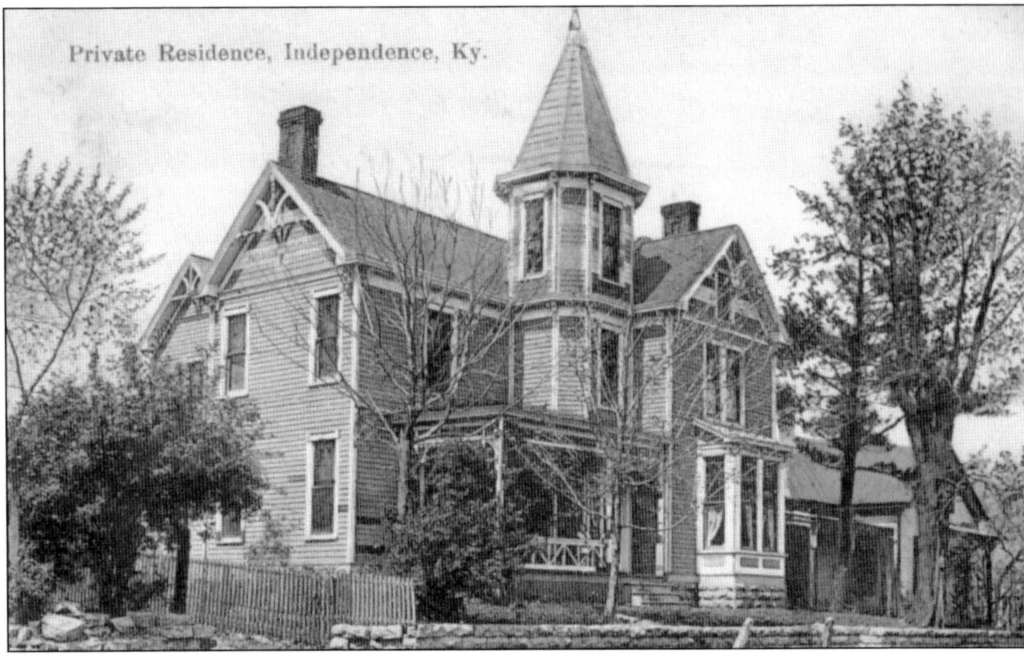

The Metcalf-Stephens House at 5241 Madison Pike is the only building in Independence listed on the National Register of Historic Places. This turreted Queen Anne frame home was constructed around 1887 by Dr. Tilford T. and Annabel Metcalf and was the St. Cecilia Church rectory from 1908 to 1914. Howard and Bessie Stephens owned it from 1914 until 1969, and their daughter, Mary Margaret Stephens, then owned it. This pre-1908 postcard states on the back "Hello Marie, The house you see is the place we are boarding at. fine place Walter." (Jerry Schneider.)

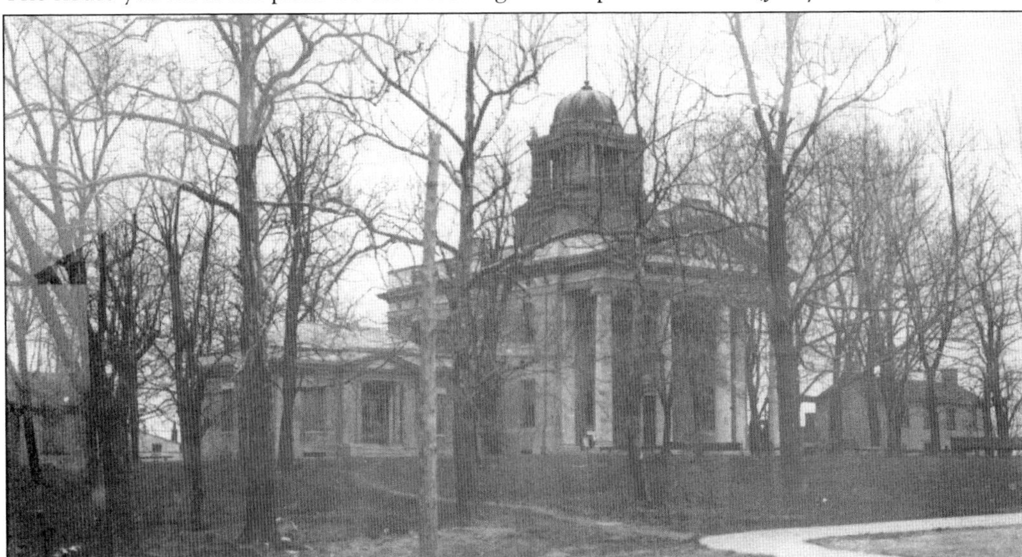

Here is the current Kenton County Courthouse with the jail to the right in a photograph taken by W.H. Folmer in 1920. The courthouse was dedicated on October 21, 1912, and cost $35,000 to build. This Beaux-Arts design with a Roman portico remains in everyday use by the public, proclaiming "KENTON COVNTY COVRT HOVSE" across the portico. The use of the Roman "V" for "U" confuses many. (Kenton County Public Library.)

Two

FARM LIFE

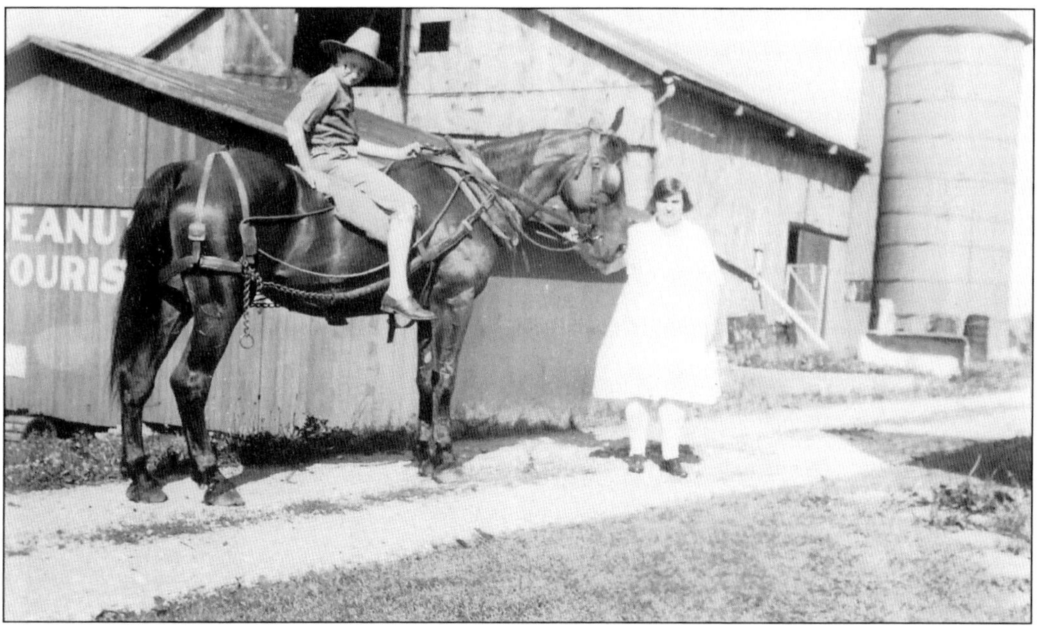

Charlie and Mary Stephens operated Peanut Charlie's tourist camp and their adjoining 87-acre farm, known as Sunshine Farm. It is currently Liberty Orchard subdivision on Madison Pike. Here Leslie Huffman rides a mule held by Mary Stephens in the 1920s. The sign advertising Peanut Charlie's is partially visible on the left. This image shows a full working farm with barn and silo. (Bob and Thelma Gibson.)

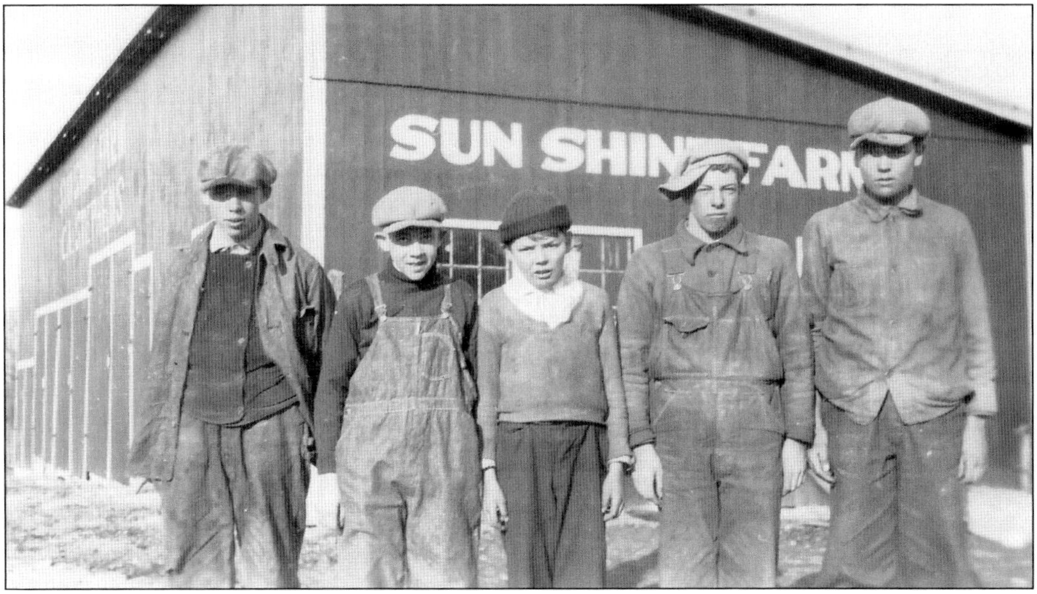

The back barn proclaimed the name of Sunshine Farm in the 1930s. Agriculture was the major part of the local economy of the area in the early 1900s. The primary farming activity was dairy farming, with many sheep, pigs, and poultry. Hay, corn, wheat, and tobacco were also grown. The typical farm would have several kinds of animals and crops. Agricultural specialization of only one or two farming activities was yet to occur. (Bob and Thelma Gibson.)

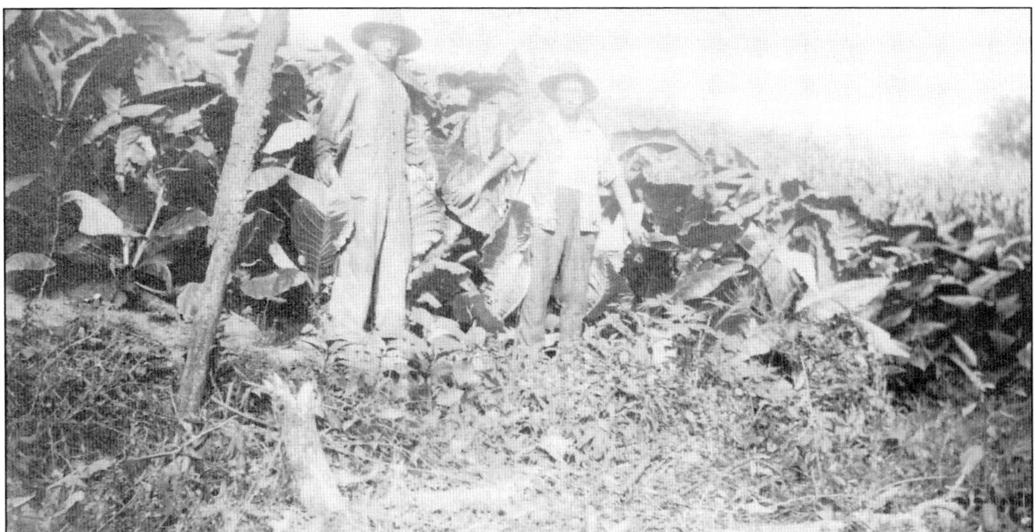

Lester (left) and Charles Stephens are in their tobacco field, ready to cut in 1923. Tobacco was not raised in Kenton County to any great extent before the 1920s. It became more widely raised in the 1930s and 1940s. Raising tobacco was, and still is, extremely labor-intensive. It was harvested by hand, cutting each stalk and impaling six on a stick, which was then hung in the barn to dry out. About eight weeks later, it was taken from the barn and each leaf stripped off by hand, tied in bundles, pressed, and taken to the tobacco warehouse for sale by the pound. Because it was stripped in early winter, barns had a "stripping room" to keep the workers warm. (Bob and Thelma Gibson.)

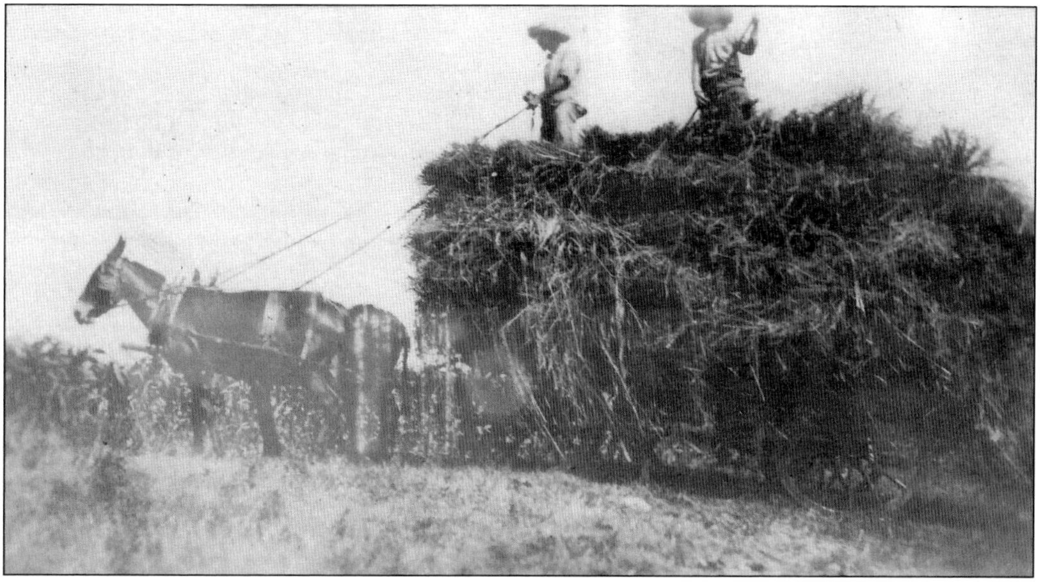

Charles (left) and Lester Stephens harvest hay at Sunshine Farm in the early 1920s. The hay was put on the horse-drawn wagon by hand with pitchforks and put in a haystack to feed the animals in winter. The hay was cut and harvested up to three or four times a year. (Bob and Thelma Gibson.)

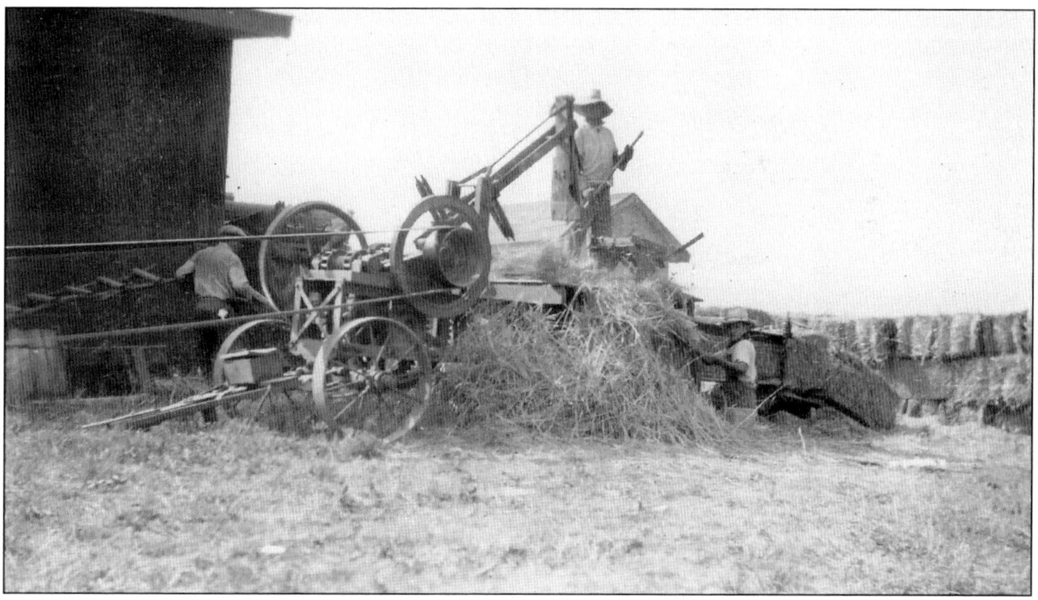

Hay harvest technology had progressed to this stationary hay baler by this 1930 photograph. Lester Stephens is on top feeding the hay in where it is bound into a hay bale, and the bale comes out on the right. The bales have been stacked to the far right and then will be stacked in the hayloft of the barn to keep out of the weather until fed to livestock. Later, pull-behind balers would gather the hay themselves in the field and make bales, which workers would load on a wagon and take to the barn. (Bob and Thelma Gibson.)

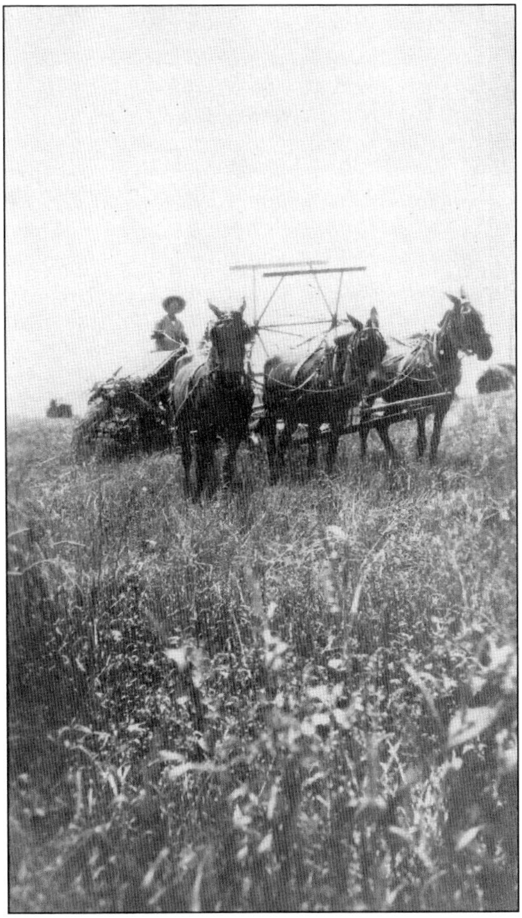

Sunshine Farm also grew wheat. In this early 1920s image, a horse-drawn wheat binder cuts the wheat and bundles it. Then workers would put it in shocks (large tied-together bundles that stood up) for a week to dry and haul the shocks to a threshing machine. (Bob and Thelma Gibson.)

Here is the wheat threshing machine on Sunshine Farm in 1930. The shocks of wheat were fed into the machine, which harvested the wheat grains to make flour. The harvested wheat is in bags to the right of the worker. The leftover wheat stalks are bound into straw bales at far right. (Bob and Thelma Gibson.)

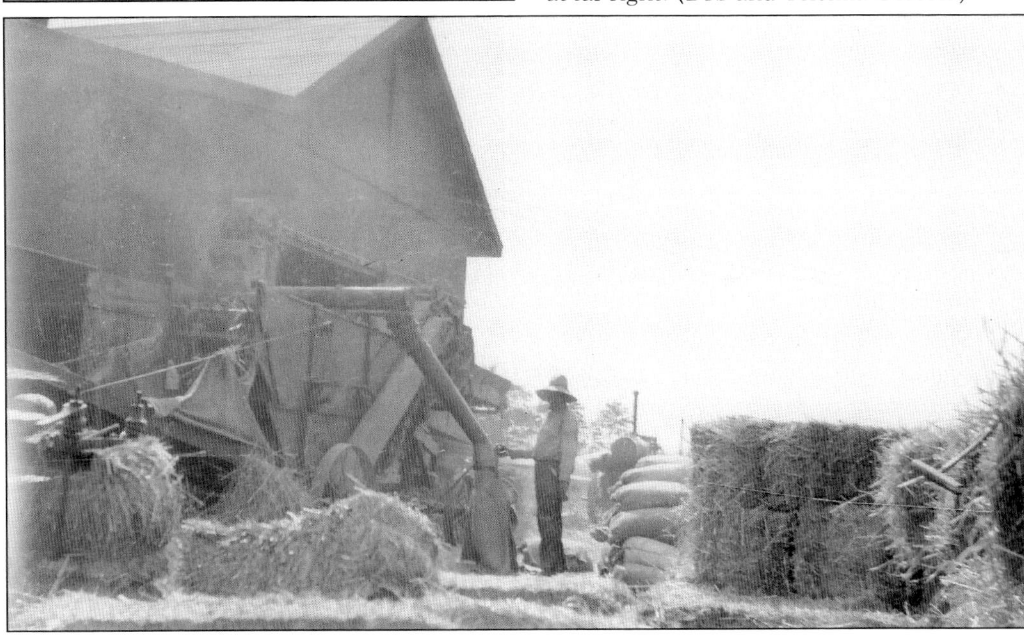

Lester Stephens admires this huge hog on Sunshine Farm in the early 1920s. Each farm usually raised a few hogs for home consumption. Farm work was never-ending, with caring and feeding animals, tending and harvesting crops, and repairing equipment and buildings. Vacations were unheard of—who would take care of the animals, particularly a herd of dairy cows that were milked twice a day? (Bob and Thelma Gibson.)

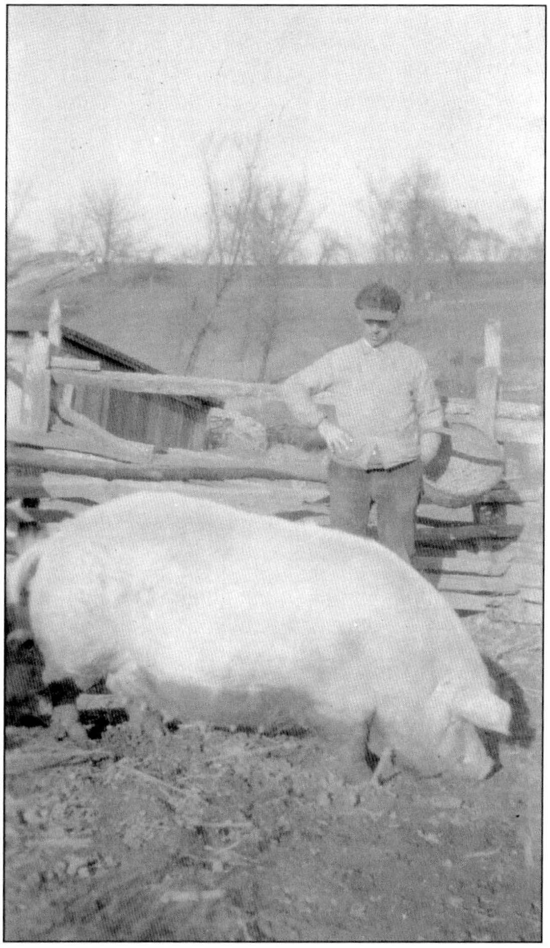

These hogs at Sunshine Farm are ready to cure around 1944. Jean Gibson (left) and her cousins, brothers Billy (center) and Bob Gibson (right), pose with two embracing the carcasses. Billy and Bob were Charles Stephens's grandsons. These hogs would be for family consumption for the coming year. The inside of the carcass is held open by a stick to cool. These would be wood smoked and cured. It was always done in cold weather to prevent spoilage; note the snow on the ground. A gambrel stick was used to hang the hog's back feet on the pole. (Bob and Thelma Gibson.)

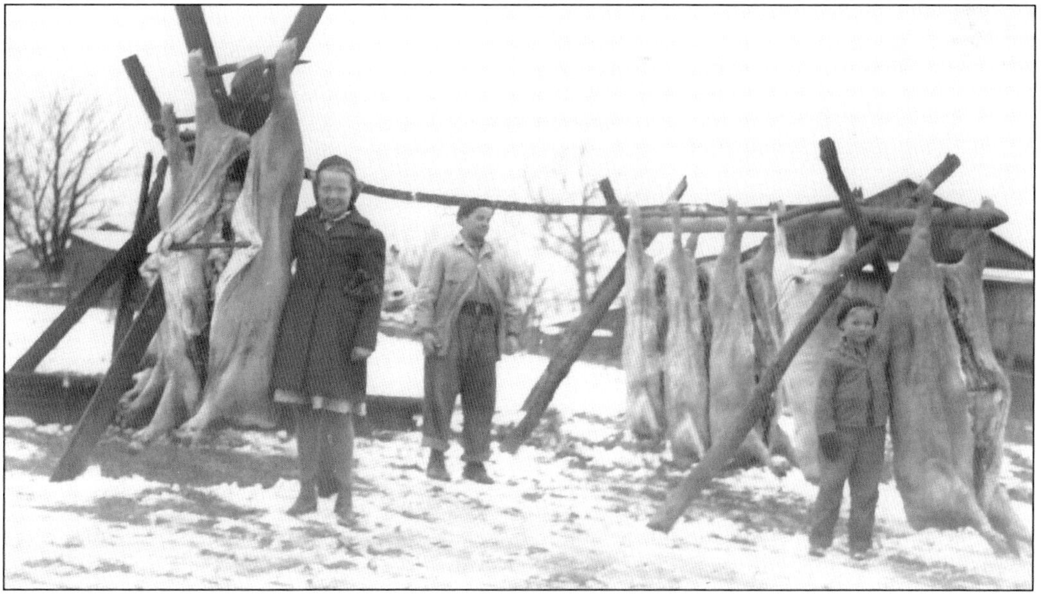

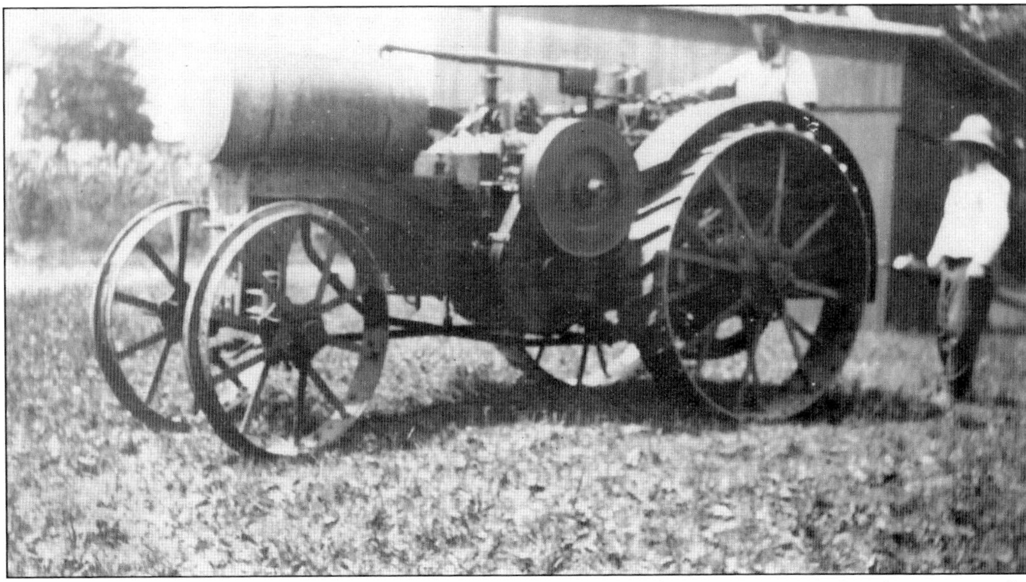

Charles Stephens is on his c. 1915 Titan tractor in the early 1920s. Lester Stephens is to the right. The metal wheels were for ground only. Mechanical problems were constant on these early machines, but they helped productivity around the farm. With more tractors in use, they replaced the horses and mules, whose numbers fell throughout the county. (Bob and Thelma Gibson.)

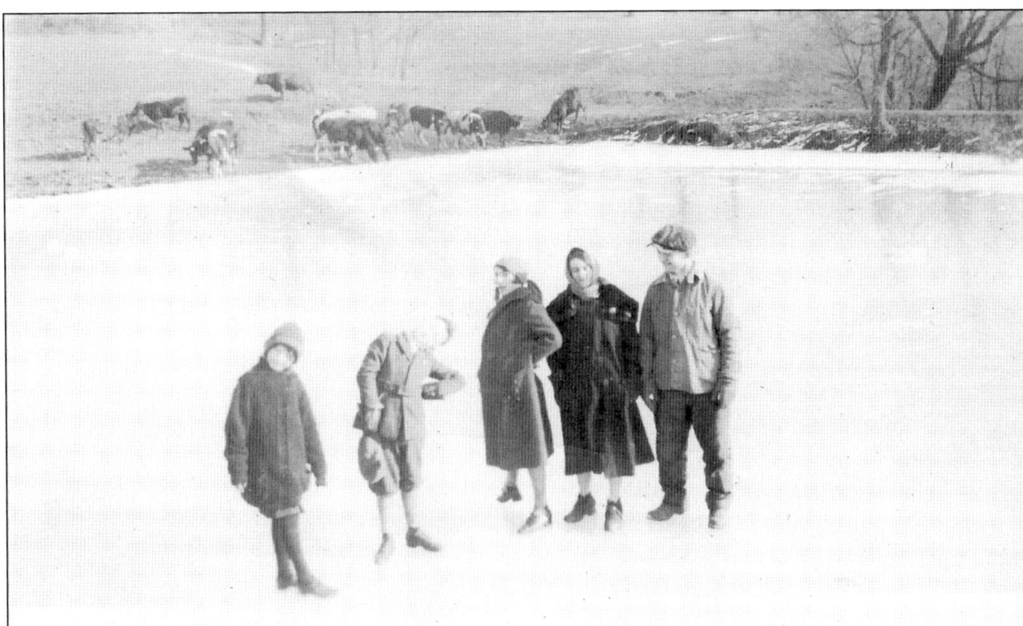

The Stephens family is on their frozen pond in the 1930s. The pond still exists in Liberty Orchard subdivision. Their dairy cows, in the background, provided dairy products for the family and most farm income. Milk trucks ran routes to pick up the milk from farmers and take it to the dairy, usually in Cincinnati. The dairy barn and milk house had to be close to the road so the truck could reach them in all kinds of weather. (Bob and Thelma Gibson.)

Ada Coleman feeds her chickens at her farm at 10669 Taylor Mill Road in the early 1920s. Every farm had some chickens for home egg and meat consumption. Their family was well-to-do; the outhouse behind her was a two-holer. (Virginia Coleman Watson.)

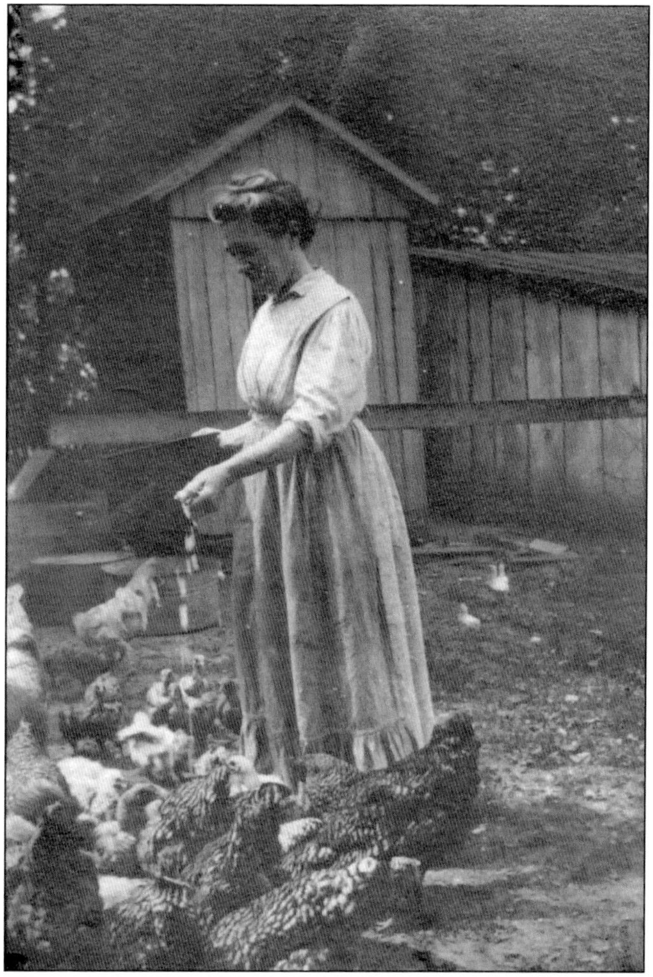

On the same Coleman farm, John Shaw, left, and Clifford Coleman show off by riding a bull in the early 1920s. Tobacco is growing to the right of the bull. John Shaw's adjoining farm is now Shaw Estates. Bulls do not like to be ridden (as anyone who has seen a rodeo would know). The bull has a ring through his nose, and this image was probably taken for sheer novelty. Do not try this at home. (Virginia Coleman Watson.)

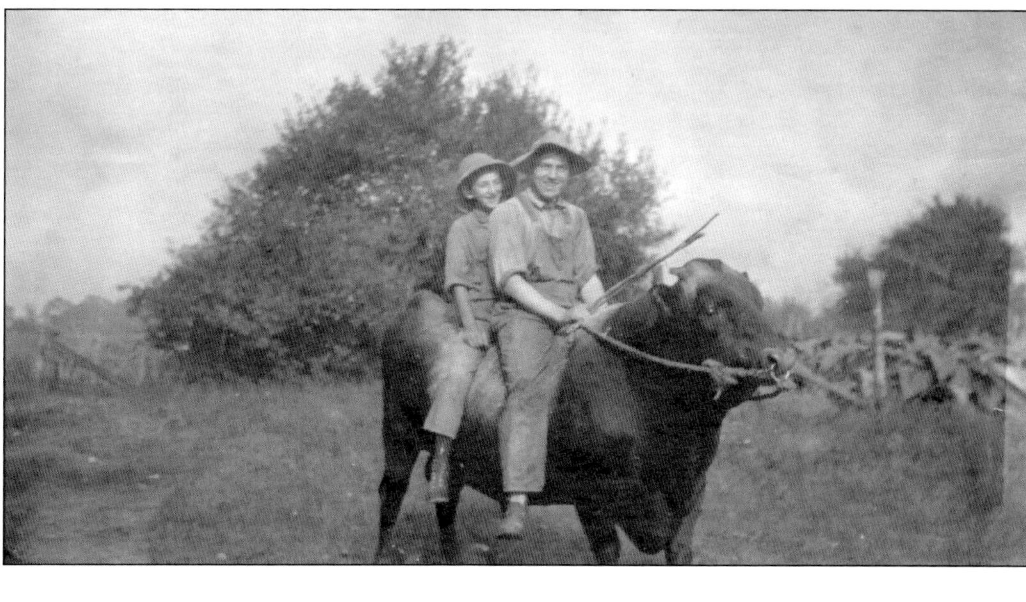

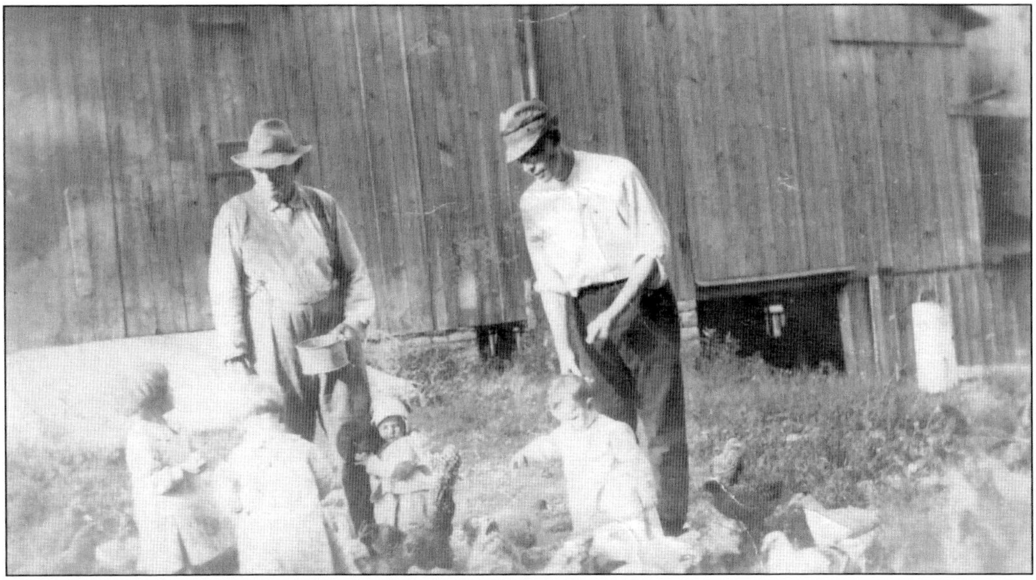

Feeding the chickens about 1921 on the Coleman farm are, from left to right, sisters Dorothy, Sally, and Virginia Coleman and cousin Ruth Coleman. The men behind are Charles Coleman, left, and his son Harry. The barn still stands at 10669 Taylor Mill Road. (Virginia Coleman Watson.)

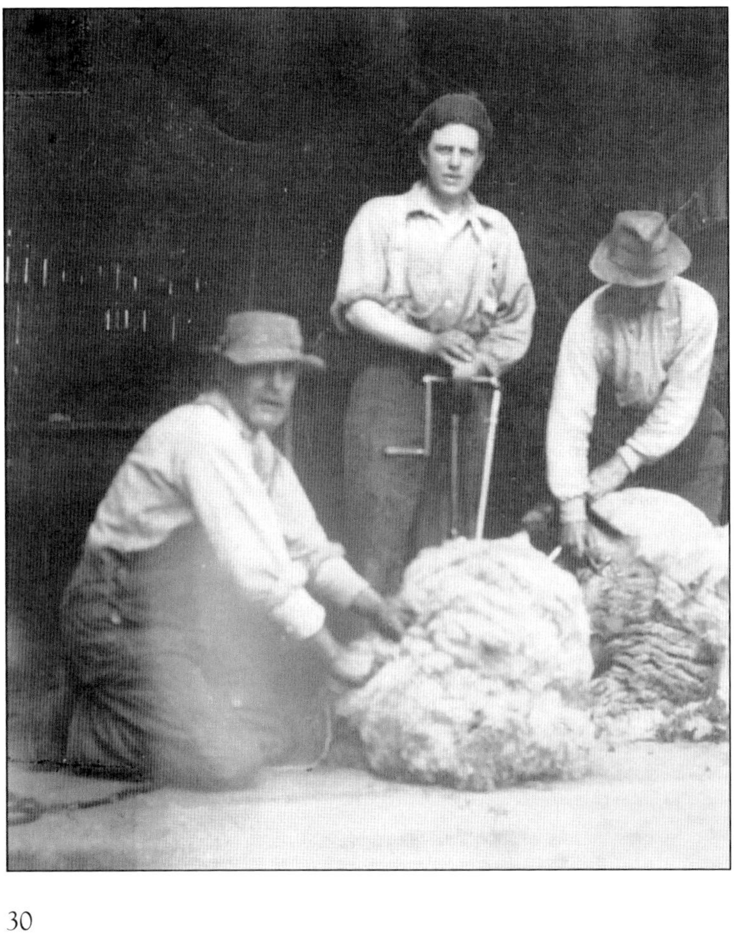

Clifford Coleman stands between two workers as they shear the wool from his sheep. This image from the early 1920s is in the same barn as above. The Kenton County Wool Association had 150 members in the 1920s. (Virginia Coleman Watson.)

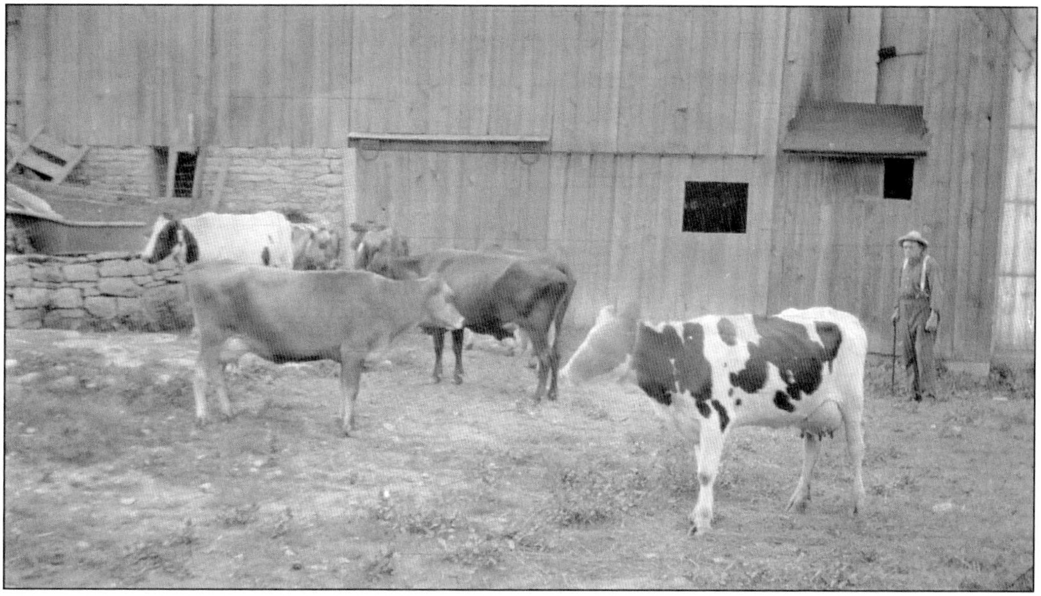

Charles Coleman stands with his cows around 1921 by the same barn as on the opposite page. He was the representative from Kenton County in the Kentucky legislature during 1887–1888. He died in 1924 at the age of 70 and is buried in Independence Cemetery. His son, Dr. Clarence Coleman, was a four-time mayor of Frankfort. (Virginia Coleman Watson.)

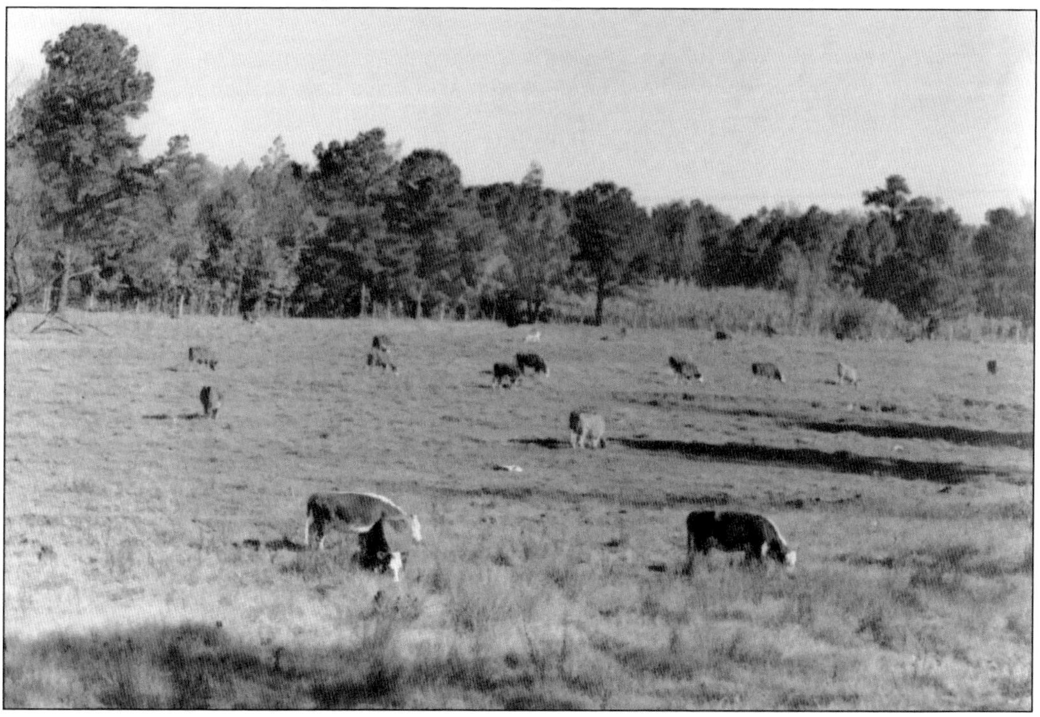

Beef cattle began to increase and dairy cattle decrease as the 20th century progressed. Here a herd of Polled Herefords (beef cattle) graze at the Ella Carroll farm at 11247 Madison Pike. "Polled" means without horns. Some Herefords do not have horns, a trait which they pass on to their calves, and this is preferred because they are easier to handle. (Karen Fisk Koch.)

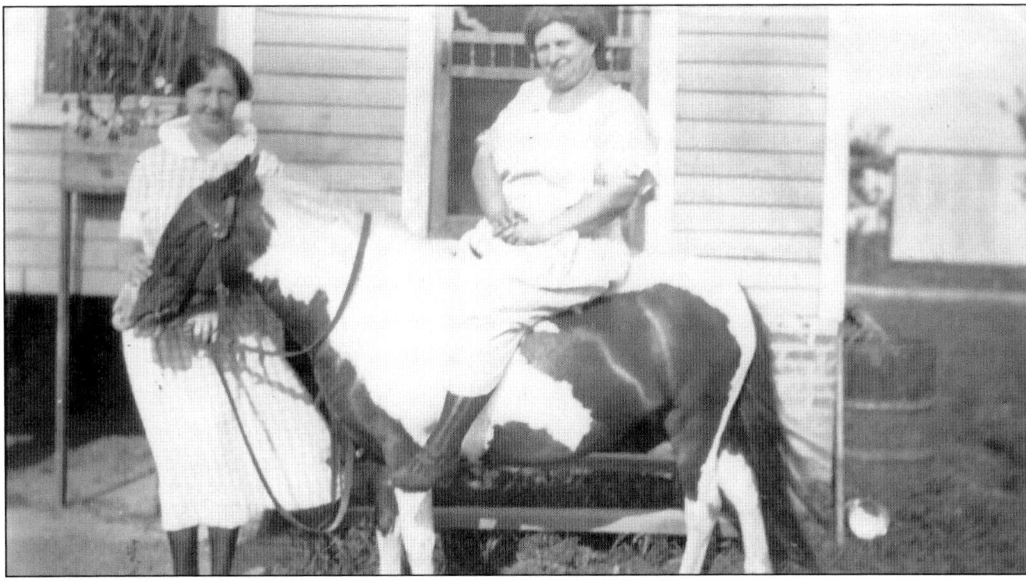

Elizabeth Rothmann poses on a pony in the 1920s in front of her house at 1791 Shaw Road. The house and farm remain in existence. She and her husband, Charles, operated Rothmann's Grocery at 5261 Madison Pike from the 1920s to the 1940s, and it continued operating until 1992. There appears to be a chicken in the barrel on the right. The lady on the left is unidentified. (Jerry Schneider.)

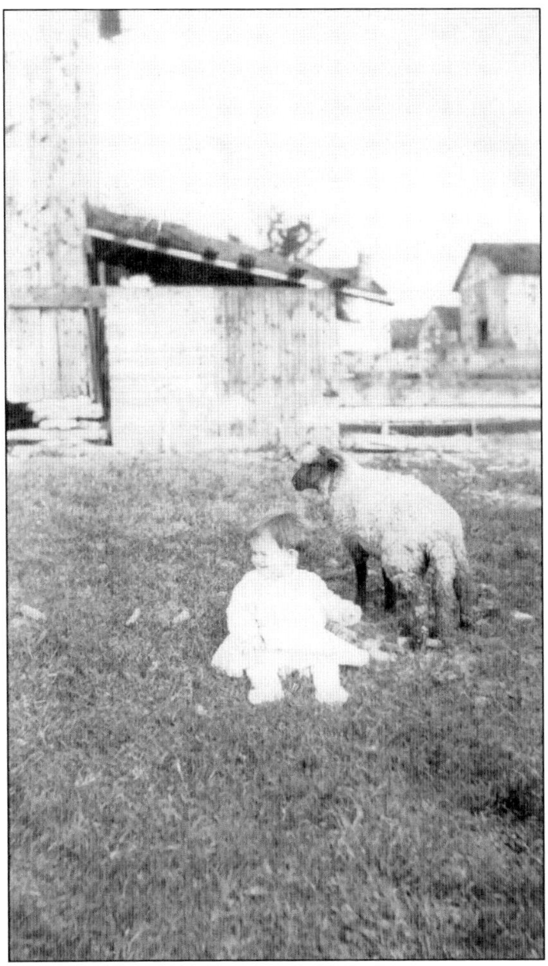

Dorothy "Dot" Kenney (Schneider) enjoys a day on her grandparents' Rothmann farm in 1919. Almost all of the area outside of downtown Independence was farmland in the early 1900s. There were about 7,000 sheep in the county at this time. Dot married Harold "Hank" Schneider, and they operated Independence Hardware in the 1950s and 1960s. (Jerry Schneider.)

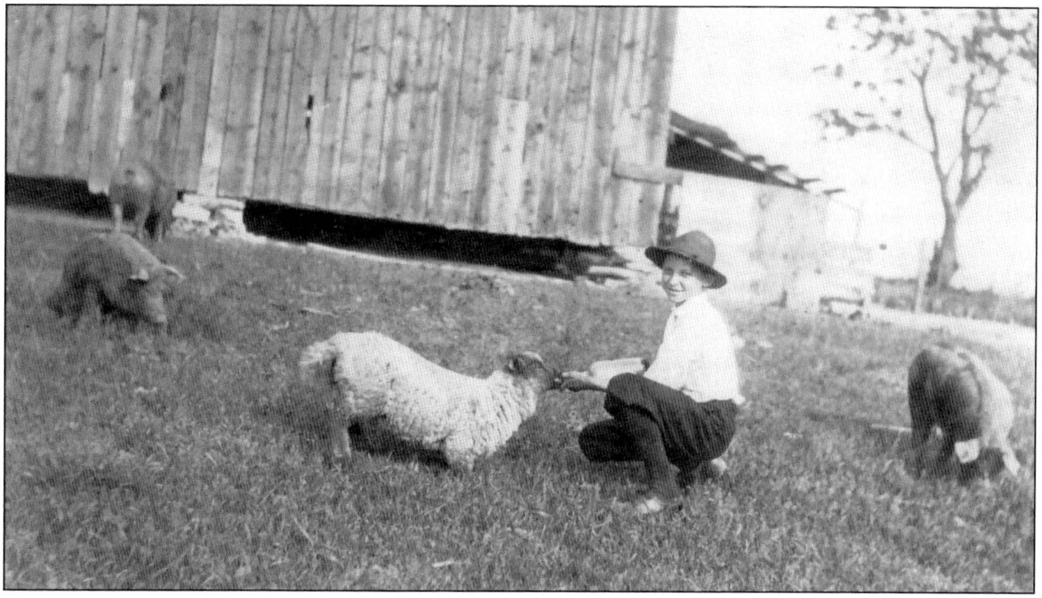

Charles Reinhold Rothmann bottle feeds a lamb in 1919 at the Rothmann farm. Three pigs roam the lot with him. He was the son of Charles and Elizabeth Rothmann. The lamb assumes what would be a nursing posture with its mother. Each animal was valuable, and farmers did what was needed to make sure it survived. (Jerry Schneider.)

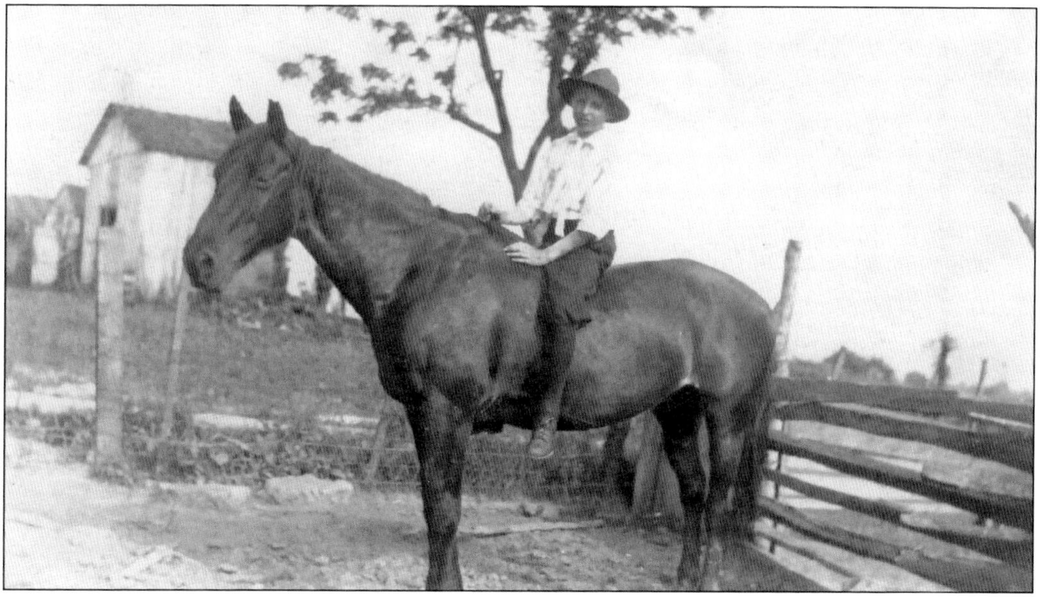

Probably the same day in 1919, Charles Reinhold Rothmann poses on a horse. Horses were vital on the farm before tractors and automobiles. They pulled all the farm equipment and hauled everything needed. If people needed to go anywhere, they rode a horse, rode in a buggy pulled by a horse, or walked. Automobiles were still scarce at this time. (Jerry Schneider.)

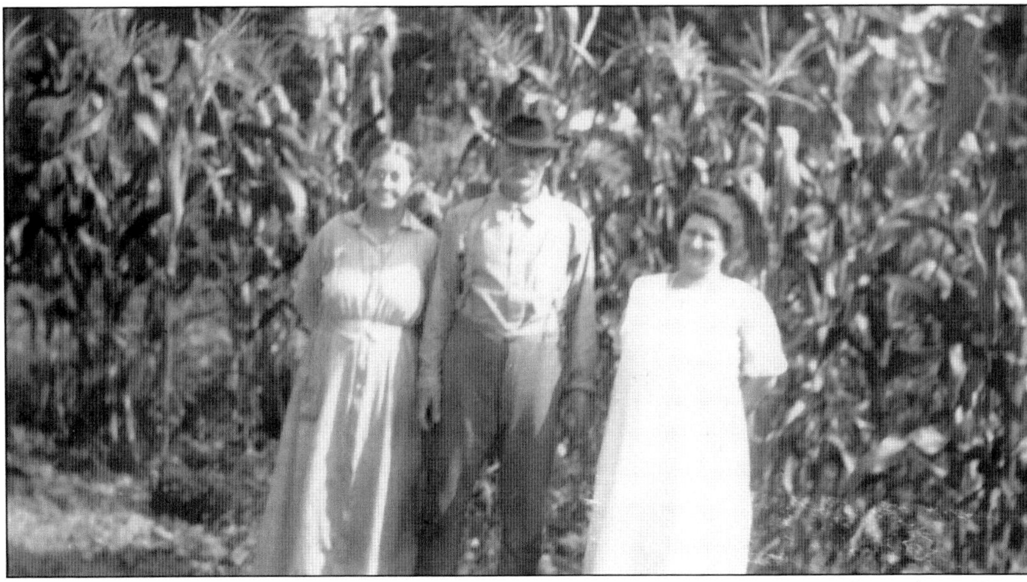

From left to right, Samuel H. and Pearl Folmer stand on their farm at 1906 Independence Road with their friend Elizabeth Rothmann, who came to visit. This 1920s image has them proudly showing their corn crop behind them. This corn would be fed to livestock and the stalks ground into silage and stored in silos for winter feeding. (Jerry Schneider.)

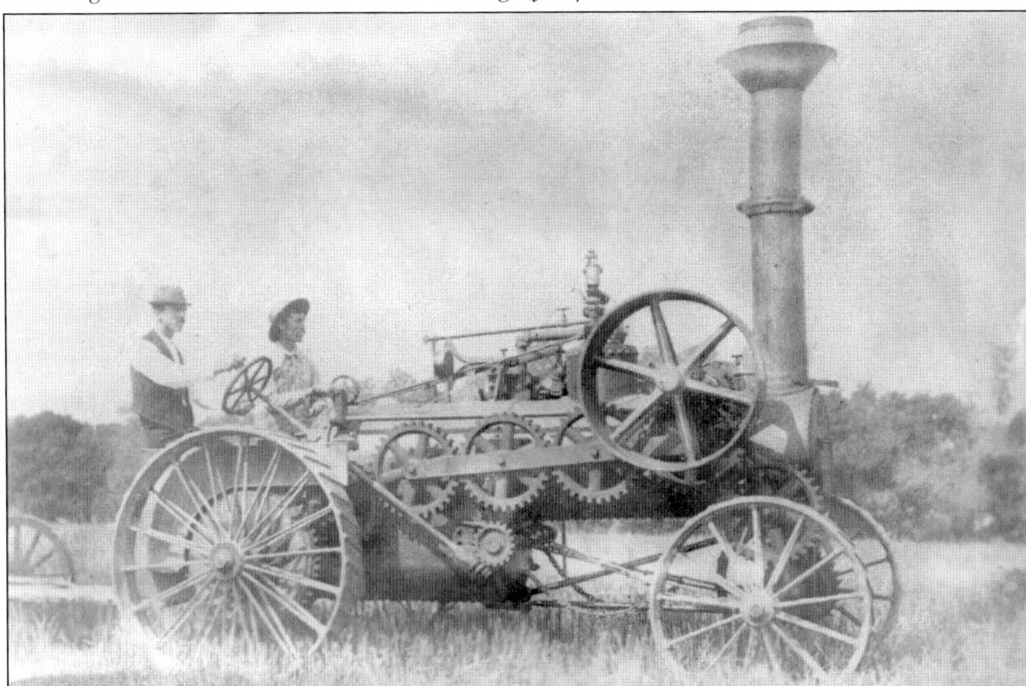

G.W. Folmer, left, and S.H. Folmer ride their threshing machine engine in the 1920s. It powered the wheat threshing machine as well as pulling it from farm to farm as they were hired by neighboring farmers. Farmers could not afford to purchase every implement and machine needed, so they would trade off equipment with neighbors or hire them to do a task that involved an expensive piece of equipment needed infrequently. (Doris Wicklund King.)

Livestock drank out of creeks and ponds when thirsty. During cold weather, when the water source froze over, farmers had to break the ice so livestock could reach the water underneath. Howard Folmer utilized a sledgehammer for this task, and the thirsty cows came for a drink in this 1930s image on the Folmer farm. (Doris Wicklund King.)

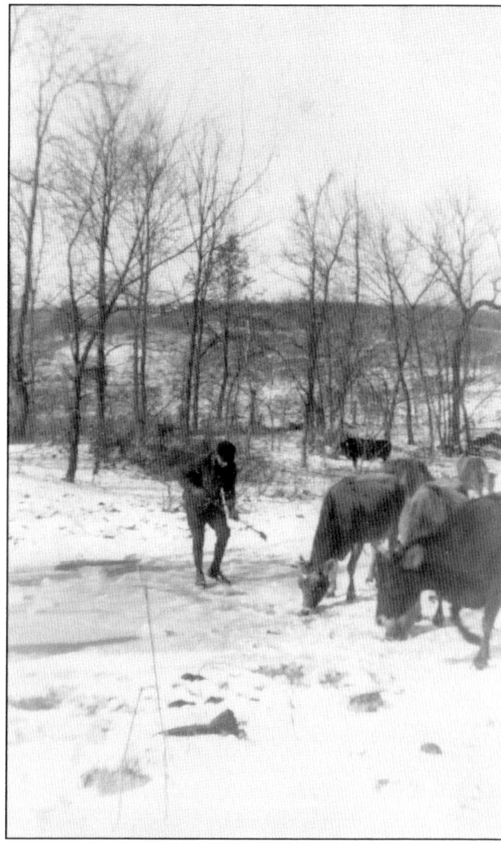

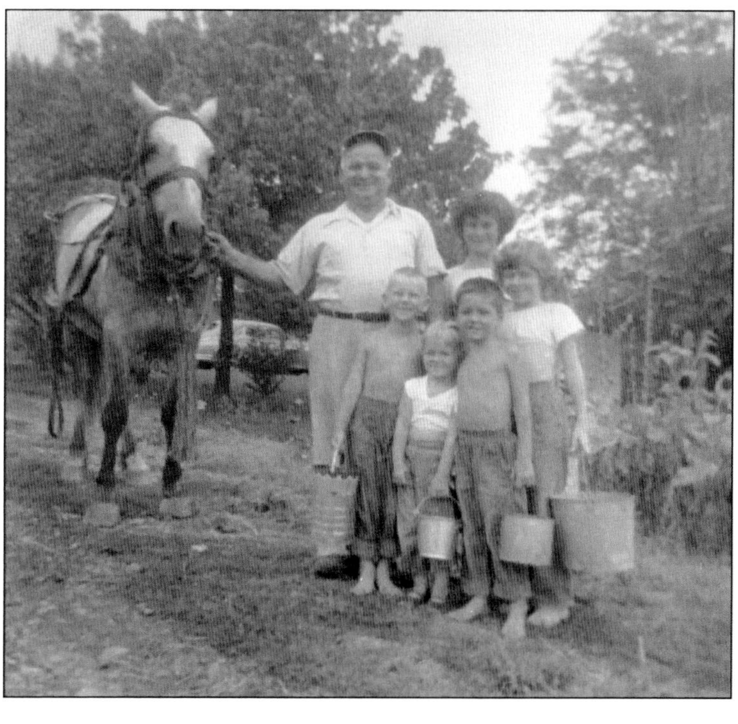

The Glass family prepares to dig potatoes from the garden on their farm at 42 McKim Drive in 1953. Shown here are, from left to right, (first row) Tommy Wichterman, Janet Glass, and Gary Wichterman; (second row) Tommy Glass, father of Janet and grandfather of the rest, Joy, and Patty Wichterman. (Janet Glass Kreidler.)

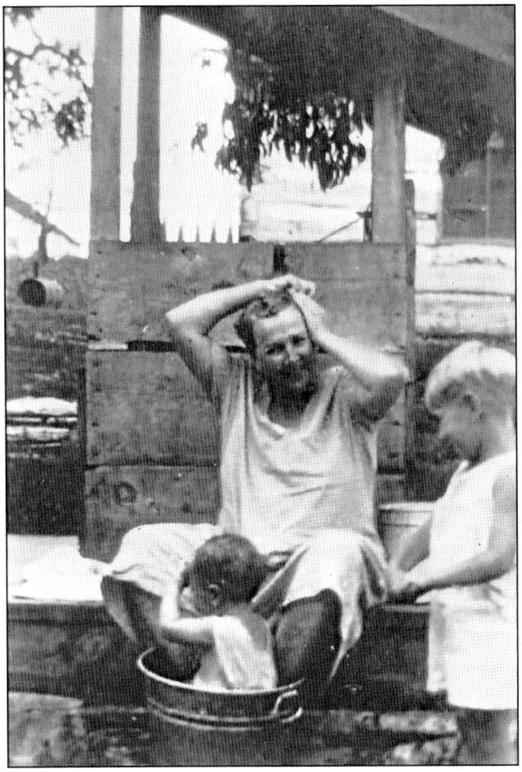

At the Hawkins farm on Fowler Creek Road, Jessie England sits on the well box and cools her feet in the tub. Her son Gayle is in the tub, also cooling off on this hot day in August 1934. Her older son, Wayne, is on the right, watching. The log cabin in the background was referred to as "the Indian log cabin" and was used as a smokehouse at this time. (Eunice Mershon.)

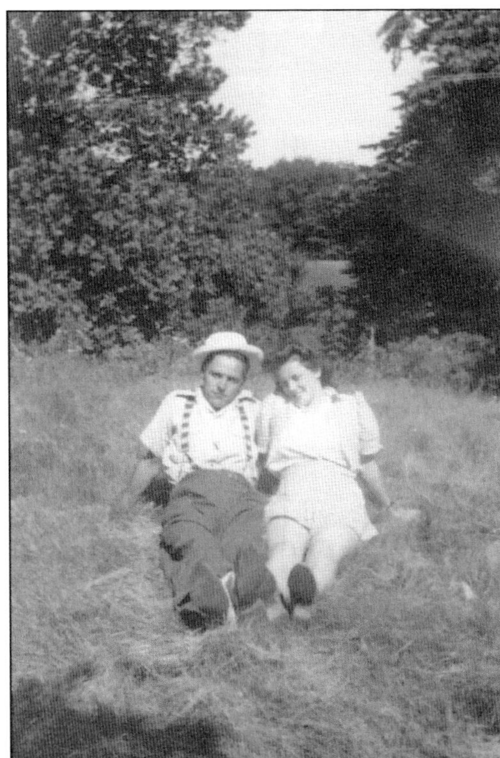

Life on the farm was not all hard work. Here Bryson Fisk goes a-courting at 11247 Madison Pike to visit the farmer's daughter, Dorothy Rankin, in 1940. They married in 1943 and had three children, one of whom is on the cover of this book. They later acquired this same farm from her family, and it remains in their family today. (Karen Fisk Koch.)

Three

To Protect and Serve

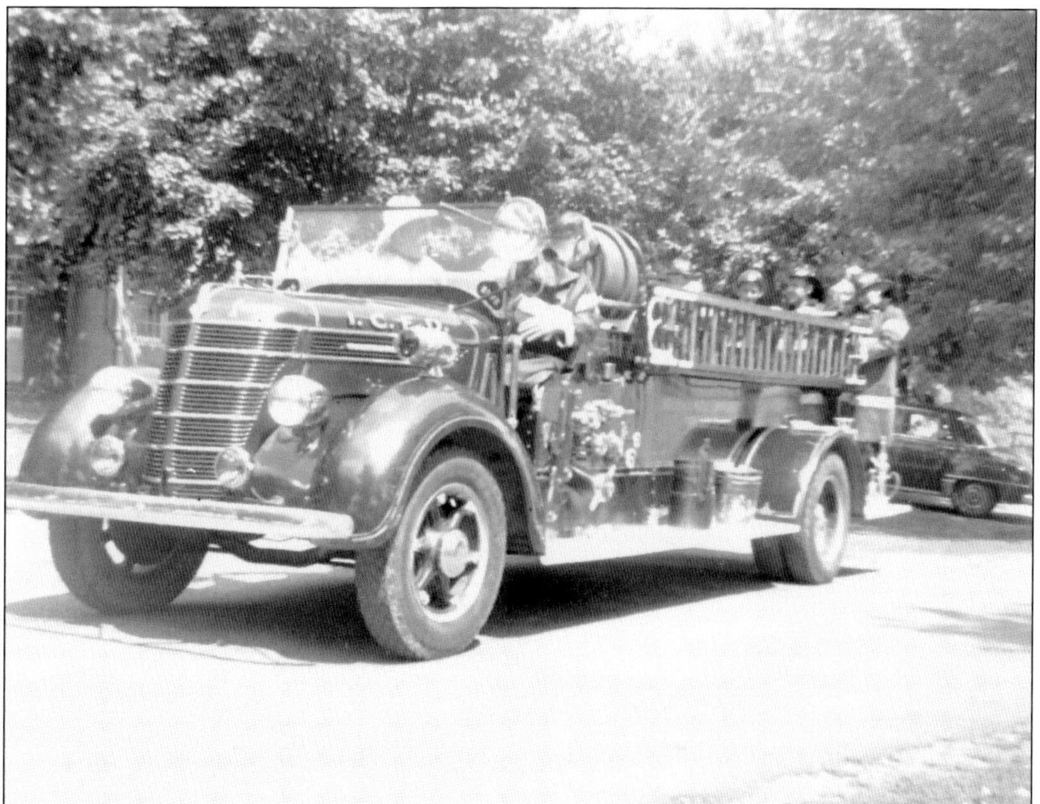

The Independence & Community Fire Department ("I.C.F.D." on the hood of the truck) was formed in 1937, and the first firehouse was constructed just south of the courthouse in 1939. The new 1936 International fire truck was purchased in August 1937 and was still in use when shown off in September 1953. (Eunice Mershon.)

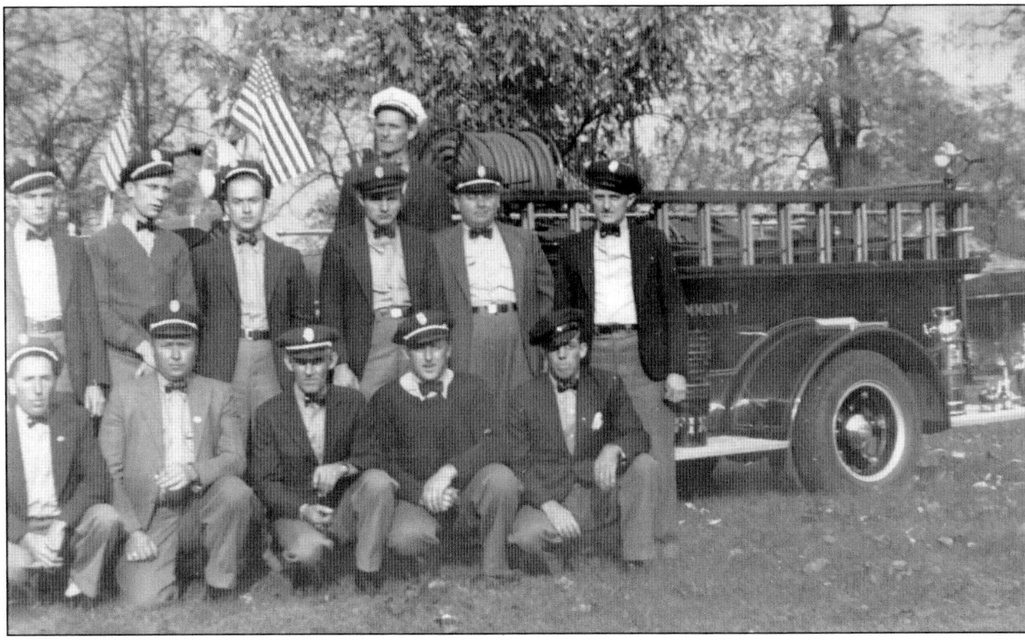

Here is the first fire department, pictured when it first formed in 1937 or soon thereafter. From left to right are (first row) Charley Houston, Ethelbert Carlisle, Ralph Ervin, John Durr, and Joe Lynch; (second row) Herman Schoborg, unidentified, Howard Clinkenbeard, Bill Guttridge, Elmer Schadler, and Skeets Holzderber. In the truck with the white chief hat is Ira Lower. (Greg White.)

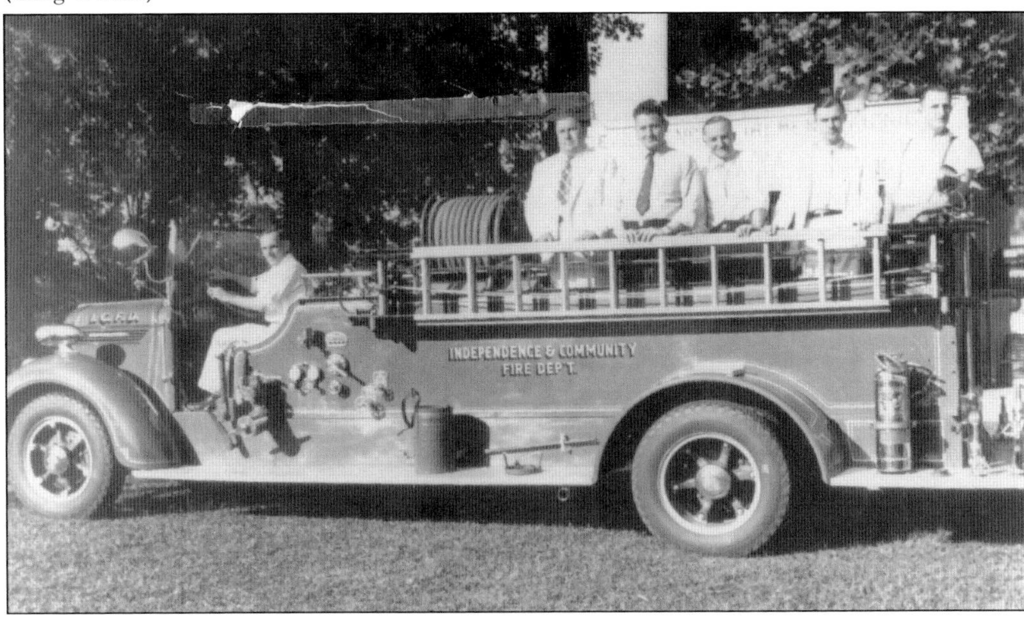

This is the same truck with the name visible on the side in 1938. From left to right are driver Ralph Ervin, Boyd Elliott, Charles Dorsey, Al Jaeger, Herman Schoborg, and Charles Holzderber. The 500-gallon storage-tank pumper was purchased from International Truck Company and equipped by Howe Company. It was stored in a garage until the firehouse was built in 1939. (Independence Fire District.)

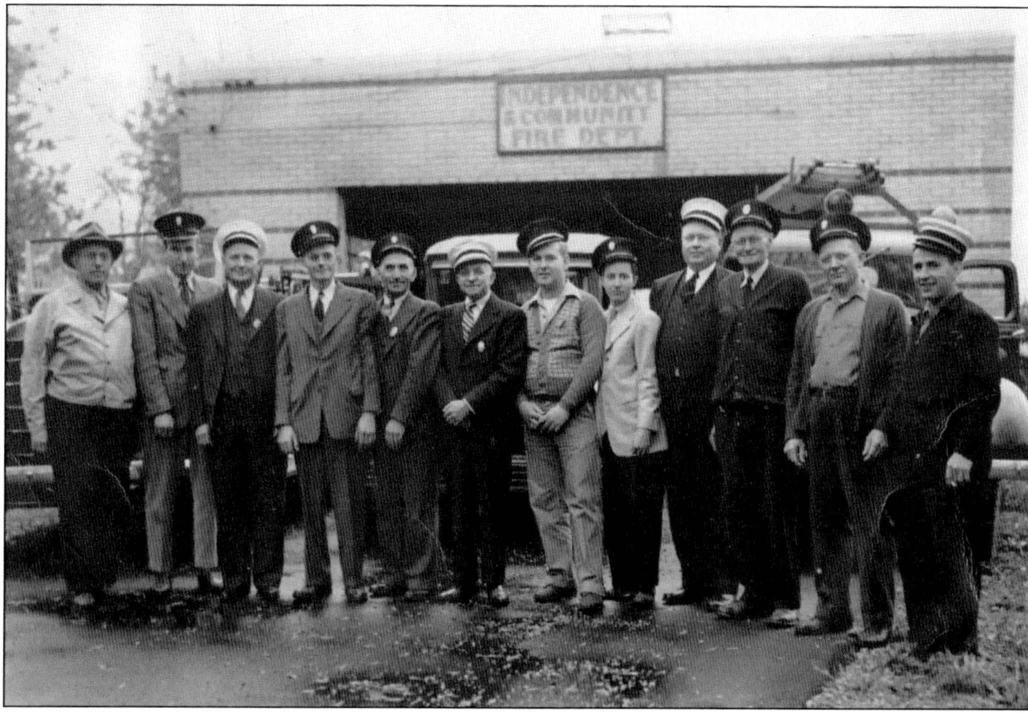

In April 1946, the department posed in front of the firehouse and their equipment. The department is, from left to right, Cliff Coleman, George Jaeger, Charles Dorsey, Herman Schoborg, Goebel Armstrong, Chief Al Jaeger, Tilford Mershon, Bill Ballard, Ethelbert Carlisle, Mike Wagner, D.T. Bagby, and Charles "Chalkie" Wilson. (Greg White.)

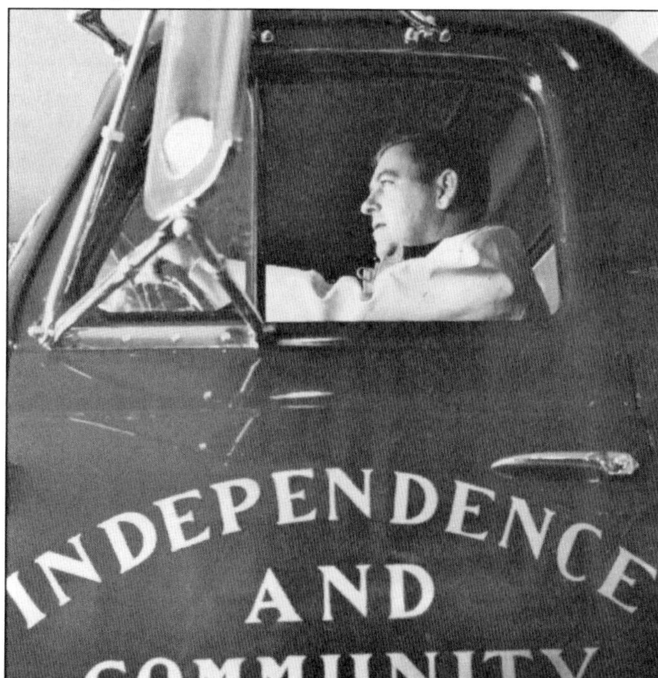

In 1961, Chief Tilford Mershon sits in the 1953 Ford fire truck; he had been chief for 17 years and had previously served as Independence trustee for 12 years. The truck could spray water at the rate of 500 gallons per minute from a front-mount pump. At the time, the department was named one of the four best fire-fighting units in Northern Kentucky. (Cincinnati Bell.)

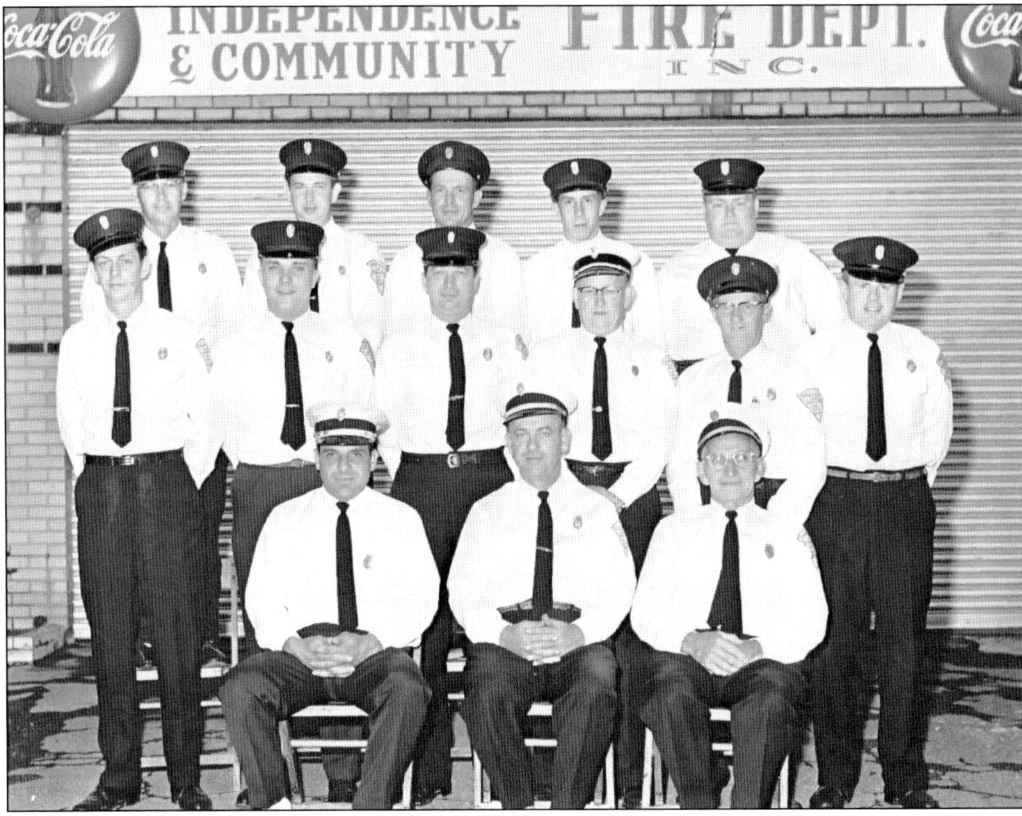

On June 18, 1964, members of the volunteer fire department pose outside in uniform. They are, from left to right, (first row) Ferd Scherder, Chief Tilford Mershon, and Goebel Armstrong; (second row) Ralph Hoppenjans, Tom Schoborg, Roy Holten, Warner Cox, Joe Caldwell, and Roscoe White; (third row) Shirley Ellison, Paul Gripshover, John Scherder, Robert Scherder, and Herbert Sharon. (Independence Fire District.)

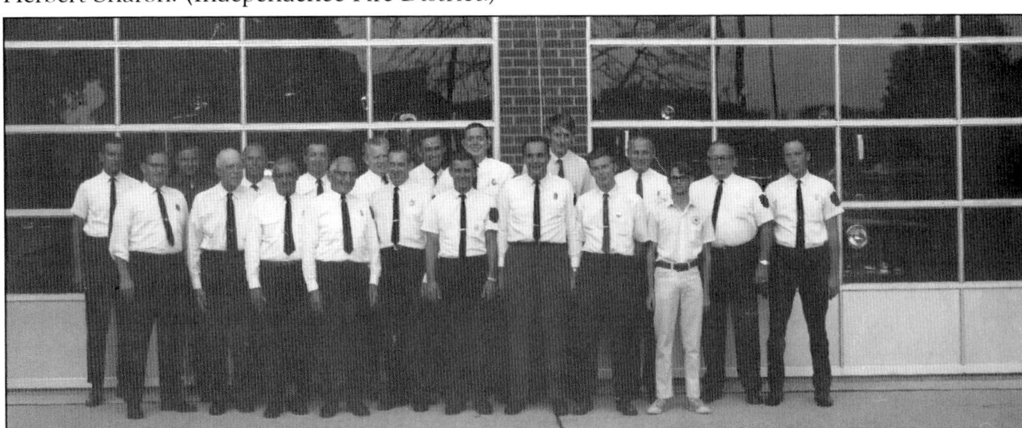

The department posed in 1970 in front of the firehouse. They are, from left to right, Hank Gripshover, Chief Warner Cox, Dennis Thornton, Cliff Coleman, Don Messingschlager, Joe Caldwell, Roy Holten, Goebel Armstrong, Roscoe White, Paul Gripshover, Joe Huesman, George Mieman, Bob Casey, Tom Schoborg, Carl Wicklund, John Jackson, Frank LeMaster, Mike Mitchell, Paul Pickett, and Randall Elbert. (Independence Fire District.)

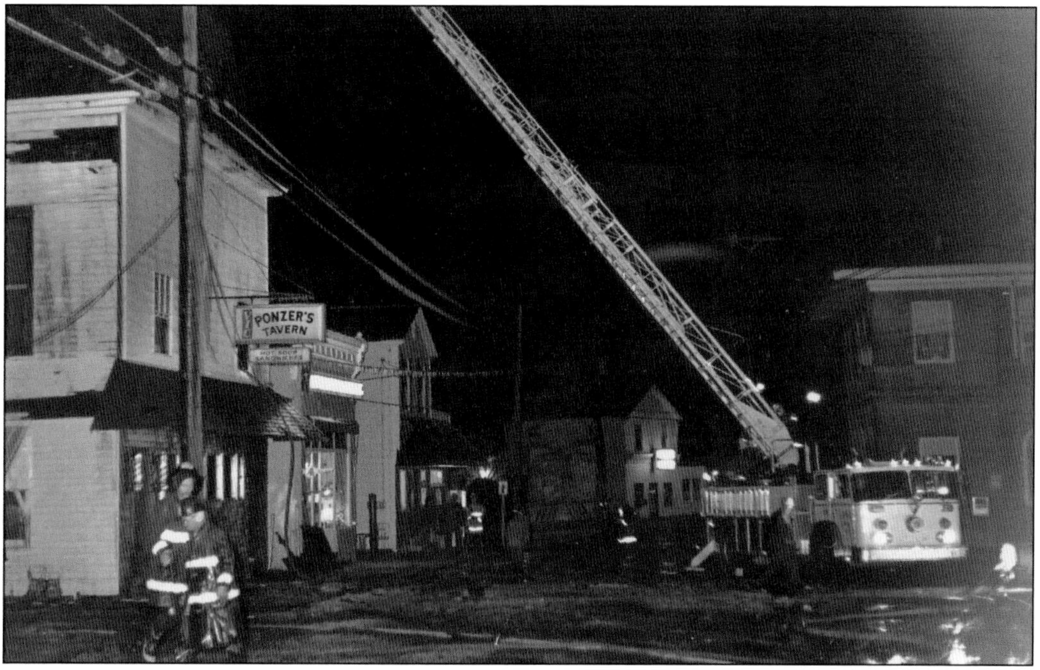

The department and three other departments responded to a fire at Vic Ponzer's Tavern, located in the Odd Fellows hall at 5265 Madison Pike downtown, in February 1976. The bank is on the right. The three-story building lost its third floor and remains two stories today. (Independence Fire District.)

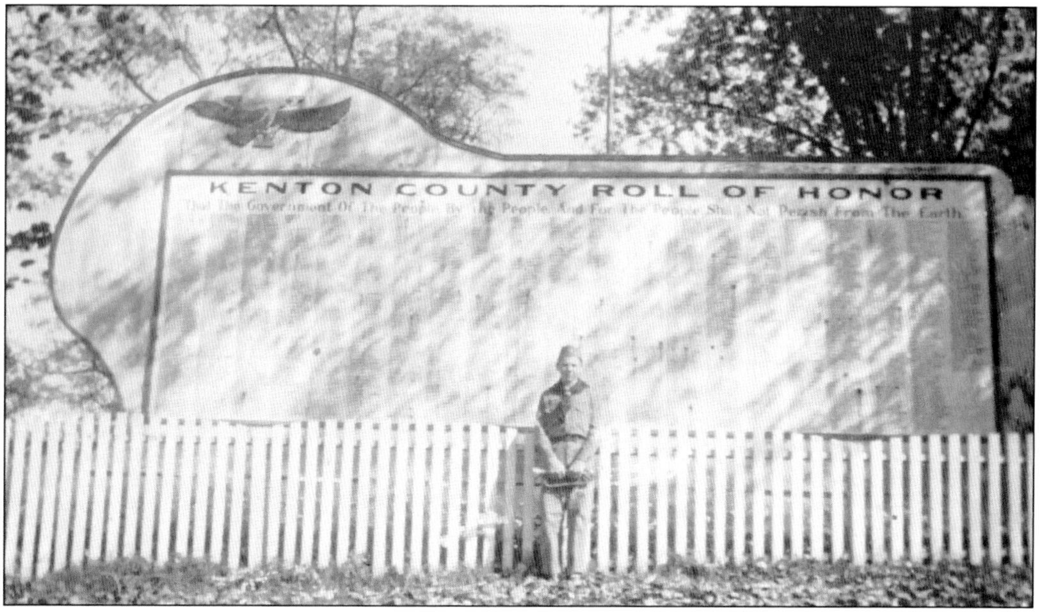

Independence of any kind would not be celebrated without the sacrifice of the military. After World War II, a Kenton County Roll of Honor billboard-type display was erected on the northwest corner of the courthouse square to honor all those Kenton Countians who served in that war. It was removed around the late 1950s. Gayle England, 17, poses in 1950 in his Boy Scout uniform with the bugle he played at public events. (Eunice Mershon.)

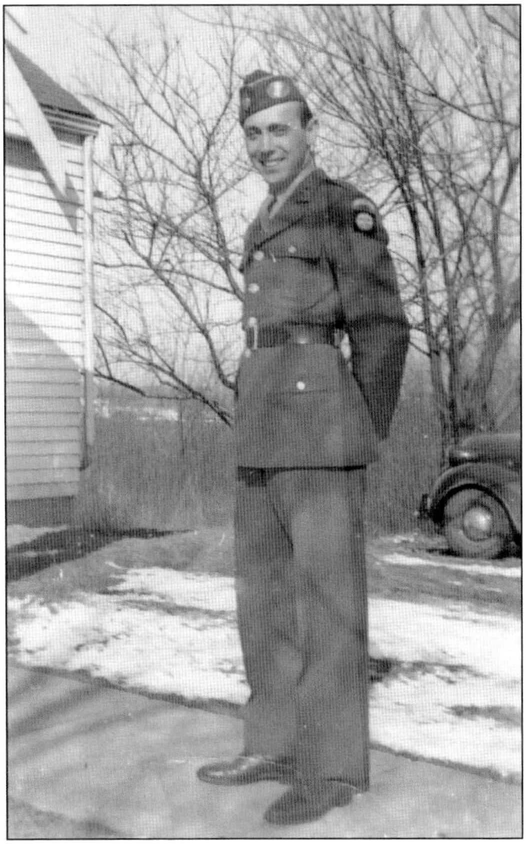

Harold "Hank" Schneider returns home to 104 McCullum Road after the war ended in 1945. He served in the Army 82nd Airborne and saw action in North Africa, Sicily, Italy, France, and Germany, and liberated or was present right after liberation of at least one German concentration camp. He participated in D-Day and was wounded three times in combat. He and his wife later operated Independence Hardware. (Jerry Schneider.)

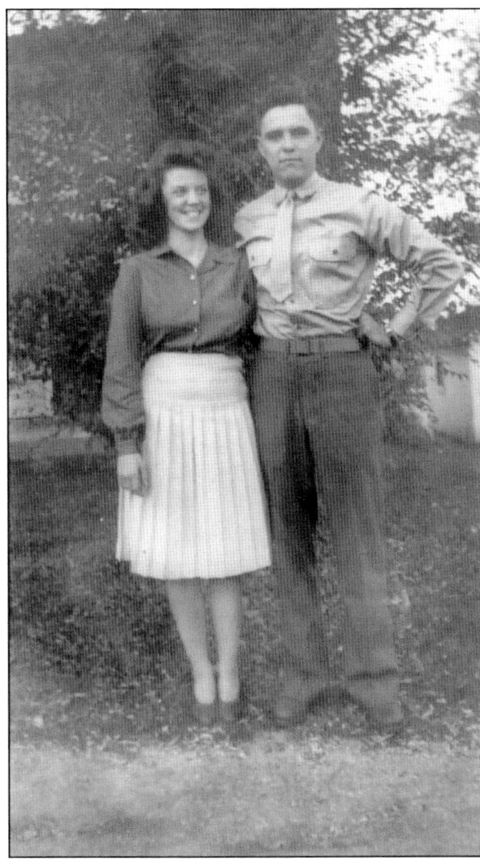

Dorothy and Bryson Fisk pose around 1943 at her grandparents' home at 11247 Madison Pike. Bryson was inducted on September 29, 1942, in the Army's 14th Brigade, 5th Regiment, as an artillery captain. He landed in France on September 16, 1944, three months after D-Day, and saw action there and in Germany. His regiment was surrounded in Bastogne, France, and saved by General Patton's forces. (Karen Fisk Koch.)

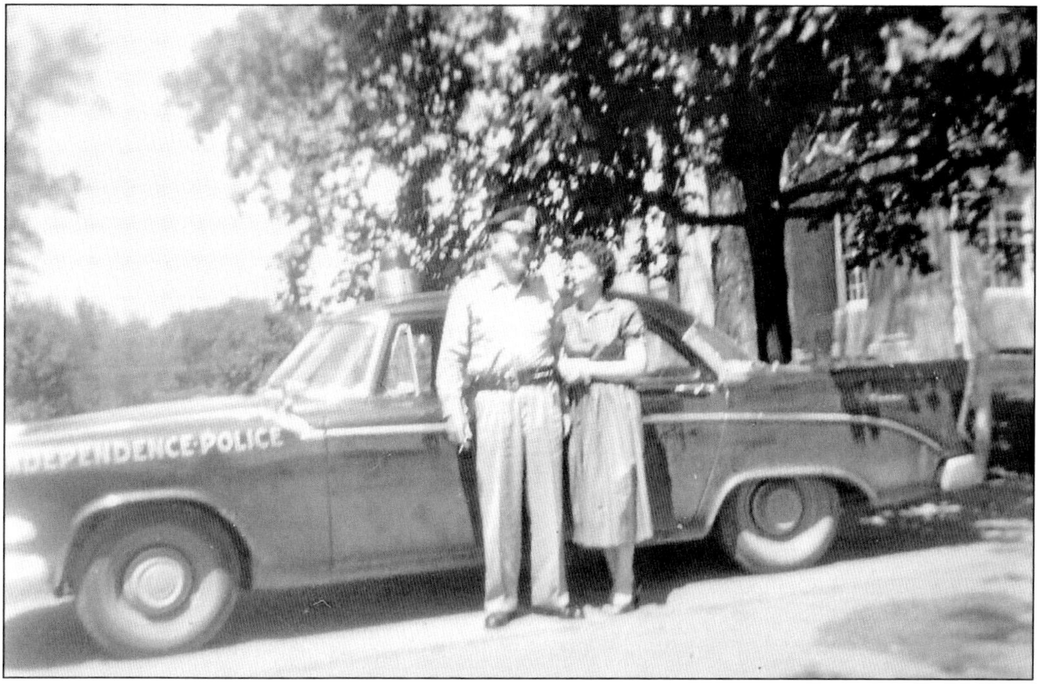

Independence police chief John Brown stands with his wife in front of his cruiser, with the courthouse in the right background. He was chief from around 1954 to 1959. Until the 1960s, Independence had either part-time officers, a full-time officer who provided part-time protection, or no officer at all. If people needed police assistance when no one was on duty, they typically tried calling the officer at his home. The Independence town marshal, Col. Nicholas Hopperton, was killed in the line of duty on November 8, 1902. (City of Independence Police Department.)

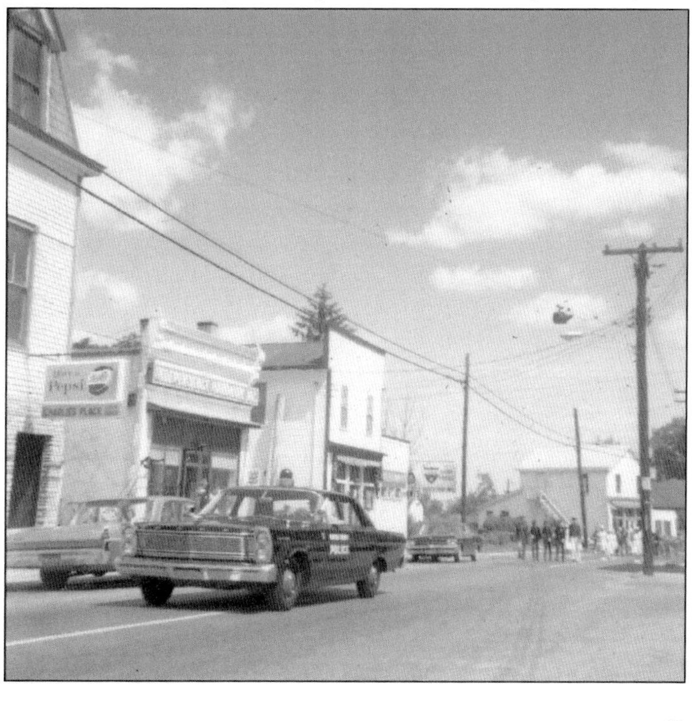

When Independence police were not on duty or able to respond, the Kenton County Police provided back up. A Kenton County police cruiser participates in this May 30, 1965, Memorial Day parade. The sign on the left reads "Charlie's Place," and next to it is Independence Hardware. (Eunice Mershon.)

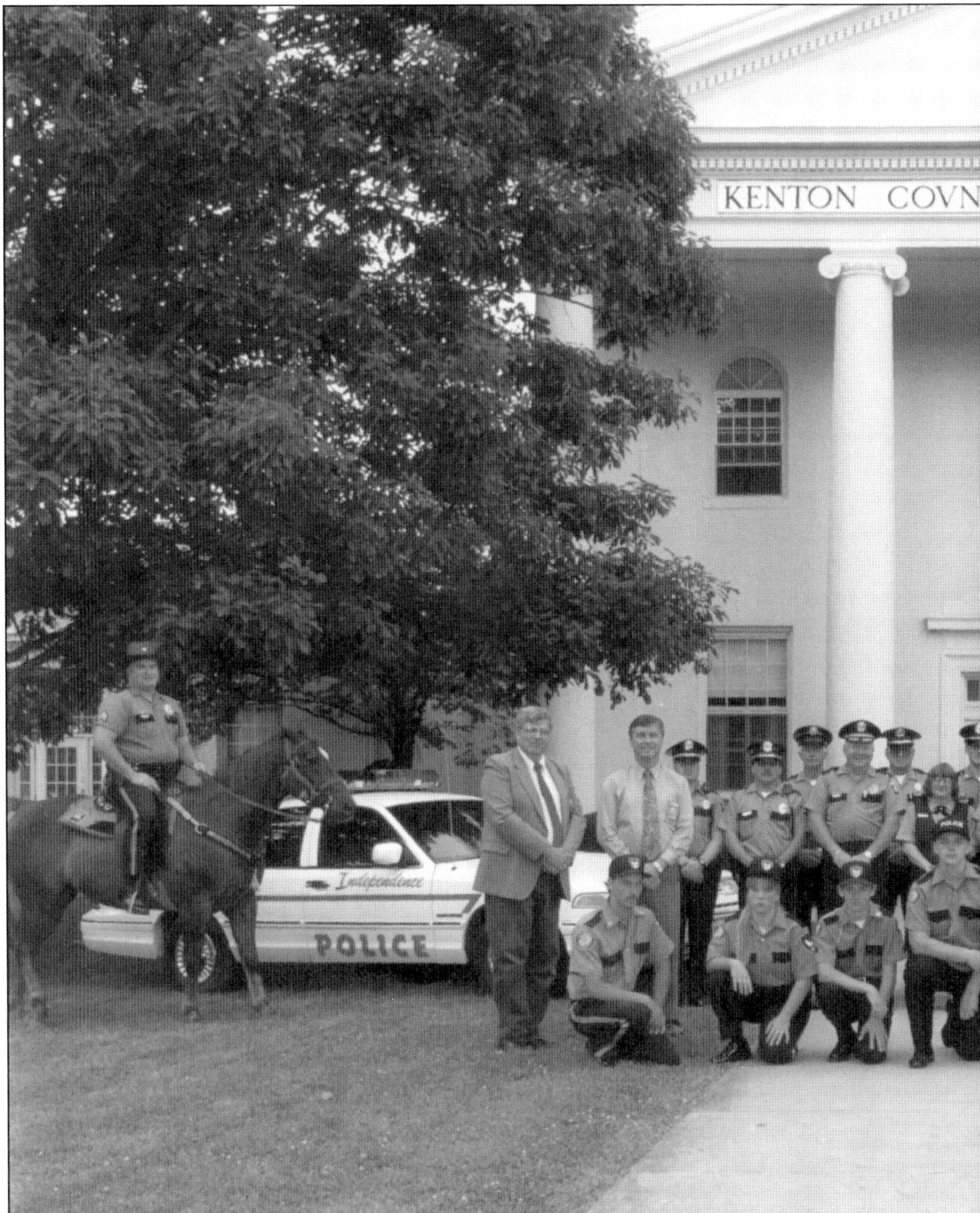

The Independence Police Department poses around 1994 along with their modes of patrol—horse, bicycle, and cruiser. This full-time professional police force provides 24/7 police protection to the large and growing city. A low crime rate is one of the many attributes attracting residents to the city. The iconic Kenton County Courthouse constructed in 1912 serves as the backdrop of this photograph. Pictured from left to right are (first row) unidentified Teenage Police Explorers; (second row) Brian Butler on a horse, chaplain Rev. Charles Steeger, chaplain Bill Risher, Anthony

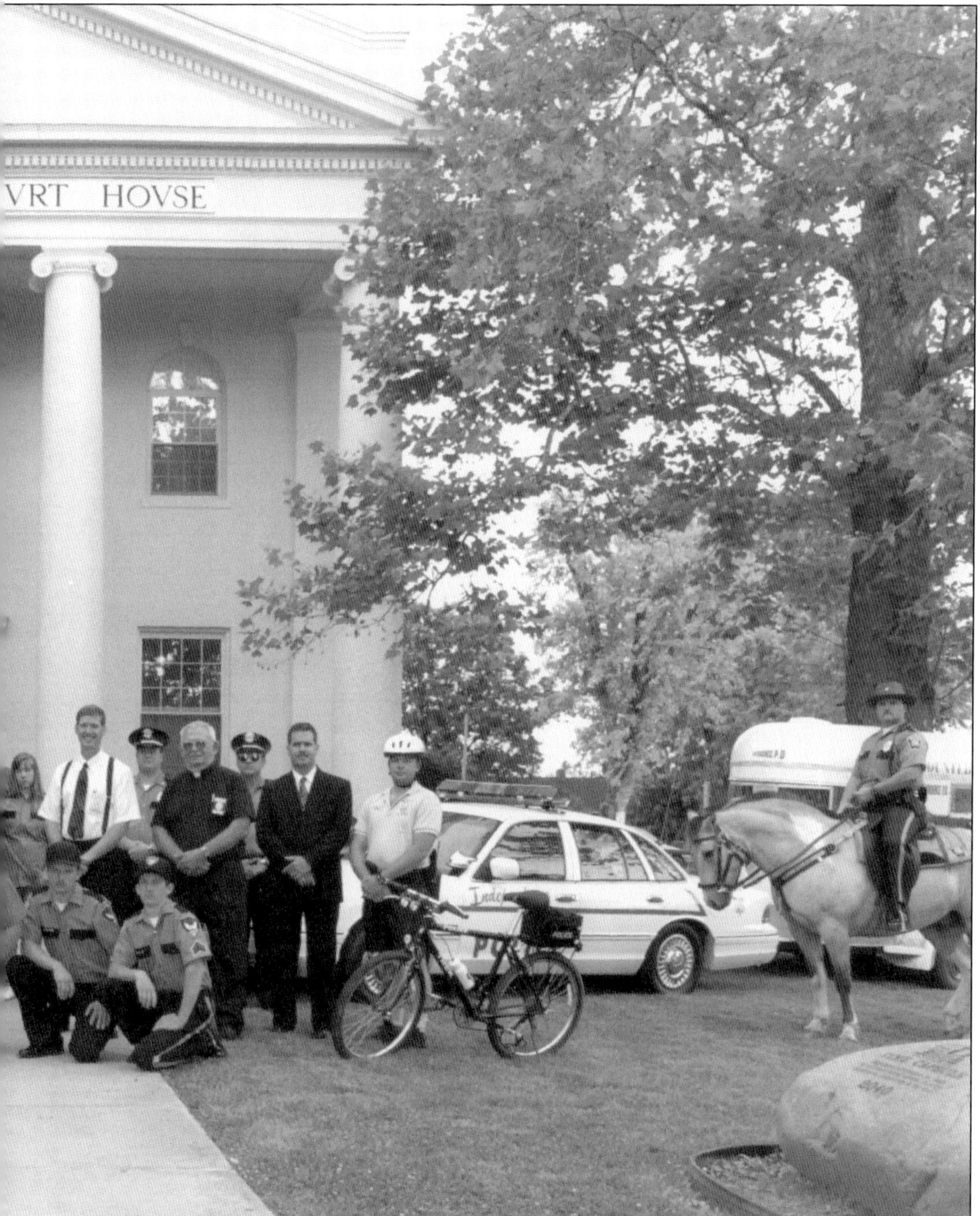

J. Lucas, Mark Hampton, Howard Goodrich, Chief Charles T. Donaldson, Bill Breeze, secretary Nancy Slusher, Todd Massey, Capt. Bill Howard, an unidentified Teenage Police Explorer holding the reins of the horse, chaplain Rev. Scott Paul, Shawn Butler, chaplain Fr. Dave Shockey, Bob Henry, Detective Rick Smith, Ed Bailey, and Phil Dunford on a horse. (City of Independence Police Department.)

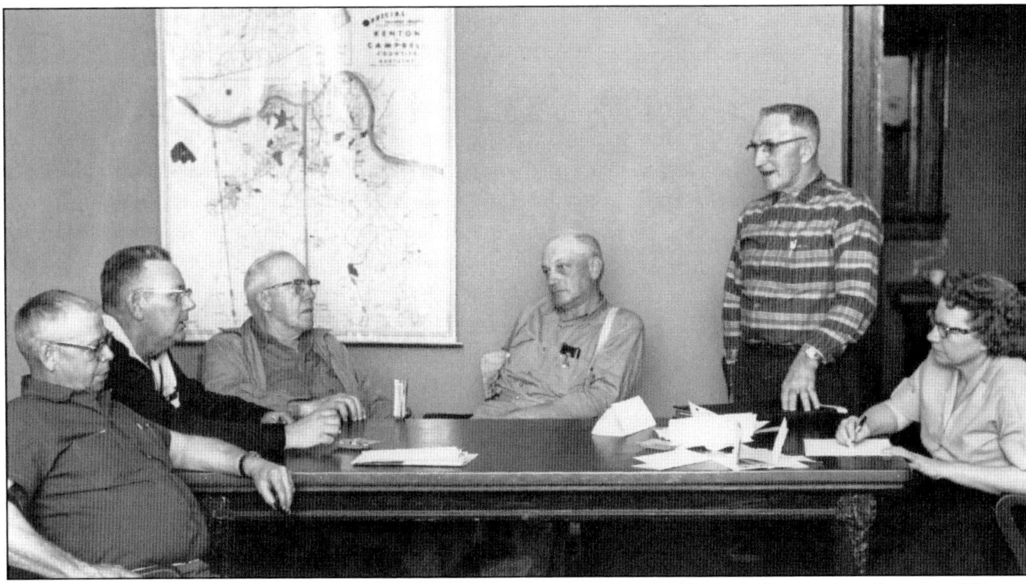

The Independence Board of Trustees is shown in session in 1961. From left to right, they are Harvey Stewart, Bill Steiger, Clifford Coleman, William Bach Sr., chairman Goebel Armstrong, and city clerk Virginia Coleman Watson, daughter of Clifford Coleman. They met in the courtroom of the courthouse on the second Monday of the month and were the equivalent of today's city council. (Virginia Coleman Watson.)

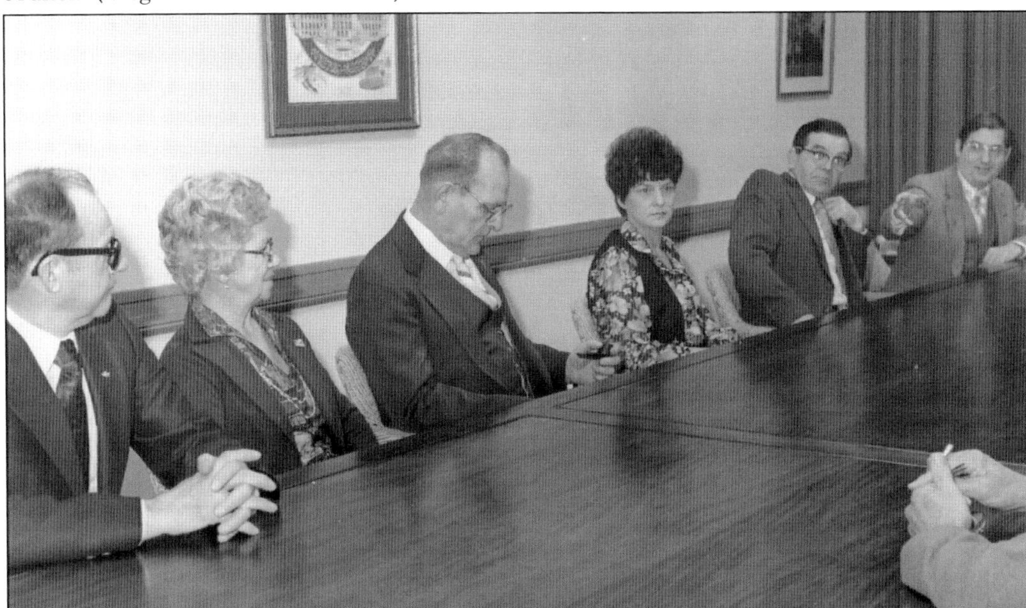

Independence City Council went to Frankfort in the 1970s to sign papers for a loan from the state. From left to right are council members Ken Blake, Dolores Richardson, Preston Tillett, Teresa Wishman, Mayor Marion Schadler, and city attorney G. Wayne Bridges. Not pictured, but also on council and present, were Norb Schoborg and Jack Williams. Thanks are expressed to all who have served and continue to serve this city, community, and nation in the capacities represented in this chapter. (Marion Schadler.)

Four

Faces and Places

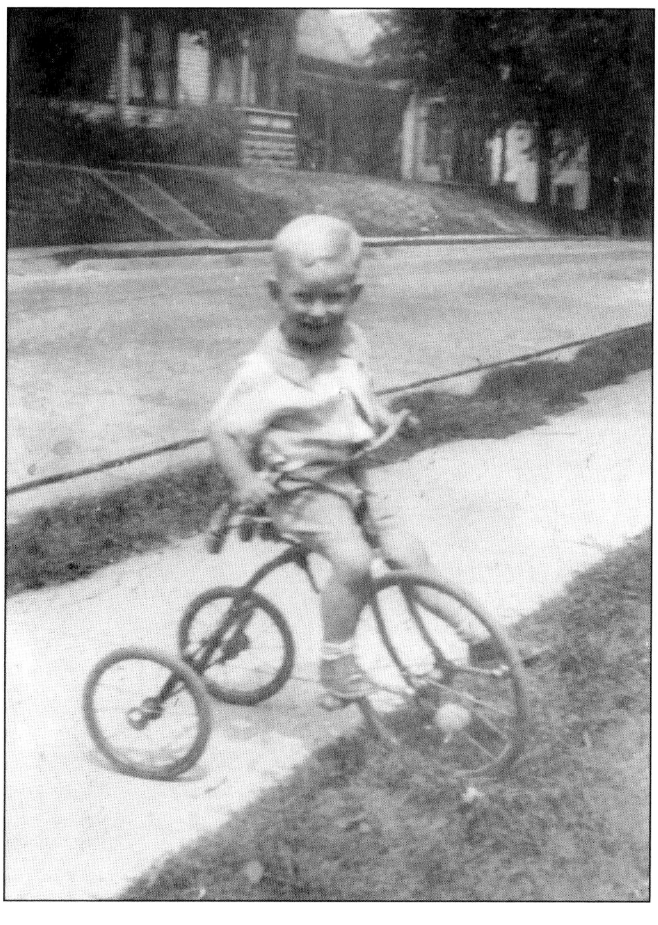

Randall Wagner takes a ride on his tricycle in 1931 outside his home in Independence. The Metcalf-Stephens House at 5241 Madison Pike is behind him to the left. He was the Independence mail carrier from 1951 to 1985, and for the first seven years, he was the only carrier needed. For the tireless efforts of Randall and his wife, Patsy, in support of Simon Kenton athletics, they are two of the four namesakes of the Cook-Wagner Fieldhouse, dedicated to them on February 21, 2011, and located on the Simon Kenton High School campus. (Randall Wagner.)

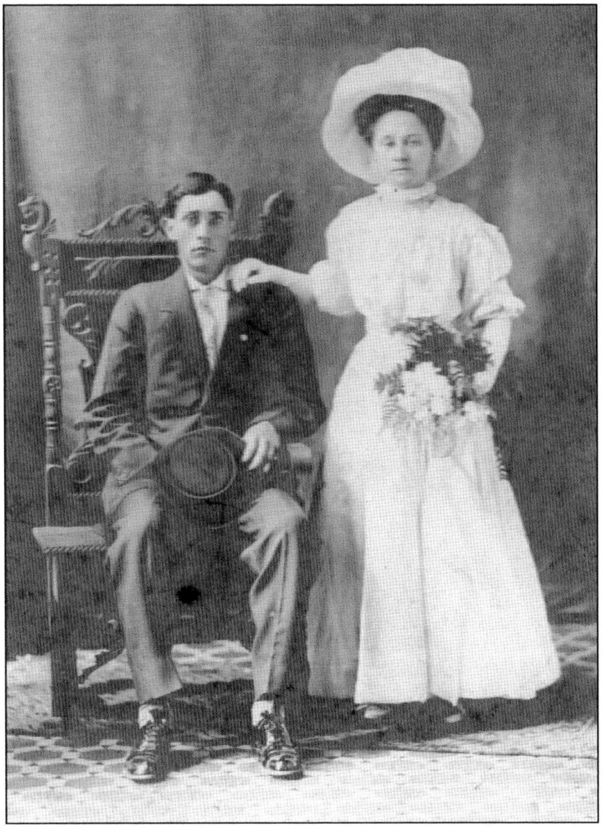

Apple Acres on Independence Station Road was owned and operated by Bryan and Sally Terry Armstrong, shown here in their early 1920s wedding picture. This orchard and farm was later operated by their daughter, Wanda Ballmer. (J.B. Losey.)

Samuel Folmer took this image of the building of the Louisville and Nashville Railroad on a hillside on Richardson Road at an uncertain date but no later than early 1900s, probably in the late 1800s. Most of the workers shown here were African Americans. (Doris Wicklund King.)

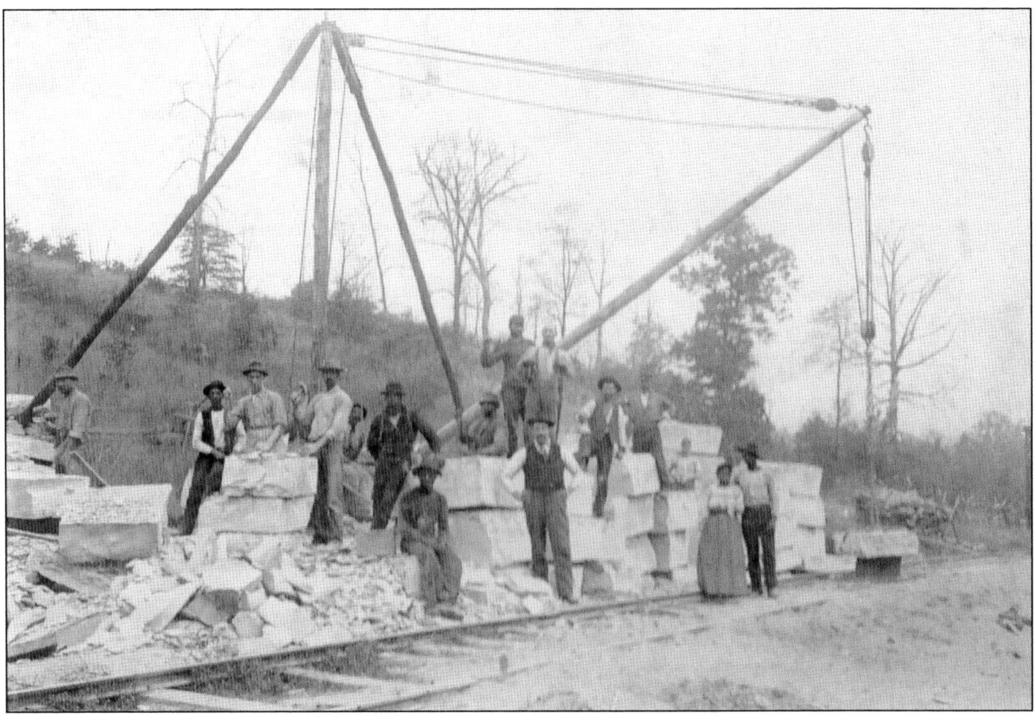

Albert Benjamin "Happy" Chandler is campaigning for the US Senate in front of the courthouse in 1938. He ran for the seat in 1938 and lost, won in the 1940 special election, and won a full term in 1942. He served two terms as Kentucky governor in 1935 and 1955 and was baseball commissioner from 1945 to 1951, overseeing the integration of baseball. The sign to his right reads "Chandler, Senator" next to a picture of President Roosevelt. He is standing on a 1937 Ford flatbed truck owned by Hobart Bridges, and the rails of it are at the bottom of the image. (Wendel Bridges.)

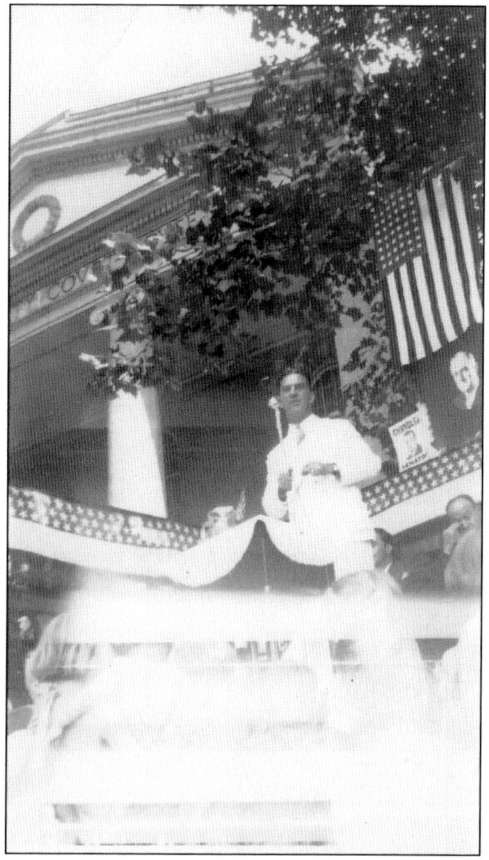

At a family gathering in the mid-1930s at the Ervin house at 5235 Madison Pike (existing) are, from left to right, (first row) Dolores Wagner (Williams), Norman Williams, Randall Wagner, Paul Keeling, baby Ted Darlington, and two unidentified children; (second row) Ted Darlington, Mildred Darlington, unidentified, Anna Laura Webster, unidentified, Dorothy Perkins, Elsie Davis Tippett, Tillie Petty, unidentified, Sadie Wagner, Mildred Riley Thornton, Floyd Armstrong, Lillian Smith, Emma Perkins, Lillian Riley, unidentified, Beulah Pickett, Russell Riley, Wanda Smith (girl, standing), Auline Ervin, and Alta Mae Keeling. (Randall Wagner.)

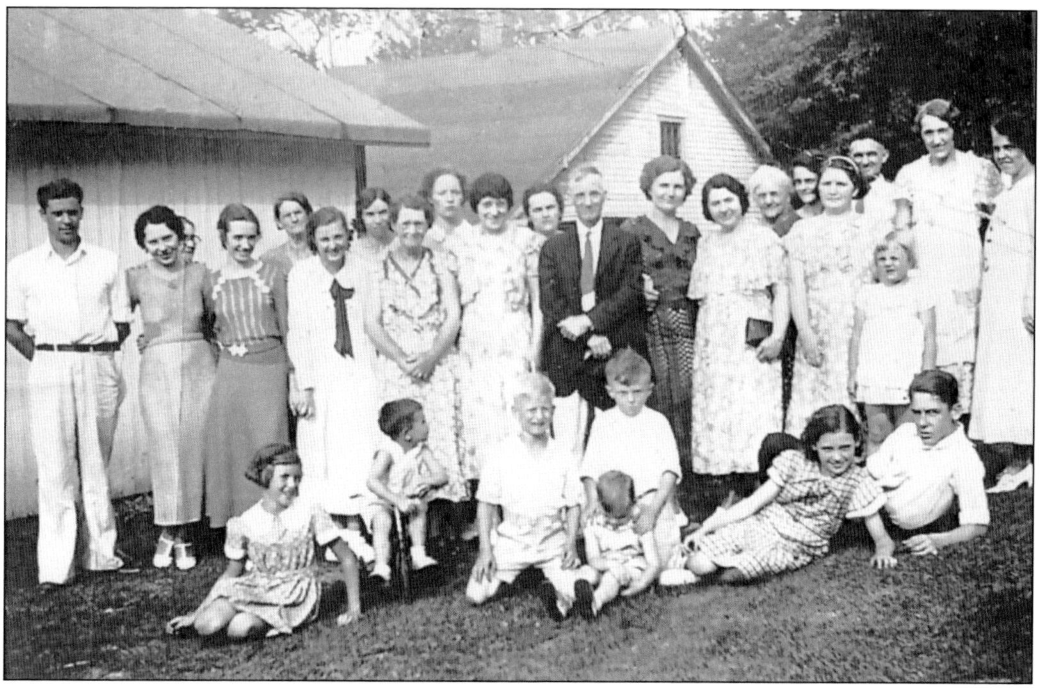

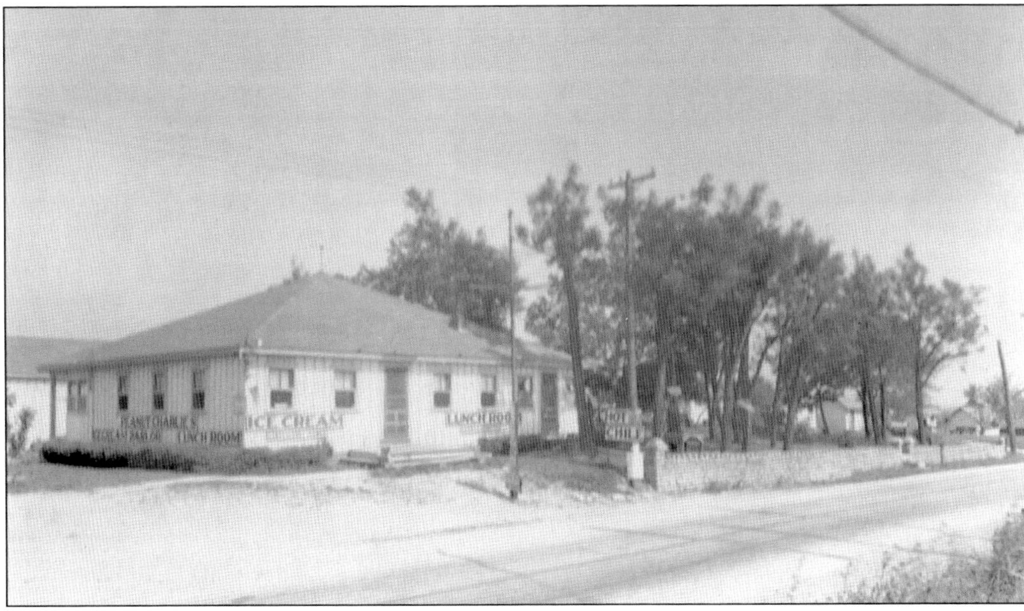

Charles and Mary Stephens operated a tourist camp for 32 years known as Peanut Charlie's about where the post office is now located on Madison Pike. Their farm is now the site of Liberty Orchard subdivision. Pictured around 1920 is the restaurant, which featured fried chicken dinners. The signs on the front read "Ice Cream" and "Lunchroom." The sign on the pole says "Hot Chili." (Bob and Thelma Gibson.)

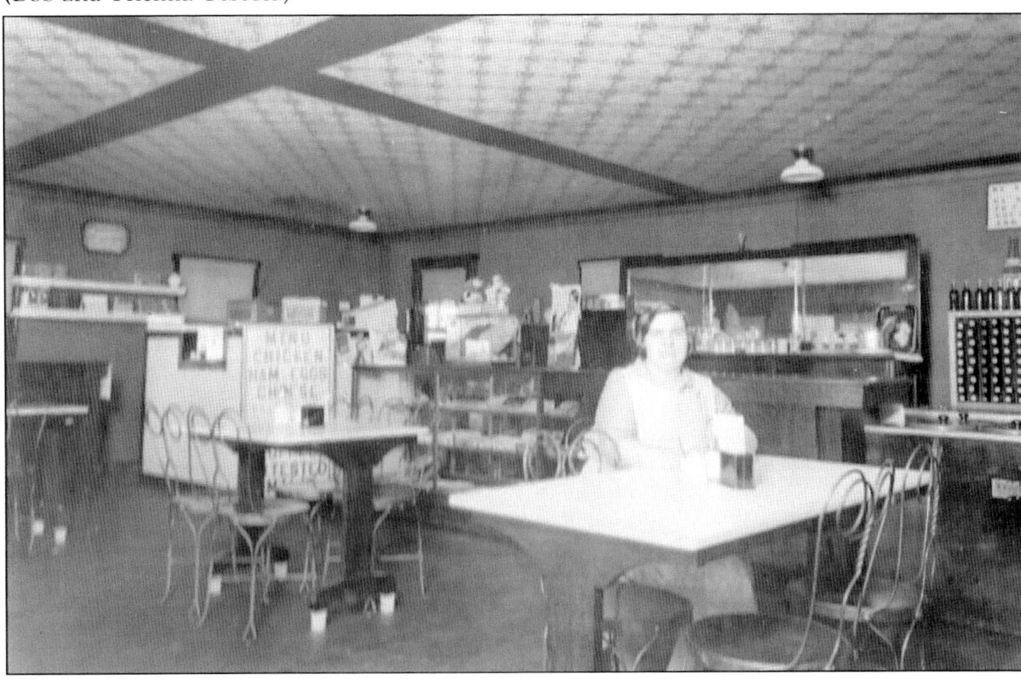

The Stephenses' daughter, Mary Esther, worked in the lunchroom store, where she is pictured around 1920. The sign at left center reads "Menu Chicken Ham Eggs." They advertised "Delightful Home Cooking," "Chicken Dinners by Appointment," and "Sandwiches a Specialty." (Bob and Thelma Gibson.)

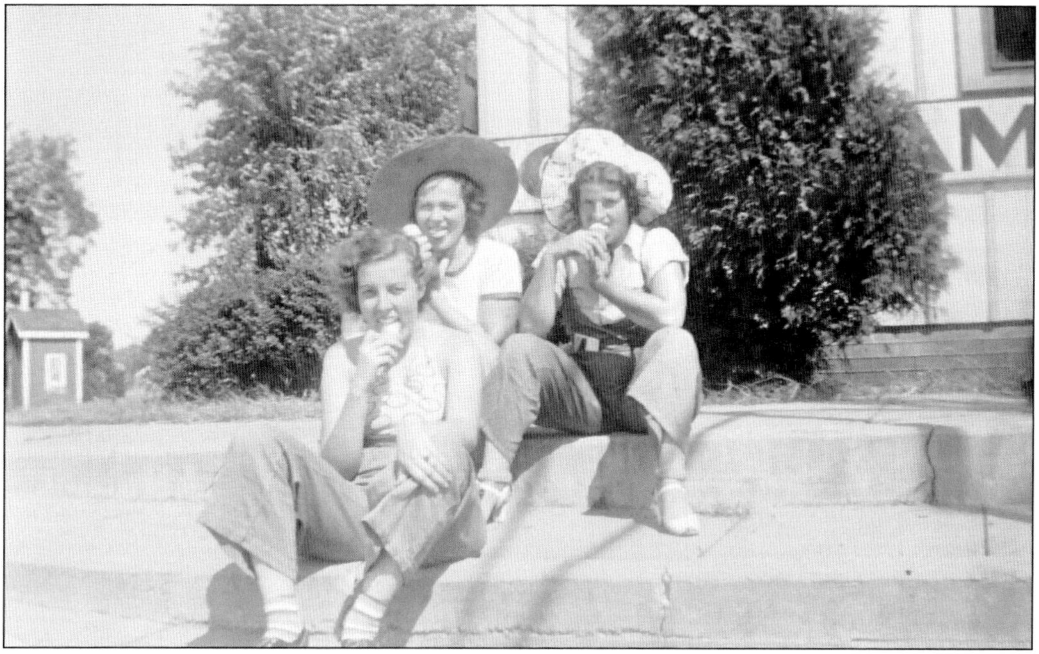

These girls—Annabelle Ballard (front), Susie Glass, and Minnie Letcher (right)—are enjoying the ice cream advertised behind them at Peanut Charlie's in the 1930s. On the far left is an outhouse. (Janet Glass Kreidler.)

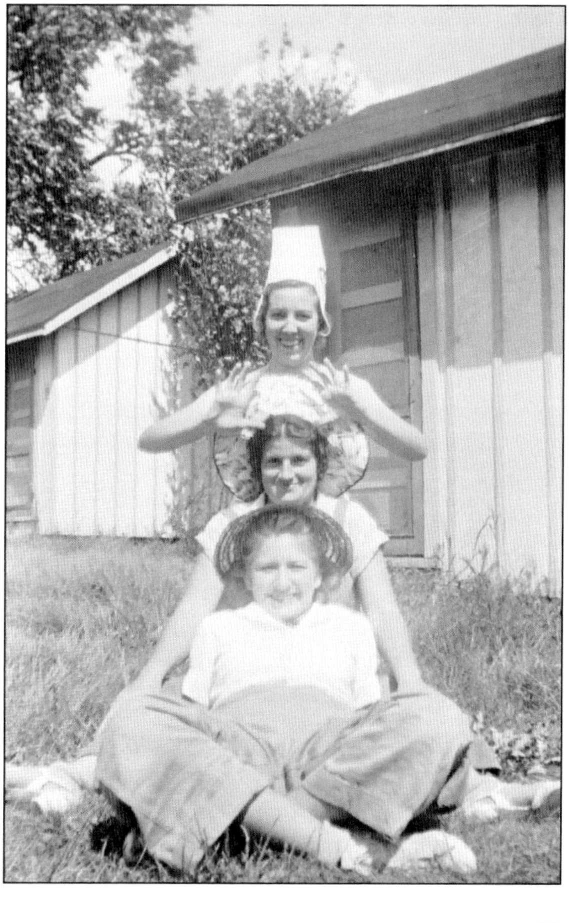

The tourist camp had 10 cabins available for travelers to rent. They advertised "Furnished Camp Rooms," "Comfortable Beds," and "Light, Heat, and Water." Some local girls pose in front of two of the cabins in the 1930s; from front to back are Anna Kathryn Glass, Minnie Letcher, and Annabelle Ballard. (Janet Glass Kreidler.)

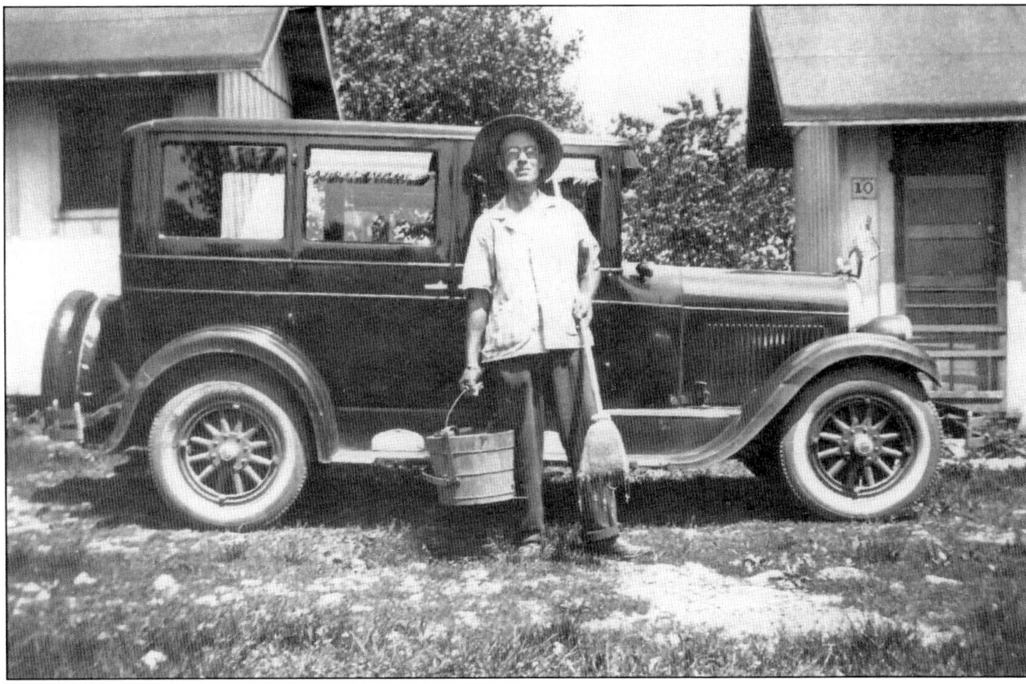

Charlie Stephens, also known as "Peanut Charlie," stayed busy at the tourist camp; here in the 1930s, he is getting ready to mop some cabins. Peanut Charlie's also featured three fishing lakes. (Bob and Thelma Gibson.)

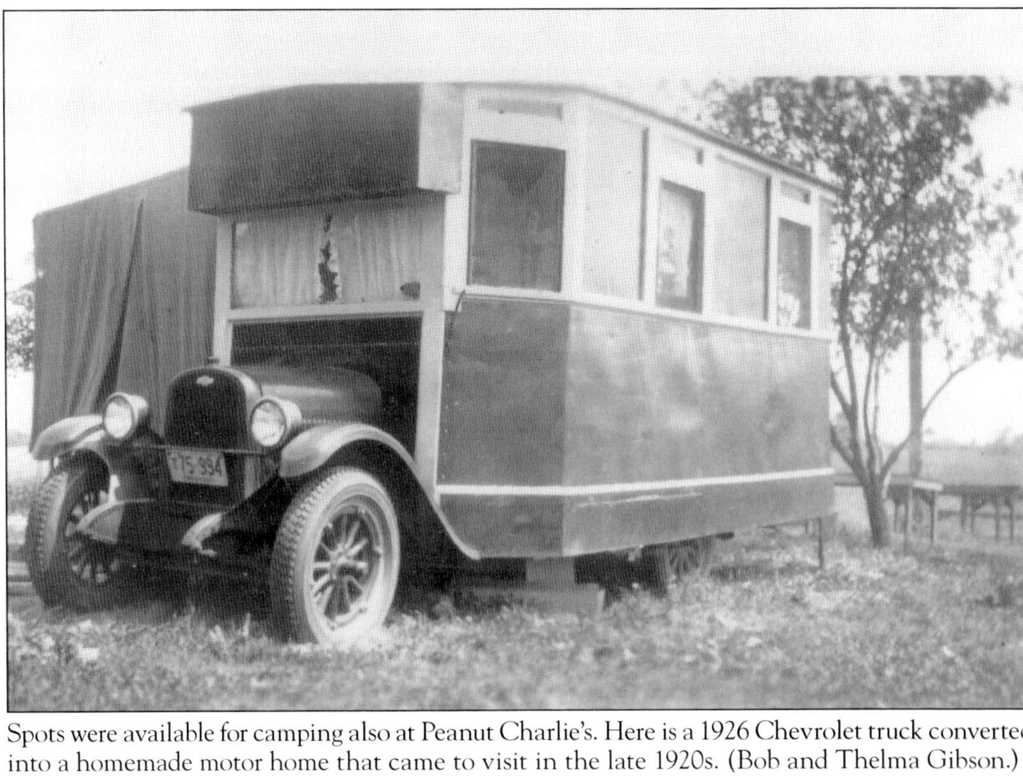

Spots were available for camping also at Peanut Charlie's. Here is a 1926 Chevrolet truck converted into a homemade motor home that came to visit in the late 1920s. (Bob and Thelma Gibson.)

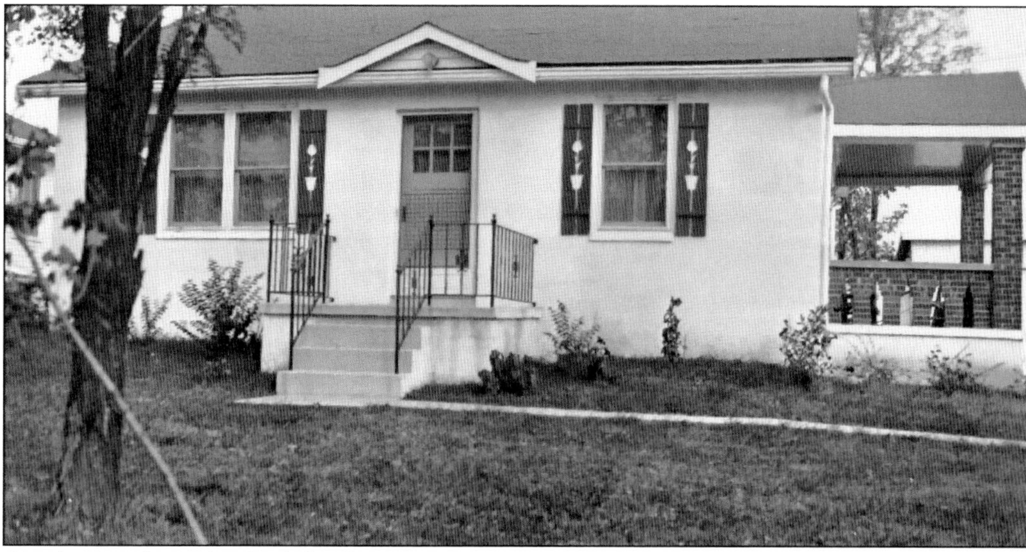

Charles Stephens finished this home at 5190 Madison Pike in 1949 and then lived there. It is shown in the early 1950s. The home was razed and a new home constructed in 2003. (Bob and Thelma Gibson.)

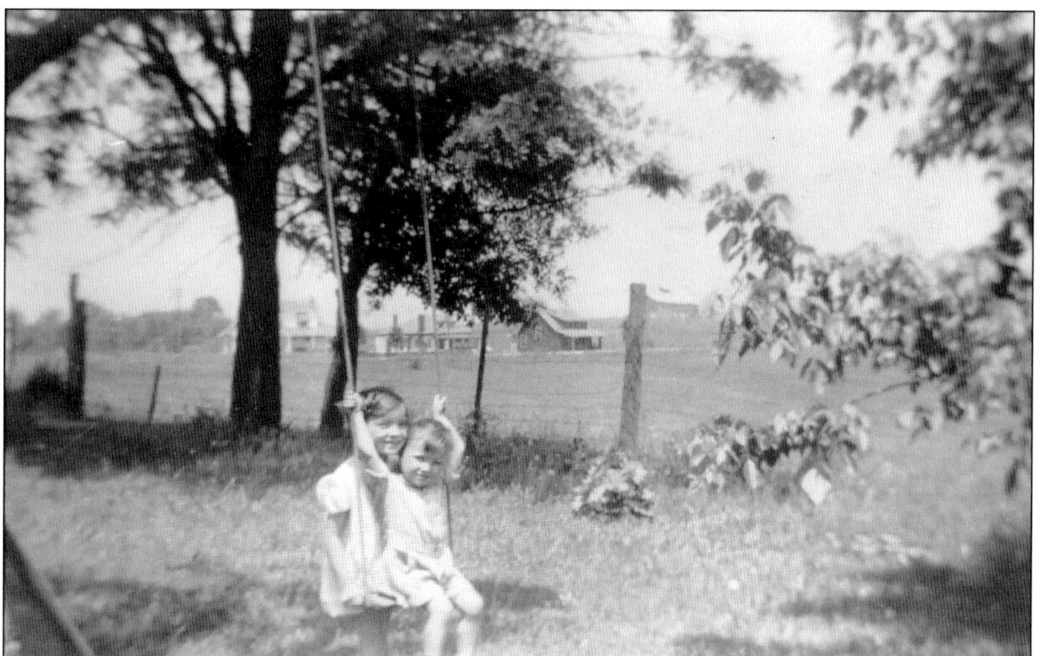

Barbara Giles (Gabbard) swings her brother Lee around 1940 at their home on McKim Drive. The Stephenses' farm is in the background. Barbara served on the Independence City Council from 1997 to 2000. She married Isaac "Ike" Gabbard, who served as mayor of Independence from 1994 to 1998 and served a term on the council from 2001 to 2002. (Barbara Giles Gabbard.)

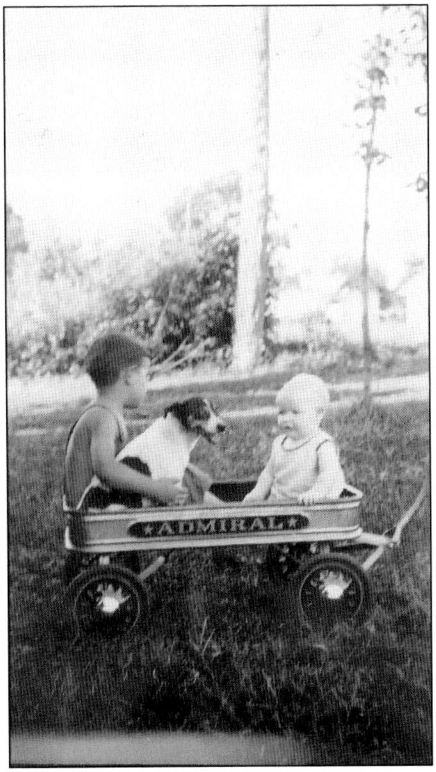

Brothers Billy (left) and Bob Gibson and their dog Spot go for a wagon ride about 1935. They are in their front yard at 5113 Madison Pike. (Bob and Thelma Gibson.)

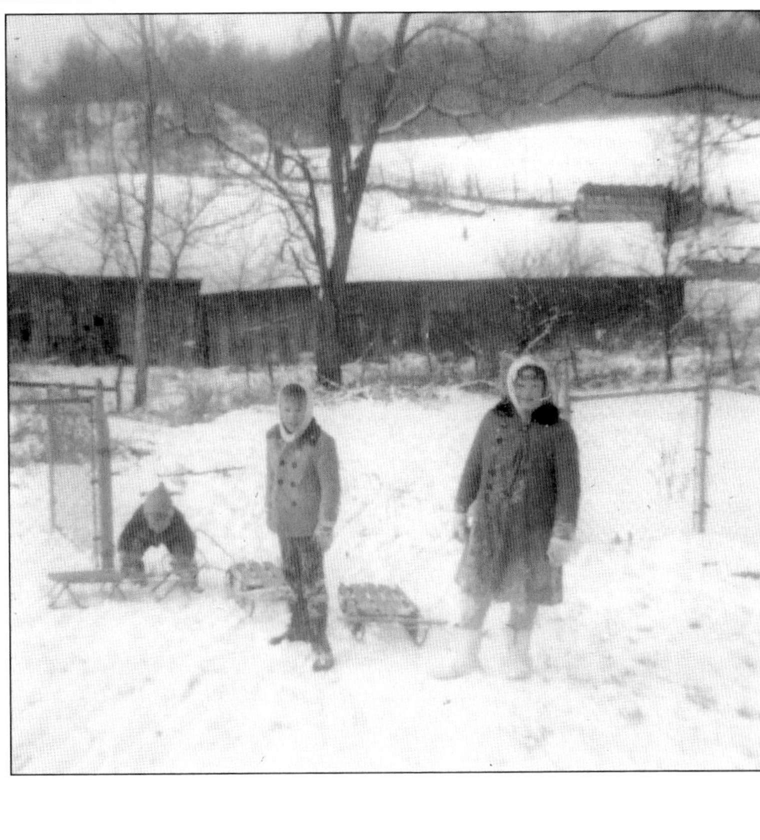

From left to right, siblings Michael, Rob, and Brenda Gibson (Harrison) play in the snow in their backyard at 5123 Madison Pike around 1970. Parents Bob and Thelma Gibson still live there. The sheds in the background are now Nicole Drive in the Independence Ridge subdivision. (Bob and Thelma Gibson.)

Playing in the side yard of the Tippett home around 1923 are, from left to right, unidentified, Arta Mae Tippett, and sister Marie Tippett. The home was torn down and is the parking lot on the south side of Independence Christian Church. The Metcalf home and barn at 5220 Madison Pike are in the upper right background. (Kimberly M. Back.)

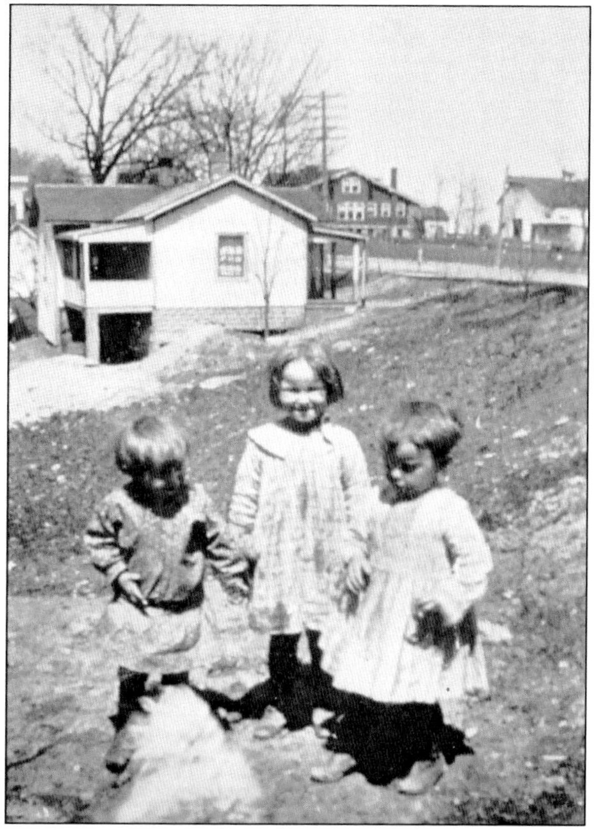

Randall Wagner, left, and Franklin Daugherty stand in front of the courthouse on a winter day in 1945. The first veterans' memorial to those serving in World War II is behind them on the left. A Kenton County Honor Roll memorial replaced it a few years later, shown on page 41. Wagner became the Independence postal carrier and Daugherty a physician. (Randall Wagner.)

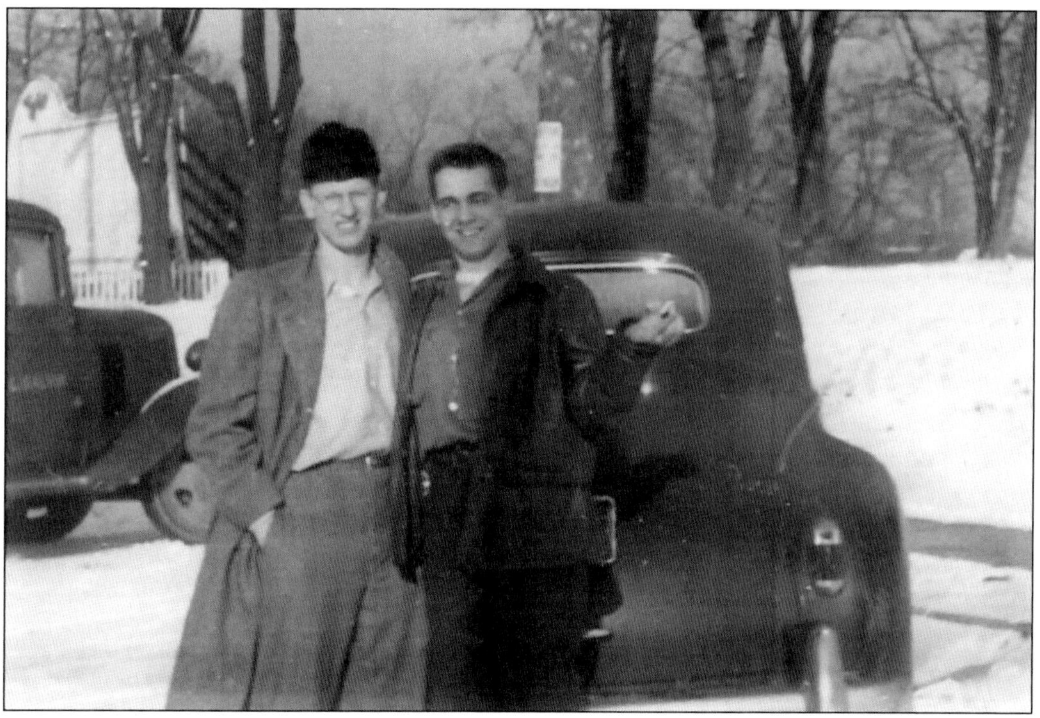

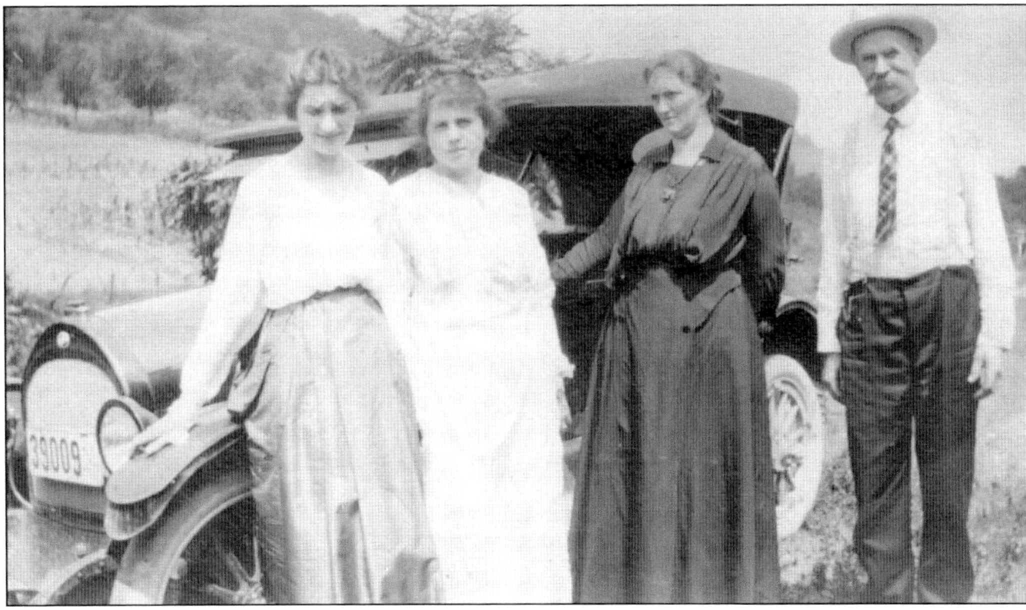

Several members of the Powers family bought this farm on the east side of the 11300 block of Madison Pike in the early 1900s. Pictured in the late 1920s are, from left to right, Albina Powers, unidentified, Mathilda Powers, and her brother Will Taphorn. (Peggy Powers Baum.)

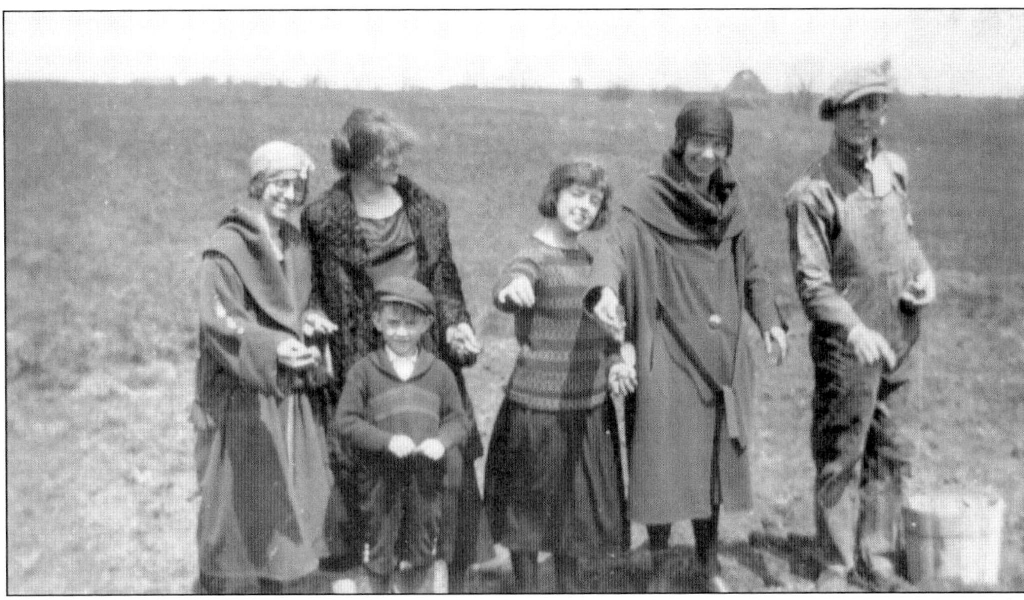

On the same Powers farm, this group is going to start sowing seed in 1925. Pictured, from left to right, are four unidentified, Marie Powers, and her brother Ambrose Powers. (Peggy Powers Baum.)

These friends are clowning at the home of E.O. Mills at 47 McCullum Road in 1928. From left to right are his daughter Margie Mills (Powers), Helen Stone (Petty), and Marie Schwall (England). They attended Independence High School together, and all three played on the 1925 girls' basketball team. (Peggy Powers Baum.)

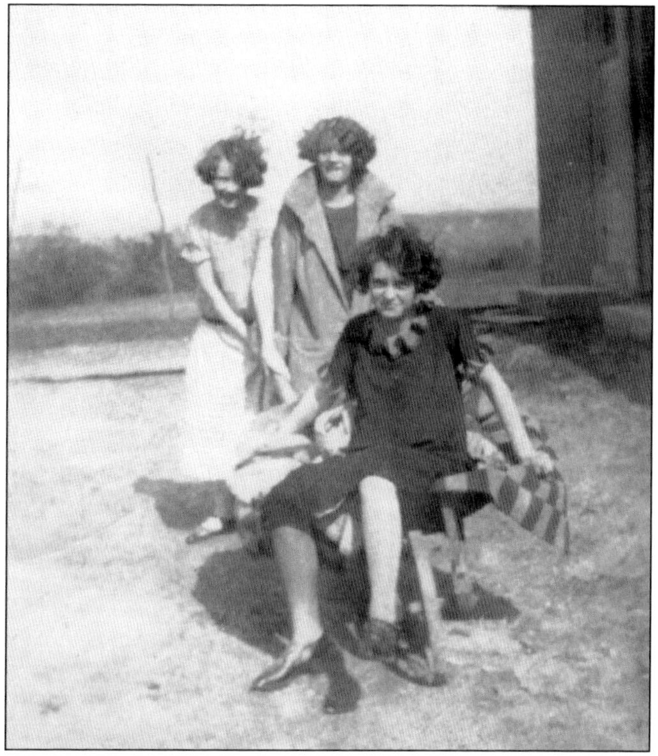

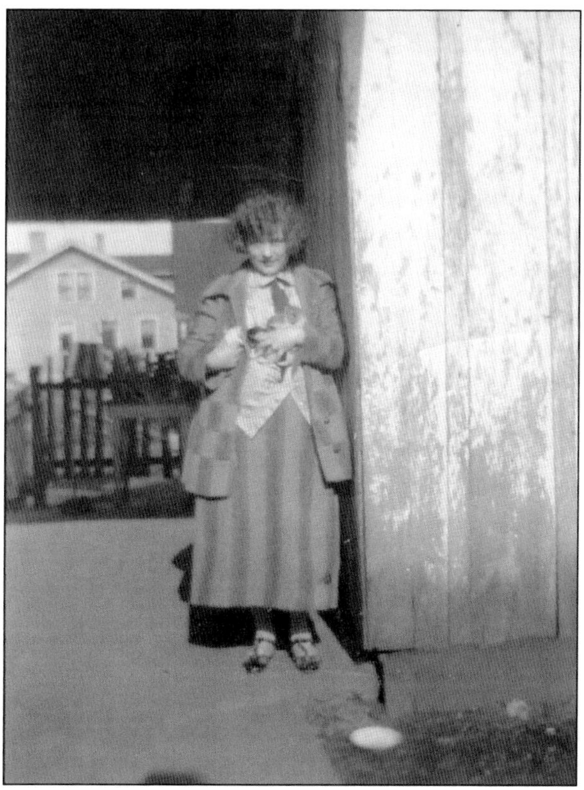

Hazel Stone (Pickett), sister of Helen (above), holds some newborn kittens in the 1920s. In the background is the home of E.O. Mills at 47 McCullum Road. She wrote a book about her life, including her time in Independence, in 1980, entitled *A Time to Keep*. In it she states she was the second baby delivered by Dr. Fred Ray, on September 18, 1904. (Peggy Powers Baum.)

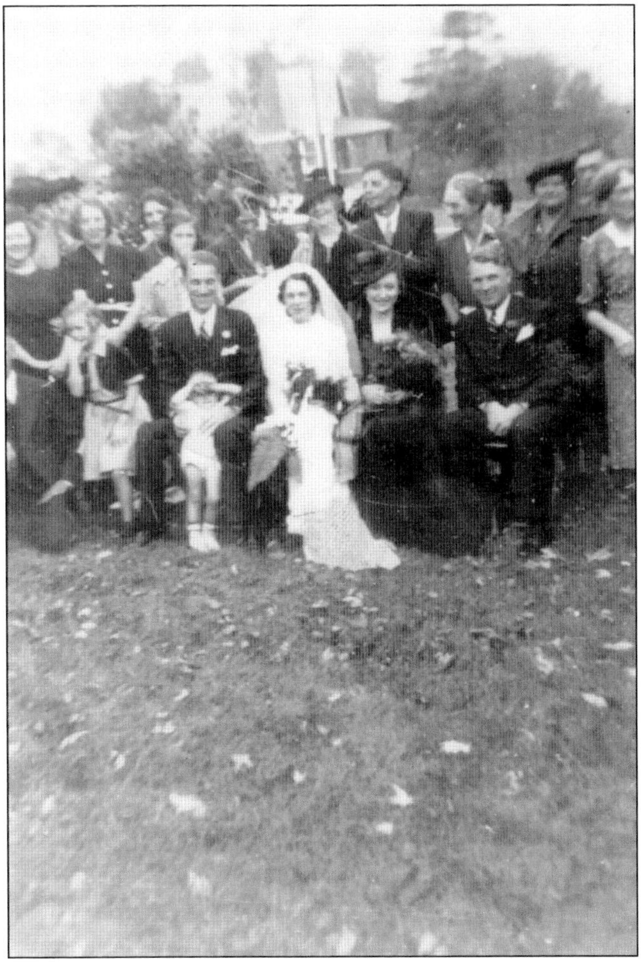

The wedding party and guests are shown at the wedding reception of Ambrose and Margie Mills Powers at 47 McCullum Road in 1939. The groom is left of the bride on the front row. The wedding was held at St. Cecilia Church. (Peggy Powers Baum.)

Enjoying a family visit around 1942 are, from left to right, (first row) brothers Rodney "Biz" and Ralph Cain; (second row) Ella B'Hymer, Caroline Cain, Wanda Garriott, Robert Cain, and Meda Garriott; (third row) Alf B'Hymer. The B'Hymers owned this home at 28 McCullum Road, still in use. (Rodney "Biz" Cain.)

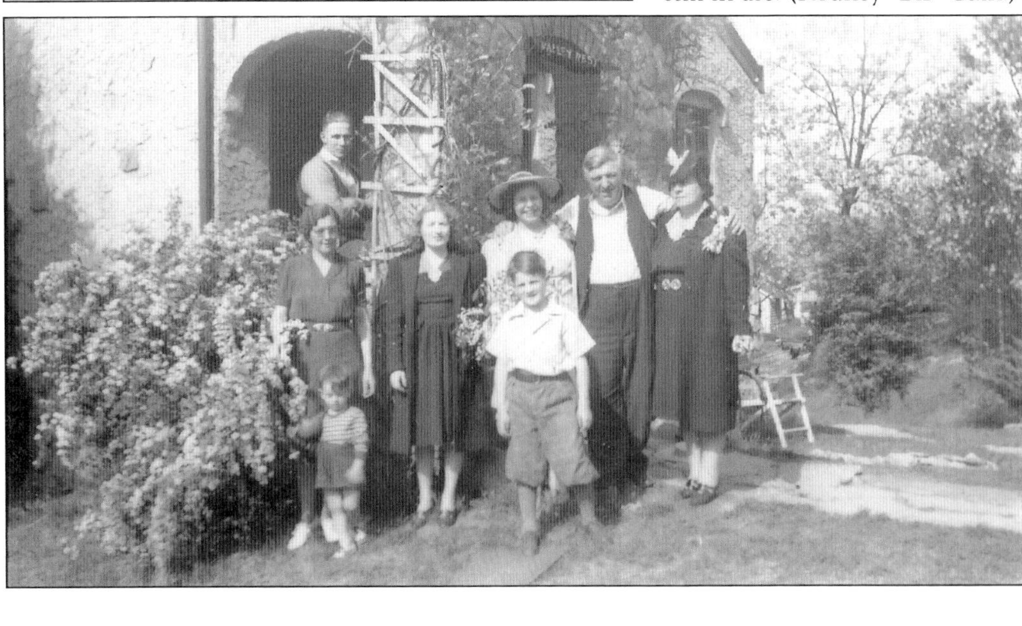

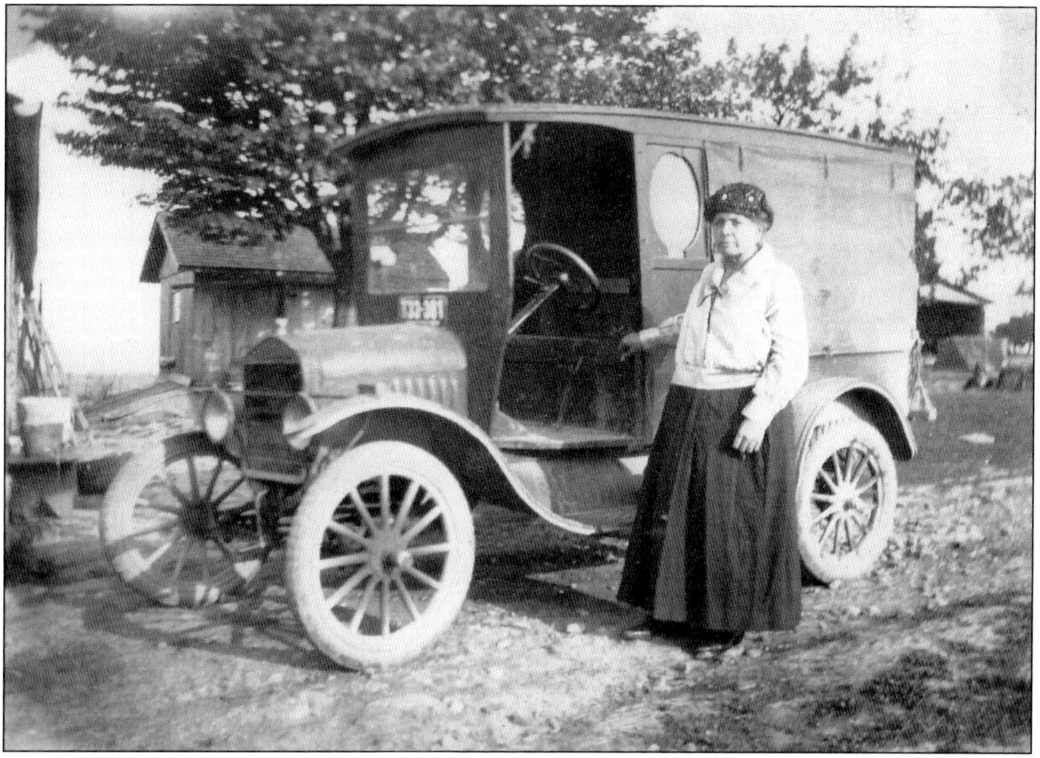

Laura Bell Webb Cain stands by a truck about 1920 at her farm at 1818 Independence Road. She is the grandmother of Rodney "Biz" Cain. (Rodney "Biz" Cain.)

Ella Mae Cain (B'Hymer) draws water from the well at the Cain farm on Independence Road in the 1920s. Water came from a cistern that drained rainwater from the roof of the home or from a well that usually had a spring in it. She married Alf B'Hymer, and they lived on Bowman Road in their later years. She lived from 1903 to 1978. (Rodney "Biz" Cain.)

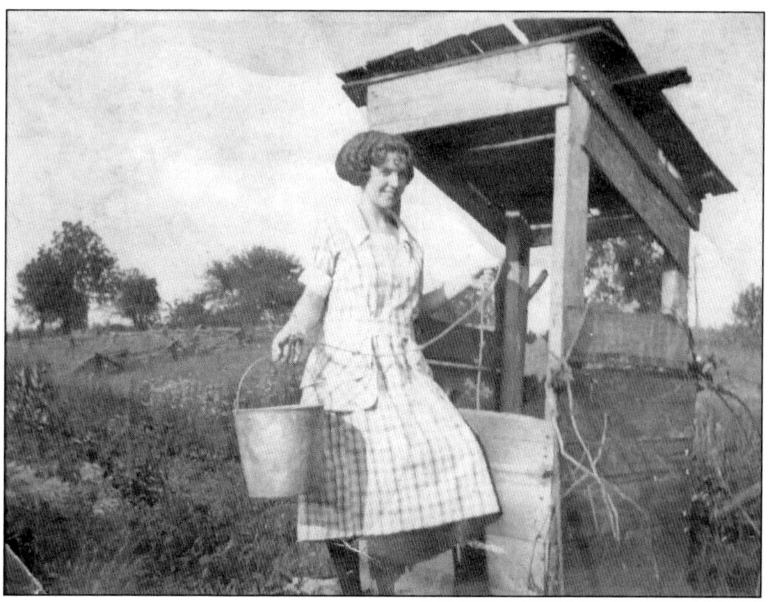

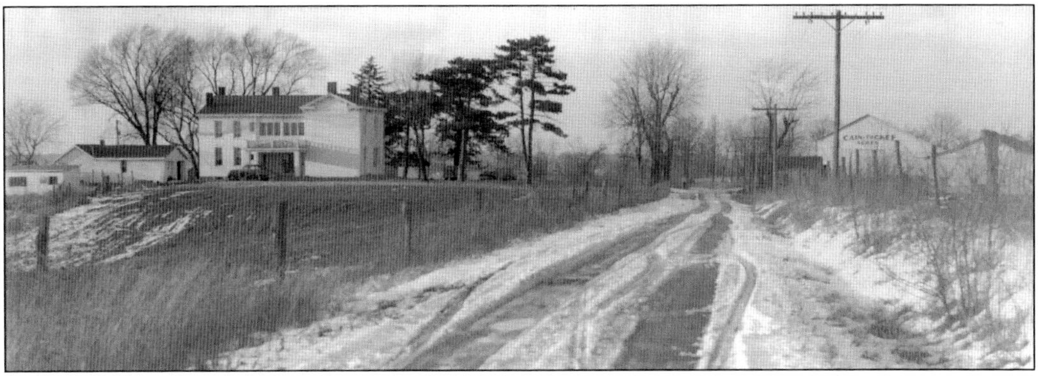

John C. Cain bought a farm at 445 Bristow Road in 1944 and named it Cain-tuckee Acres, pictured here in the mid-1940s. The house was built by the Williams family in 1861. Effie Hogrefe bought it in 1904 and sold it to the Cains. This brick home has walls 13 inches thick. It remains in the Cain family. (Rodney "Biz" Cain.)

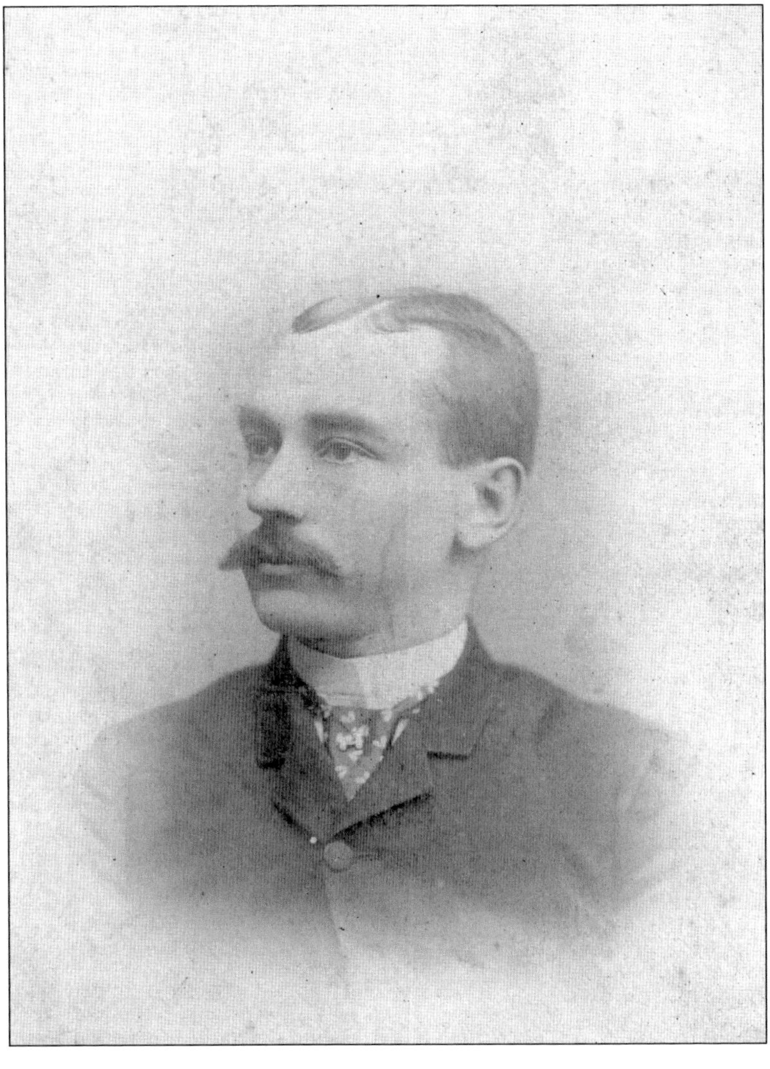

Effie Hogrefe, the second owner of the home above, is shown here around 1900. He lived from 1871 to 1945 and is buried in Independence Cemetery. He was a farmer, and Hogrefe Road is named for him. (Senator Katie Kratz Stine.)

Pictured around 1927 at the home at 445 Bristow Road are, from left to right, Effie Hogrefe, Minnie V. Daugherty, her aunt Marie Hogrefe, and unidentified. Effie Hogrefe hand-carved the solid cherry banister and hand-turned the spindles on the front staircase in this home. (Senator Katie Kratz Stine.)

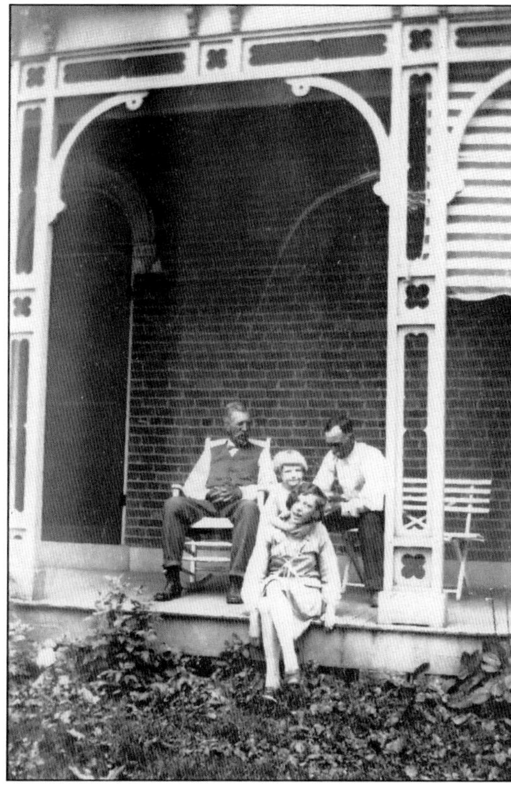

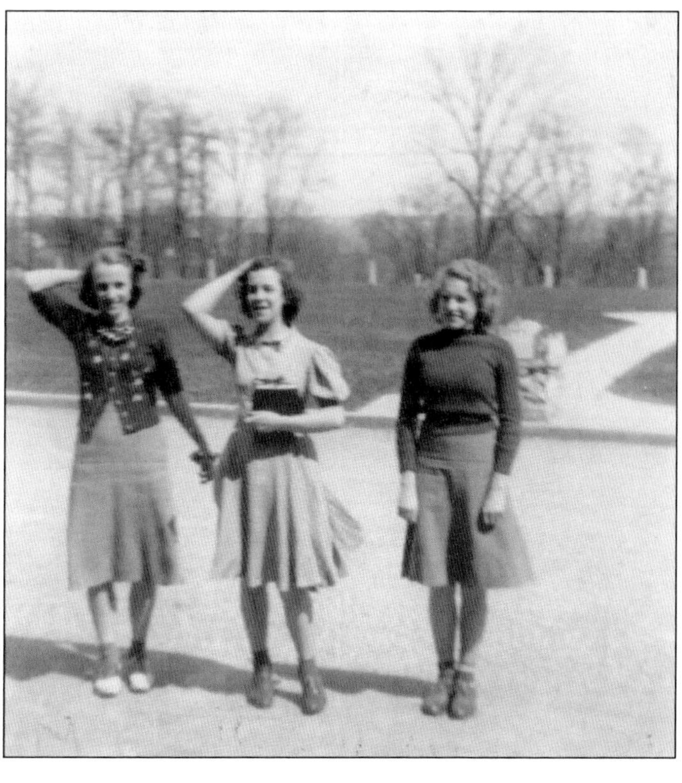

These schoolgirls in front of Simon Kenton High School around 1940 are, from left to right, Minnie V. Daugherty (Kratz), Wanda Colclough, and Virginia Klein. Daugherty graduated from the University of Cincinnati medical school and practiced for a time with her husband, Robert Kratz, in Independence. Their daughter is Senator Katie Kratz Stine, currently Kentucky Senate president pro tempore, Senate District 24. (Senator Katie Kratz Stine.)

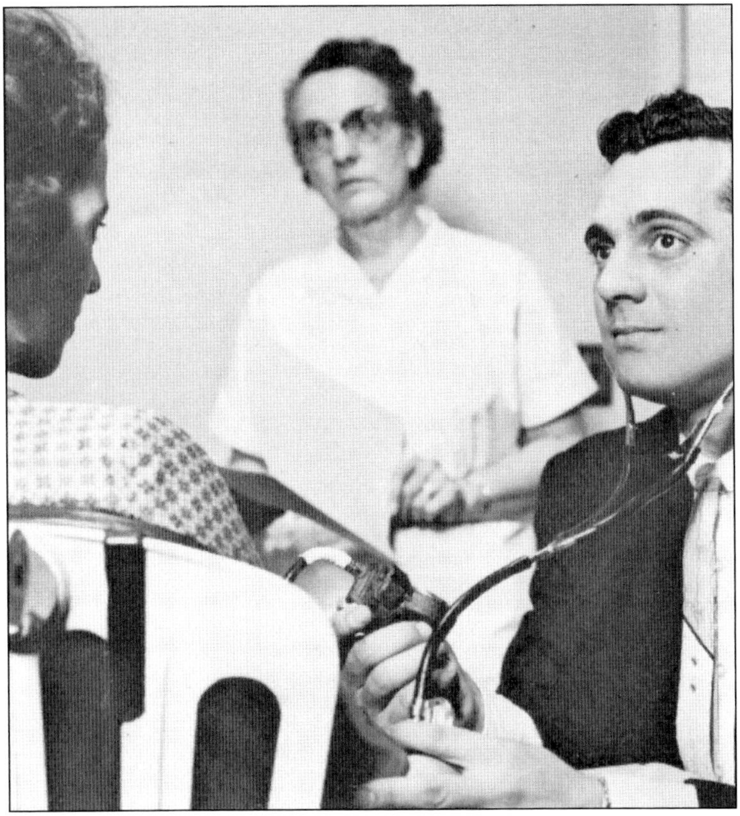

Dr. John Franklin Daugherty was the third generation of his family to practice medicine in Kenton County. At the time of this 1961 image, he traveled 150 miles a day to see 65 patients. He was one of two physicians in the city at that time. His mother, Virginia Hogrefe Daugherty, behind him, also worked in his office. (Cincinnati Bell.)

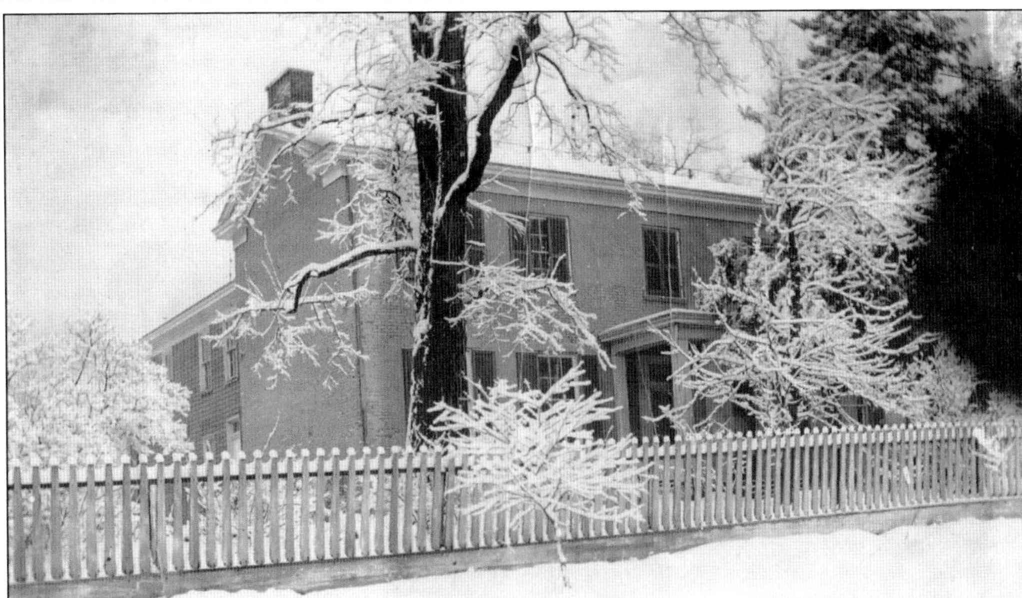

The old Folmer home at 1906 Independence Road was built around 1848 and was torn down in 1969 to construct a new home. Daniel Folmer bought this eight-room brick and frame home in 1858, and the property remains in his family. This image was taken in the 1940s. (Doris Wicklund King.)

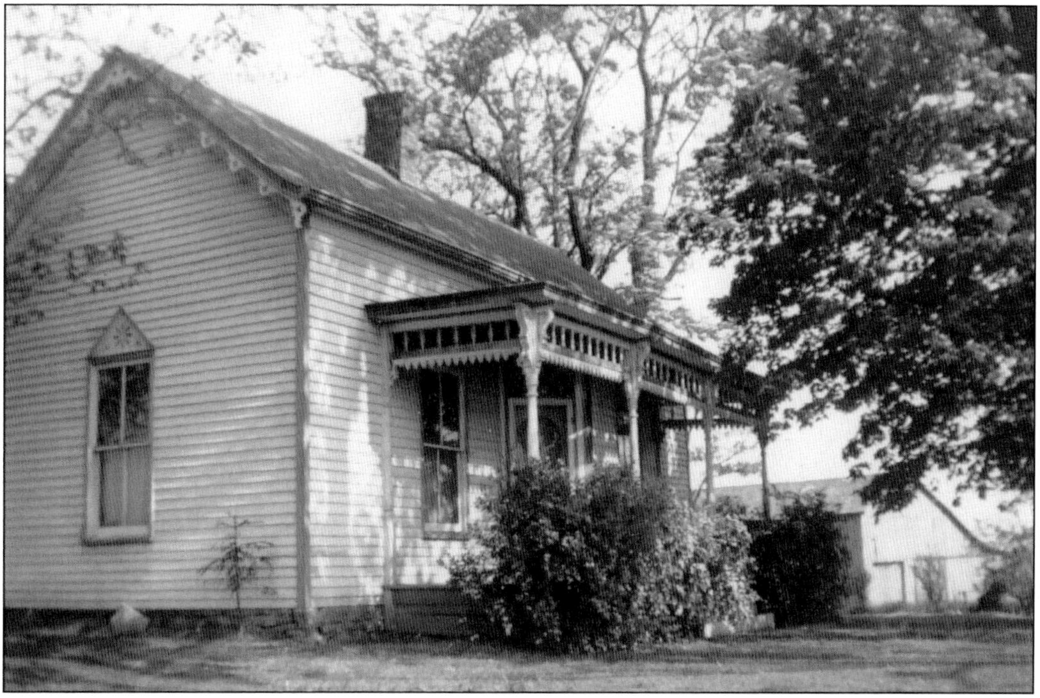

This home at the Rankin/Fisk farm at 11247 Madison Pike was constructed in the late 1800s. The barn to the south is on the right. The home was deemed sufficiently historic that the Route 17 widening, completed in 2008, avoided taking it. This image was taken on June 17, 1950. (Karen Fisk Koch.)

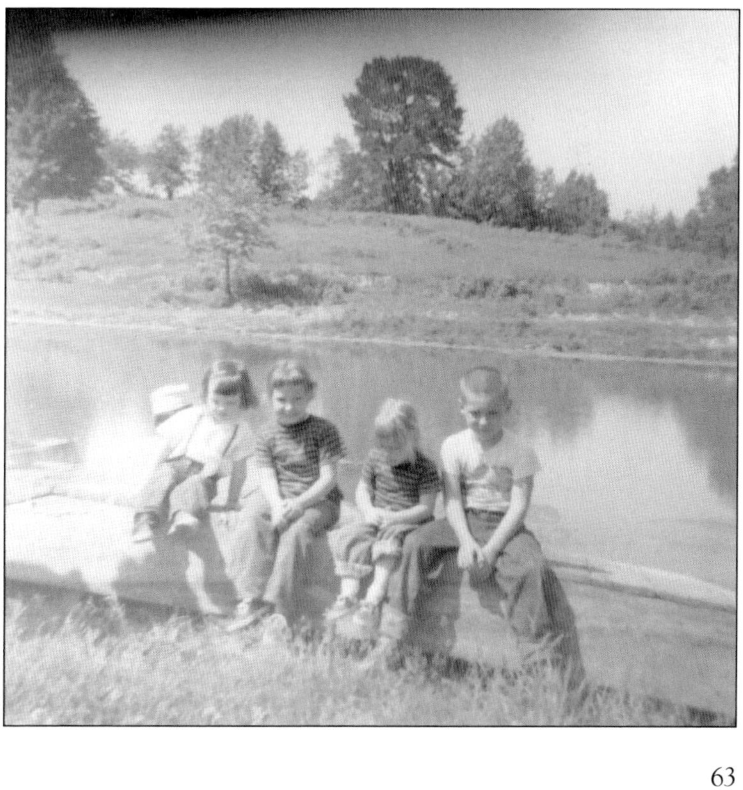

On the same Fisk farm around 1958 are, from left to right, Karen Fisk (Koch), Cheryl Osterbrook (Peebles), sister Vicki Osterbrook (Smothers), and Karen's brother, Bryson "Skip" Fisk. The lake remains on the property, as does Karen Koch. (Cheryl Osterbrook Peebles.)

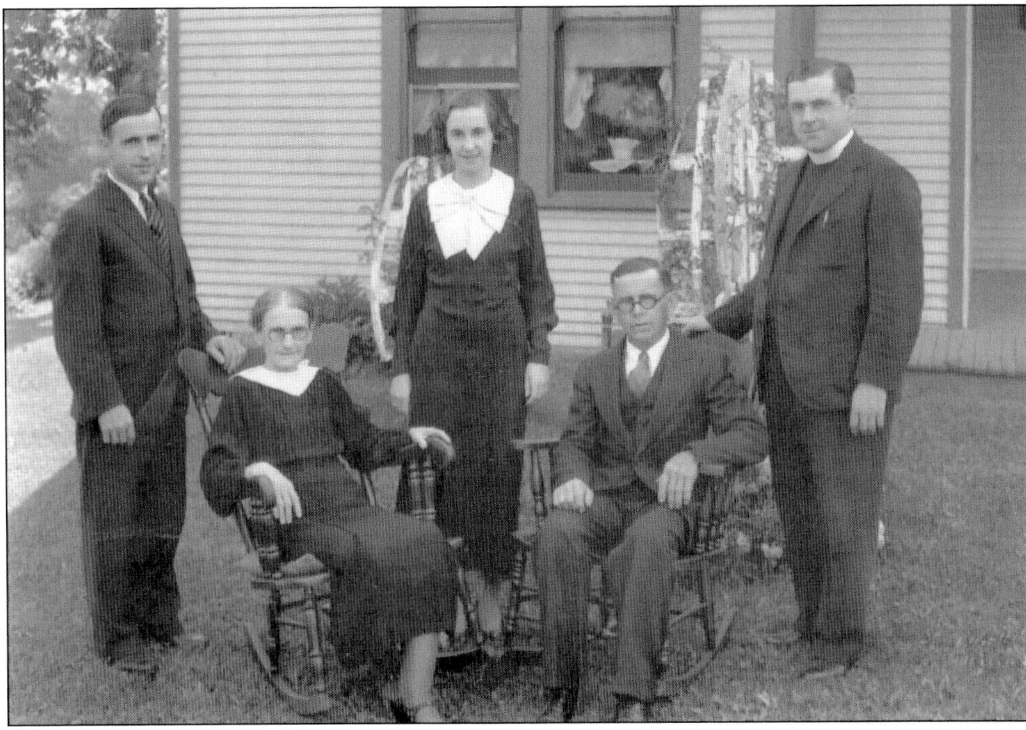

In the 1930s, the Wilson family lived on Madison Pike just north of Independence Christian Church, which eventually bought the house for a parking lot. From left to right, they are (standing) Charles "Chalkie," Mary Ellen (Huesman), and Father Leo; (seated) parents Mary and Charles. Leo, as an altar boy in 1919, reportedly failed to extinguish the fire in a censer at the first St. Cecilia Church, and the church burned to the ground. (Al Meese.)

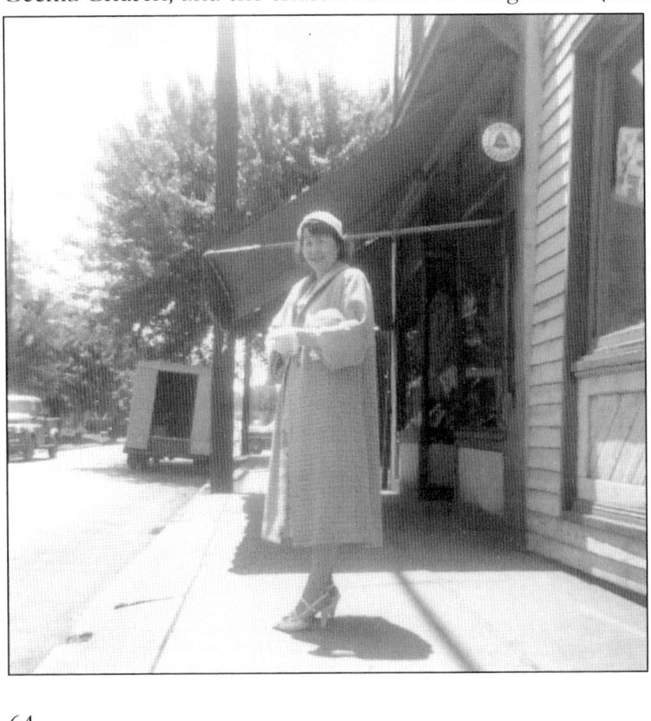

Margaret Gadker Wilson stands in front of Wilson's Department Store, which she owned with her husband, Charles "Chalkie," at 5285 Madison Pike in the 1940s. Wilson's had a variety of goods, including clothing and shoes. They bought it from Carrie Schoborg and operated it into the 1970s. (Brenda Schoborg Hopkins and Jean Wilson Smith.)

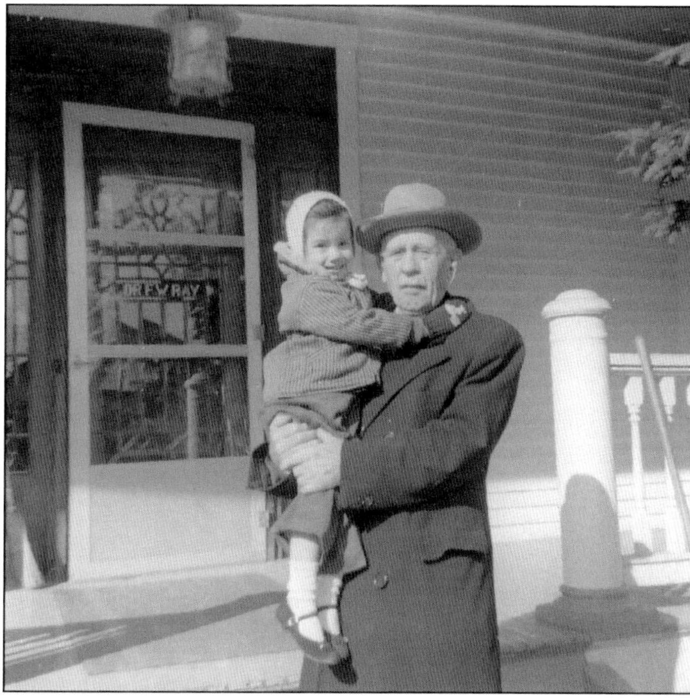

Dr. Fred W. Ray stands in front of his home at 5293 Madison Pike with his great-granddaughter, Jennifer Russell around 1957. Dr. Ray lived from 1872 to 1965. He emigrated from Staffordshire, England, and was naturalized in 1900. He married Emma Colclough (1876–1952), and they had two children, Margaret and Harold. (Elizabeth Russell.)

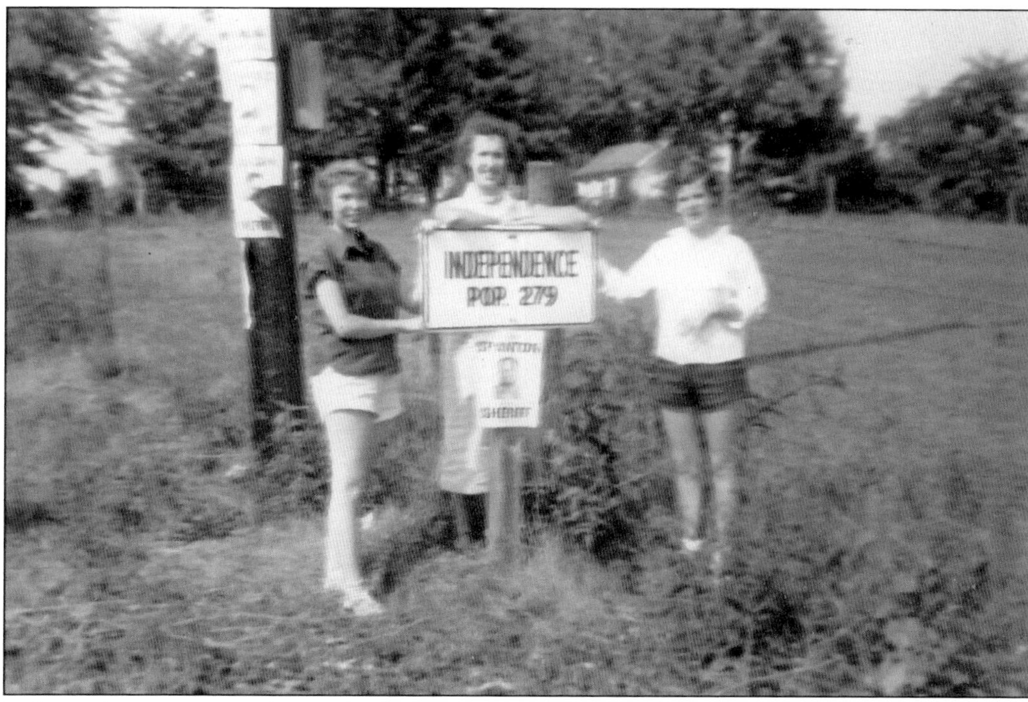

Independence was not always the large, growing city it is today. In 1953, this sign graced the southern entrance to Independence on the east side of Madison Pike across from 5323 Madison Pike. The census figures were 285 for 1950 and 309 for 1960. The Simon Kenton juniors pictured are, from left to right, Jeannie Miller (Poe), Joan Redman (Pieper), and Betty Jo Lillard (Foster). (Mark Lillard.)

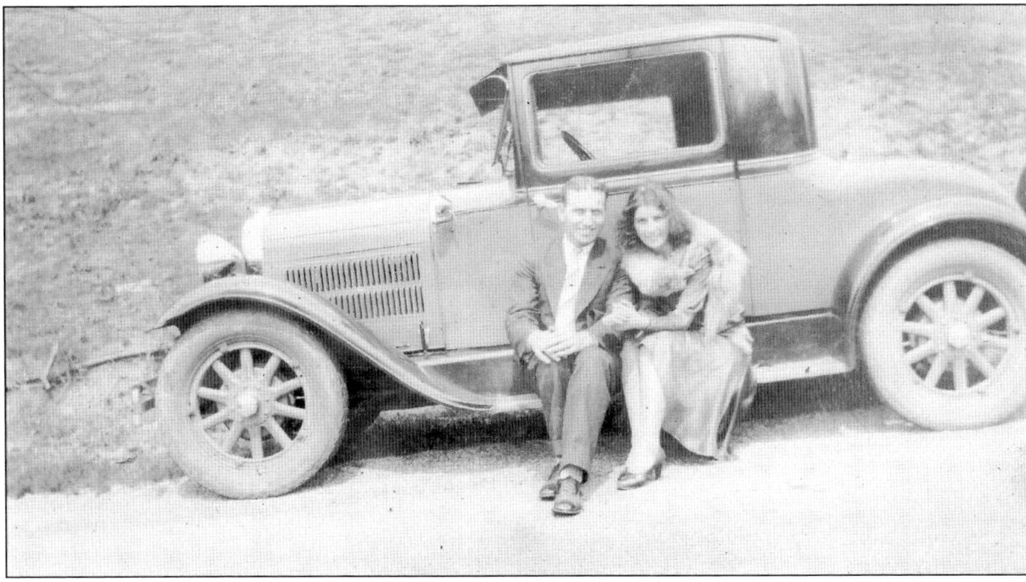

Goebel Armstrong and Irene McGrath are seated together on the running board in the 1920s. They later married. Goebel appears throughout this book, as he was active in the fire department and city government and served as chairman of the board of trustees in the 1960s (the equivalent of today's mayor). He was instrumental in initiating the policy of annexation to assure the growth and viability of the city. He was assistant fire chief at the time of his death in November 1970. (J.B. Losey.)

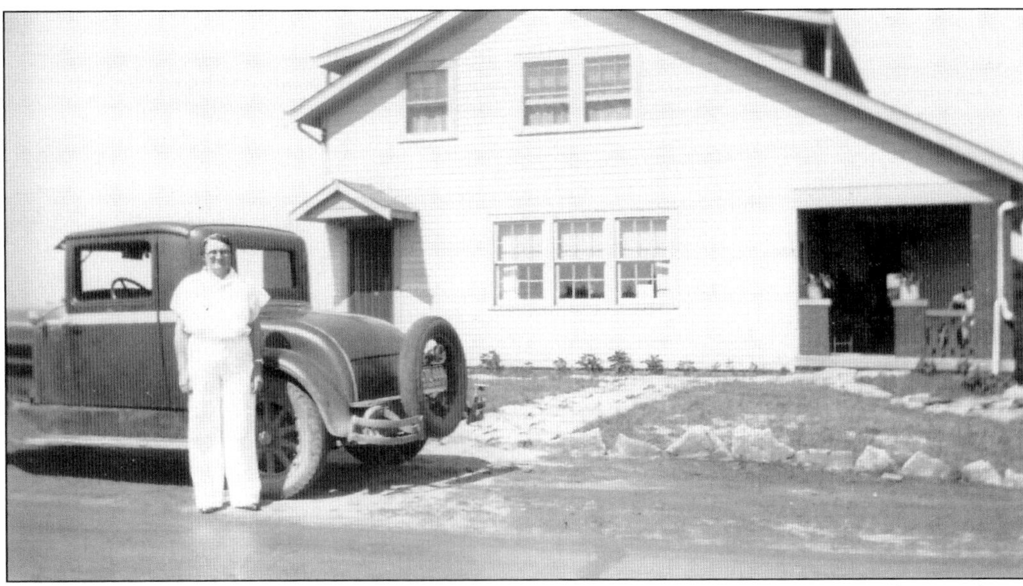

Dora "Doe" Armstrong House stands in front of the Rust residence at 5153 Madison Pike in the 1930s. She lived nearby on McKim Drive and prided herself on having the earliest produce from her garden. She worked for a time at Rothman's grocery and played Santa Claus at several churches in the 1940s. The Rusts operated a feed store across the street. The home remains today. (J.B. Losey.)

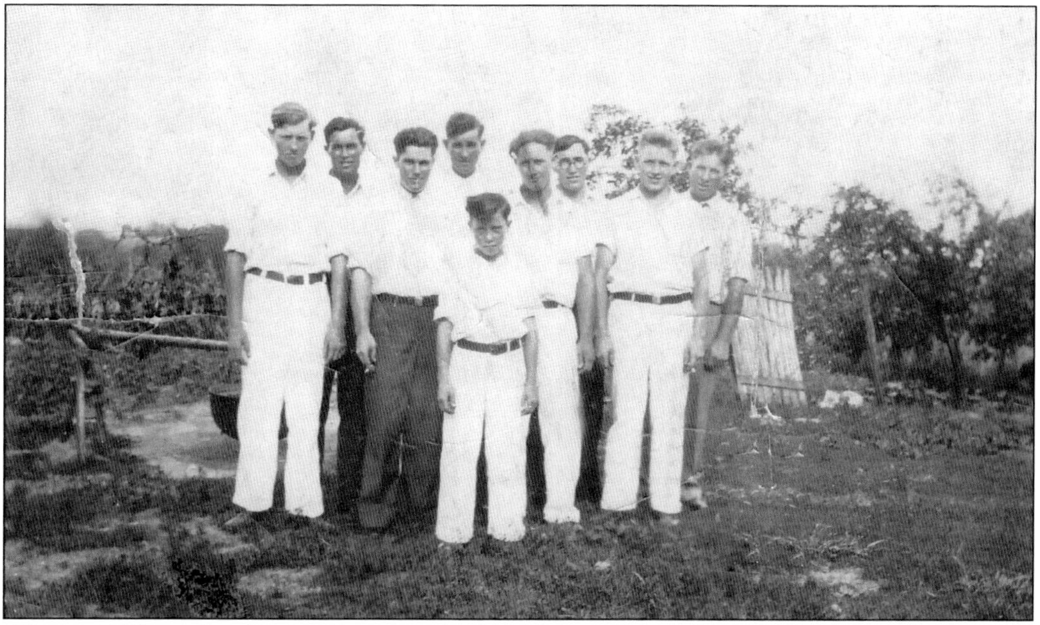

All nine Williams brothers pose on Marshall Road in the 1930s. From left to right, they are (first row) Charlie; (second row) Remley, Gilbert, Harold "Pat," Raymond, Elmer, Earl, Clifford, and Hubert. (Betty Northcutt Williams.)

Four generations are standing here in 1950. They are, from left to right, Elizabeth Rothmann, her daughter Stella Kenney, her daughter Dorothy Schneider, and her son Jerry Schneider. Elizabeth Rothmann lived at this house at 5377 Madison Pike after her husband died, and this image is taken in the front yard. Behind them is the east side of Independence Cemetery. The building visible behind burned with all of the cemetery records, hindering the finding of graves. (Jerry Schneider.)

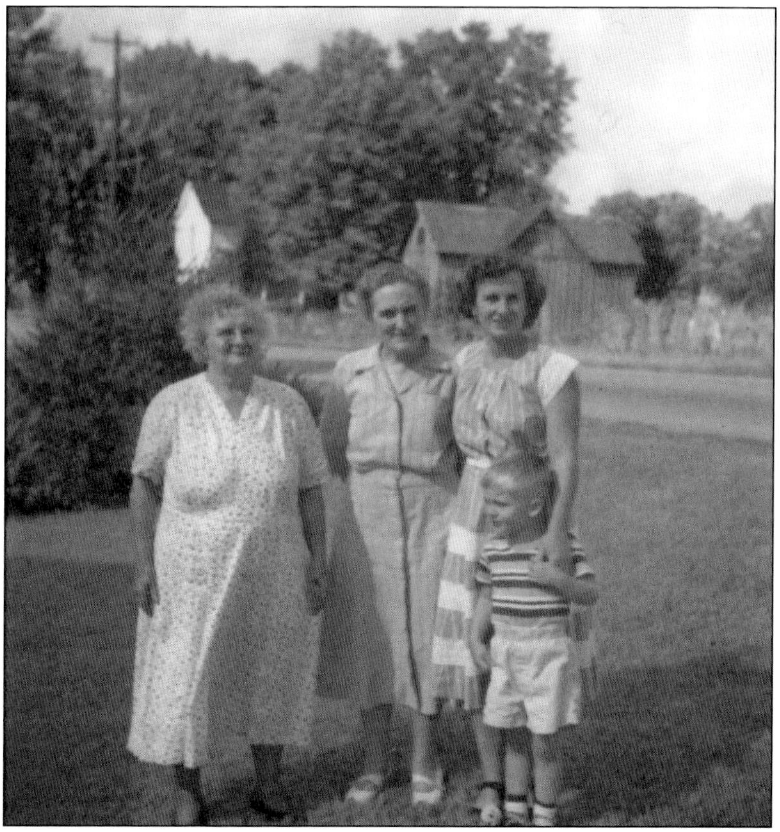

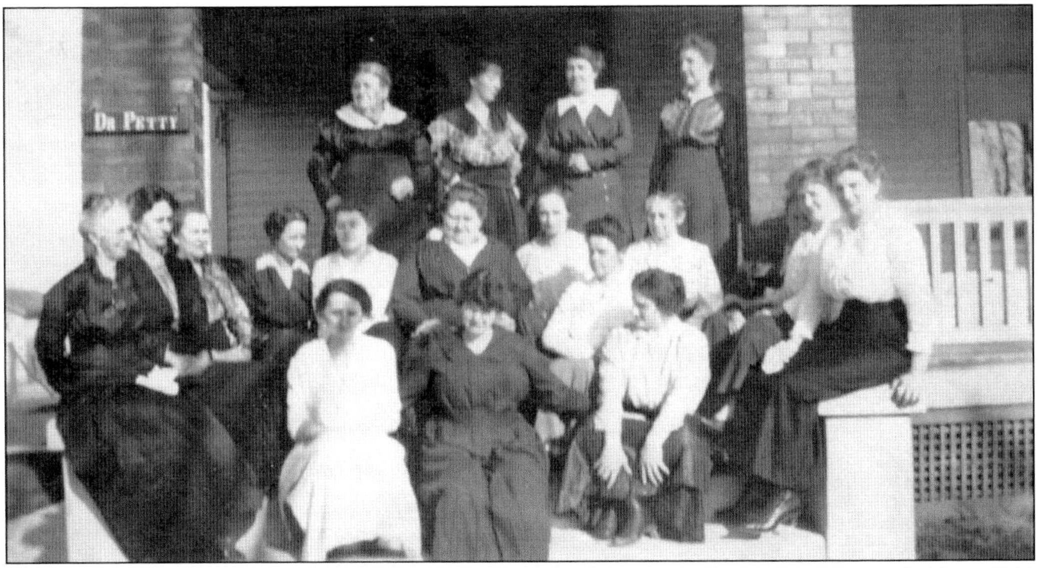

These ladies had an euchre card party at the home of Dr. Petty (see sign at upper left) at 5310 Madison Pike on July 20, 1933. The lady second from left sitting under the sign is Nellie Sweeney Mills. (Peggy Powers Baum.)

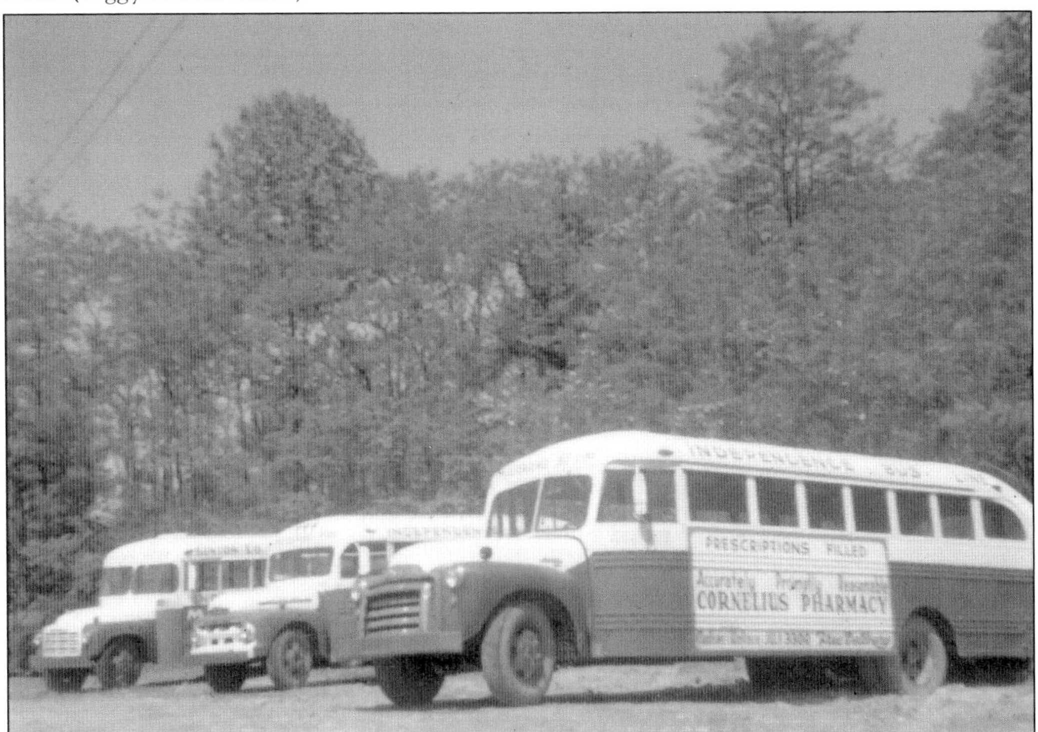

The Independence bus line was operated by Elmer Dedden, and the bus parking lot was south of St. Cecilia Church. The line ran from Fiskburg in southern Kenton County to Second and Court Streets in Covington several times a day. This image was taken on May 30, 1961. Along the roof, it reads "Independence Bus," and the sign on the side advertises for Cornelius Pharmacy. In 1956, fare from Nicholson to Independence was 35¢. (Eunice Mershon.)

Carl and Bertha Moon had five sons serve in World War II, and two perished—Calvin and Bernard. The local American Legion post is named in their honor, the Moon Brothers Post 275 American Legion. The Moons worked with both the Girl and Boy Scouts. At the dedication of the new post office on September 30, 1961, at 5279 Madison Pike, Bertha Moon poses with some of her Girl Scouts. Carl and Bertha Moon lived on Klette Road beside the courthouse and are buried in Independence Cemetery. (Eunice Mershon.)

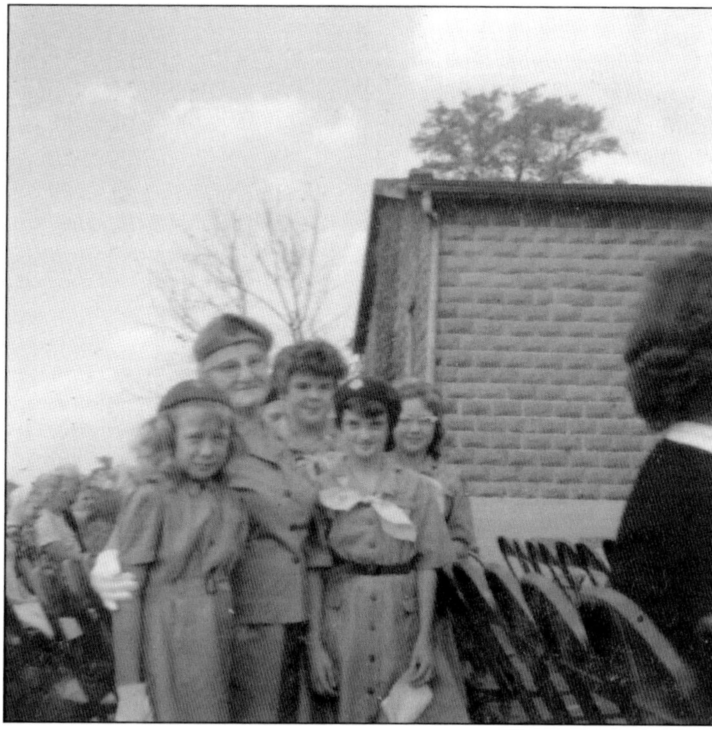

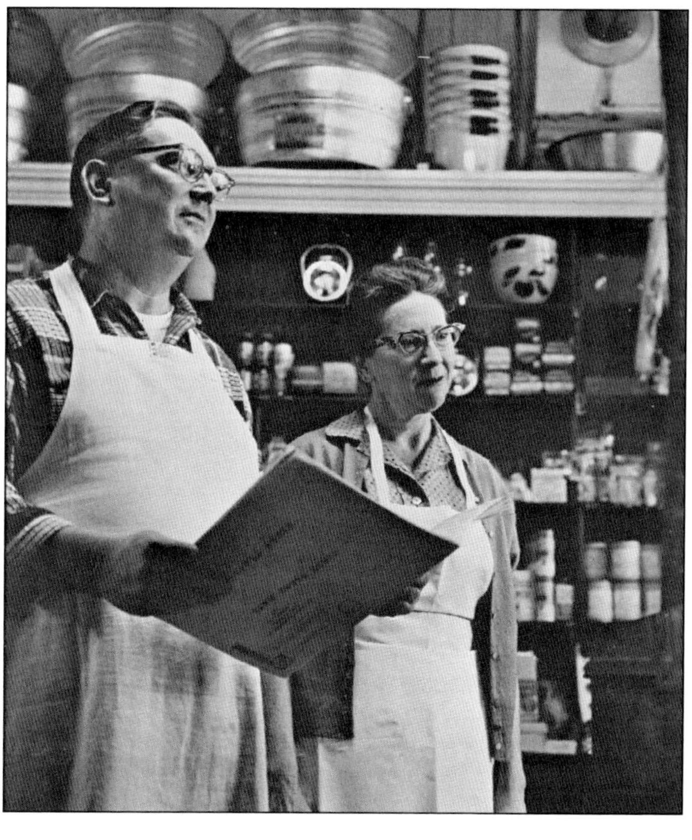

Howard A. Stephens Jr. and his sister Genevieve Galloway operated a country store heated by a potbellied stove in this May 1961 image. It was previously Schoborg's grocery and was just south of 5247 Madison Pike. Thereafter it operated as a bakery, and it was later torn down. (Cincinnati Bell.)

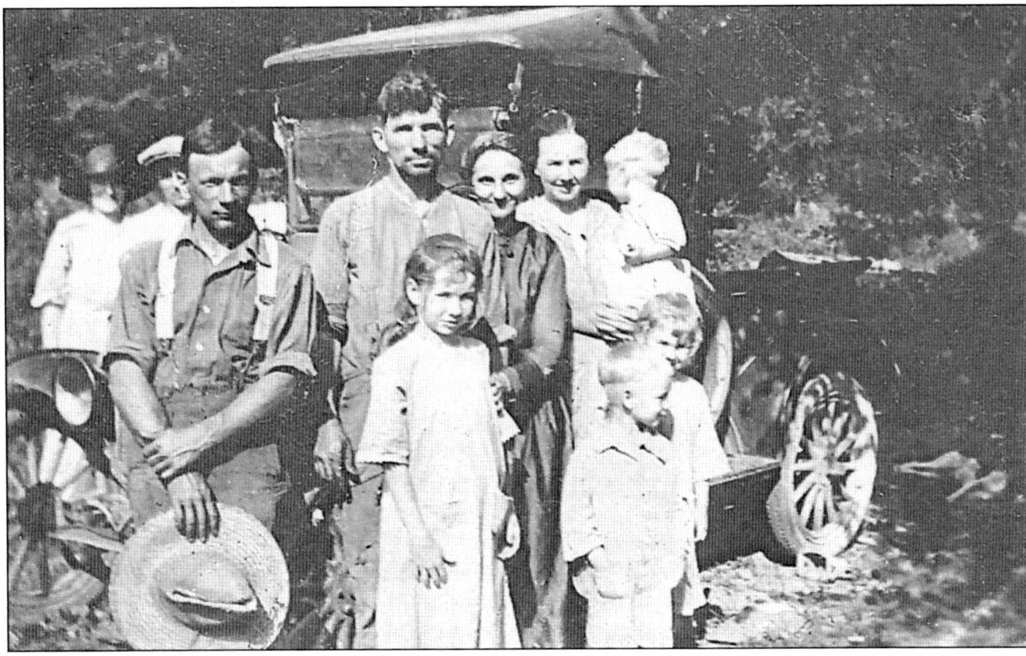

This family photograph is at the home of Ed England on Fowler Creek Road in June 1922. They are, from left to right, (first row) eight-year-old Hilda, four-year-old Harold, and seven-year-old Dolores England; (second row) Jim and Albert England, Ida Fisk, and Jessie and Floyd England; (third row) Vina and Cliff England. (Eunice Mershon.)

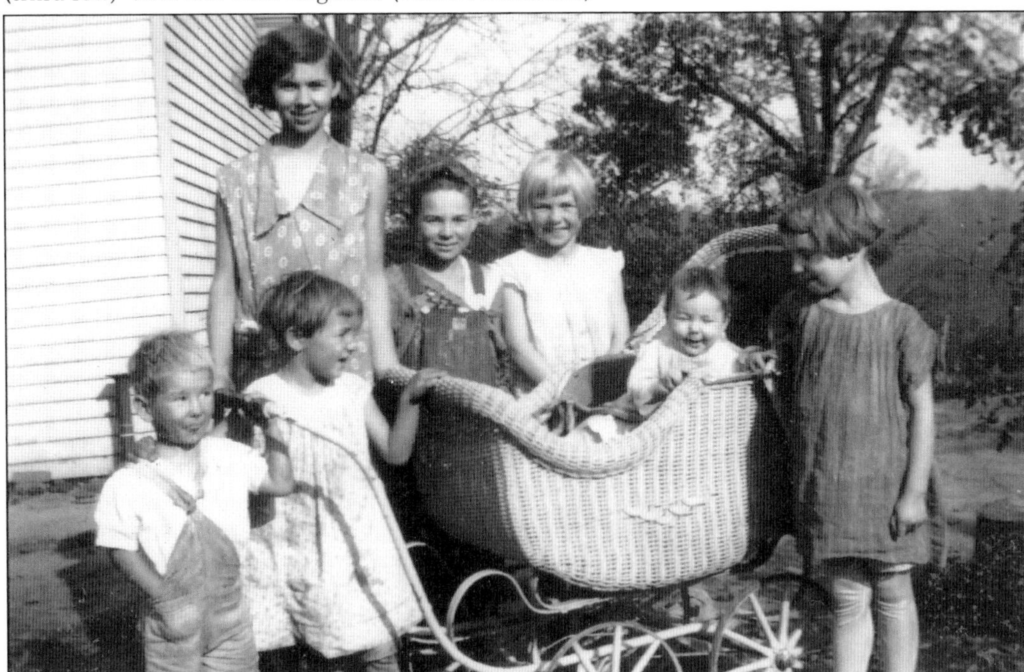

The England children, at the same farm on Fowler Creek Road in 1930, are, from left to right, (first row) Ray and Eunice; (second row) Dolores, Floyd, Betty, Wayne (in carriage), and Norma. (Eunice Mershon.)

The Schoborg family is shown outside their home at 5373 Madison Pike in 1938. They are, from left to right, (first row) Mary Lou Schoborg (Kaub), unidentified, and Rita Schoborg (Dumbacher); (second row) Margaret Flerlage Schoborg and her mother, Clara England Flerlage; (third row) Herman Schoborg. Margaret and Herman were married, and the two children are theirs. The dog is Trixie. Herman Schoborg served on the fire department for many years. The home remains today. (Mary Lou Schoborg Kaub.)

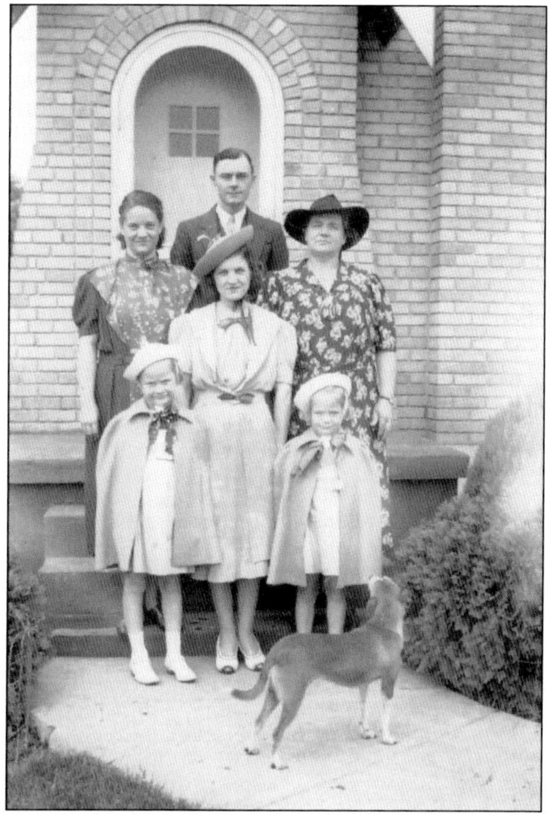

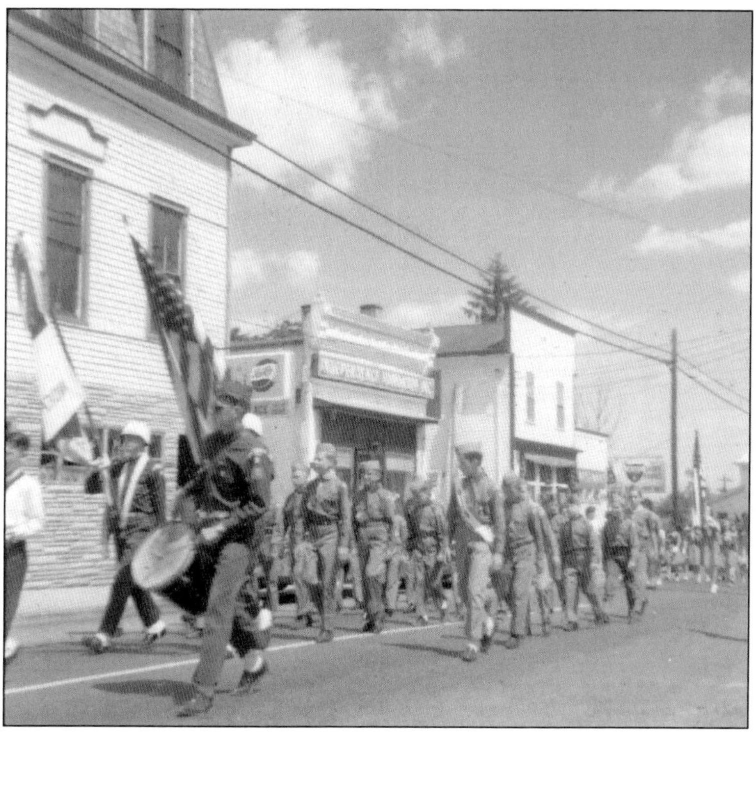

Parades through town have long entertained residents, most of whom have marched themselves at some point. Memorial Day parades have been done for decades. Here a group of Boy Scouts marches south on Madison Pike on Memorial Day, May 30, 1965. Independence Hardware is behind in the center. (Eunice Mershon.)

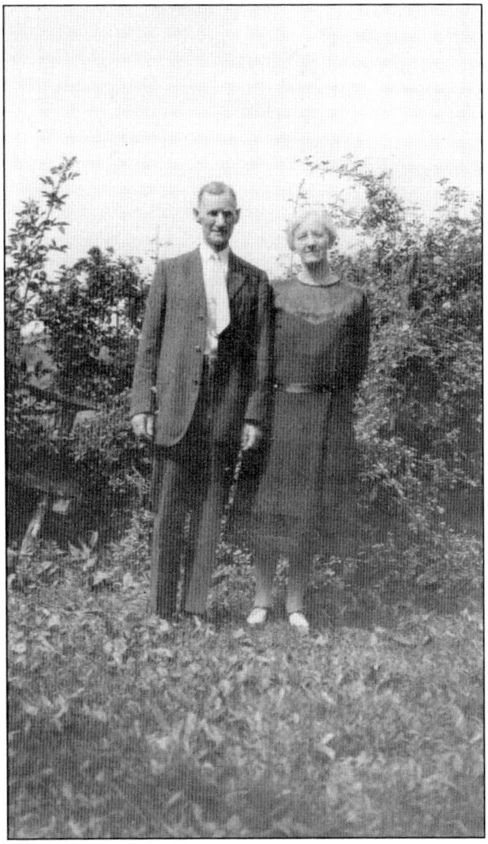

Atwood C. and Lucy Bird, husband and wife, pose at the Bird family farm on Madison Pike on June 9, 1929. He served as the president of the Bank of Independence for a time. The southern Kenton County community of Atwood is named for him. Atwood Bird lived from November 6, 1867, to June 9, 1960. (Miley Sue Bird Van Horn.)

The residence of Atwood C. Bird, built in 1910, is pictured here in the 1920s. It was demolished in 1995 for construction of the Independence Towne Center at Madison Pike and Route 536. (Miley Sue Bird Van Horn.)

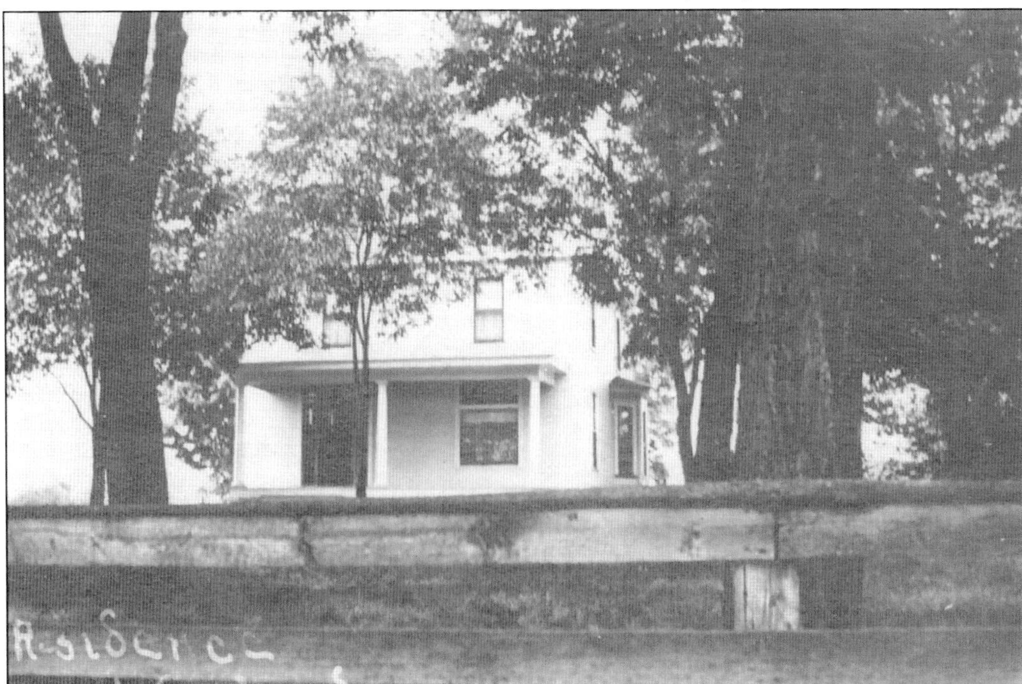

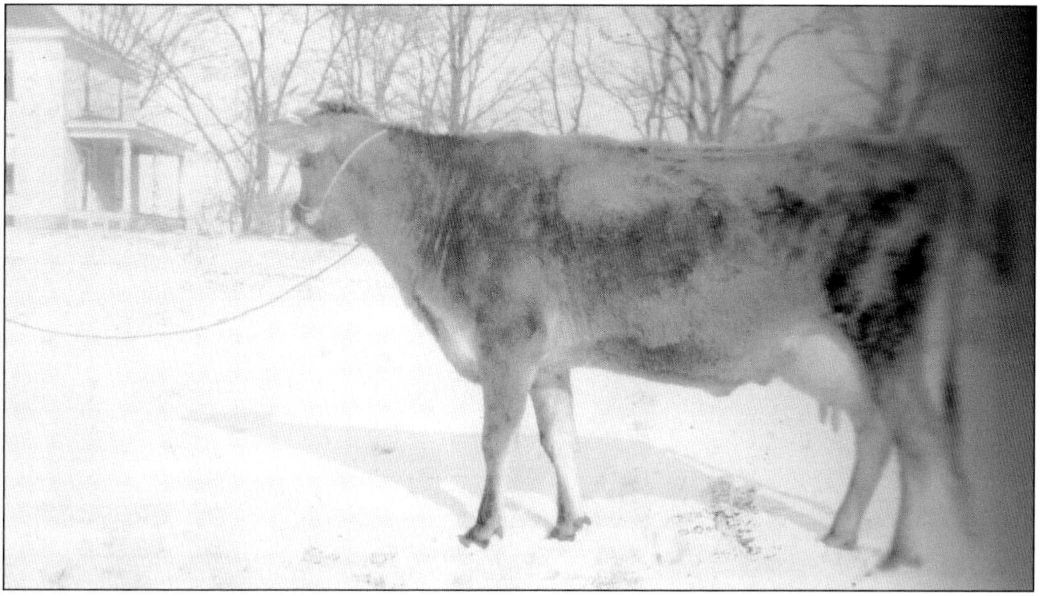

The 1926 Kenton County Extension Agent report pictured this prizewinning dairy cow owned by the Bird family. Their farmhouse on Madison Pike is on the left. This dairy farm of 238 acres raised a variety of crops and livestock over the years. (Kenton County Extension Service.)

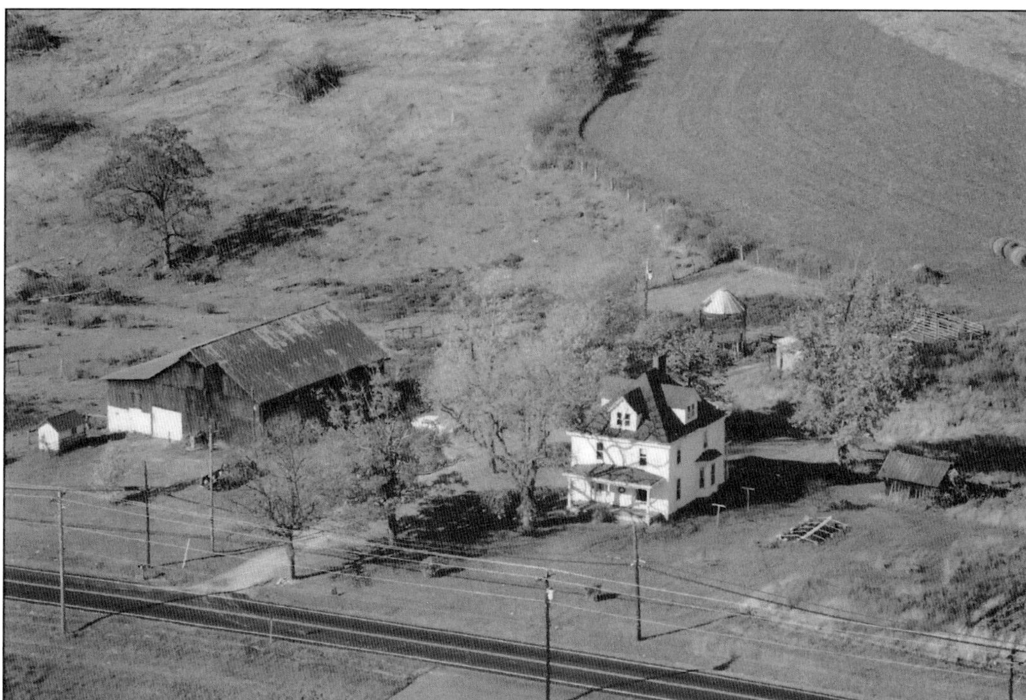

This aerial view of the Bird farm in 1994 shows the beginning of clearing and excavation work on the Independence Towne Center. The house, barn, and other structures were demolished soon after this image was taken. The last family members who owned it were Stanley Bird and T.L. Bird. (Miley Sue Bird Van Horn.)

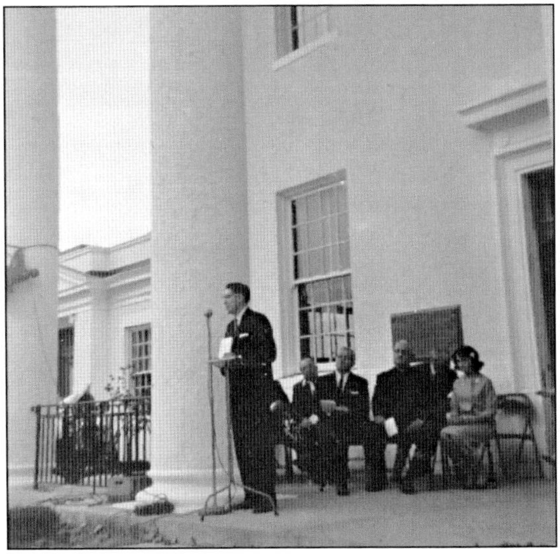

Substantial improvements, including painting it white, were made to the Kenton County Courthouse, and it was dedicated on October 18, 1964. A program with music and speakers was overseen by master of ceremonies G. Wayne Bridges, a local attorney (standing). He went on to serve as Independence city attorney from 1972 to 1990, fighting the many legal battles as the city annexed large areas. In 1986, the Kentucky Bar Association named him Outstanding Attorney. The lady seated at the right is Laine Marshall, who spoke on the history of Independence. Judge James Dressman and school superintendent R.C. Hinsdale are also seated and spoke that day. (Eunice Mershon.)

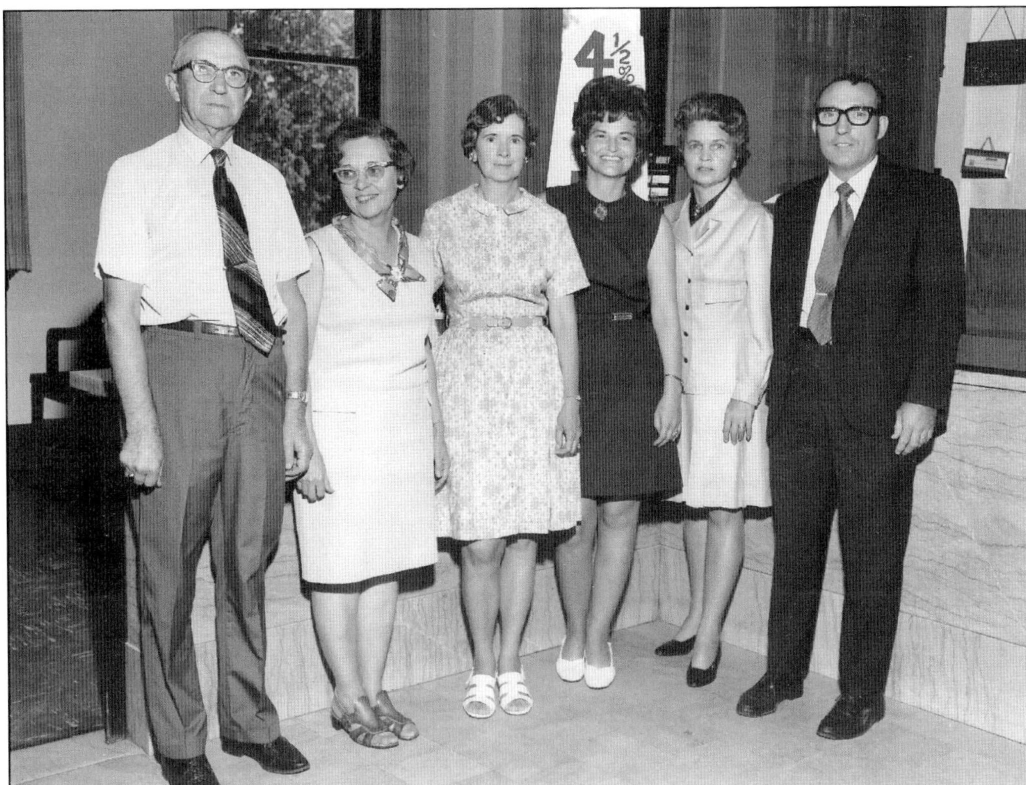

The Bank of Independence started in 1902 in the building at 5263 Madison Pike, which still reads "Deposit Bank" near the top. In 1920, it built the present building at 5262 Madison Pike. Around 1971, it merged with Peoples Liberty Bank, which subsequently merged several times. It was the only bank in town for decades and took care of the farmers and businessmen in town. In the 1960s, some staff posed inside. They are, from left to right, Pres. Raymond Giles, Mildred Wilcoxson, Edith Bach, Faye McMillan, Nina Crutcher (later Curry), and Omer Mastin. (Barbara Giles Gabbard.)

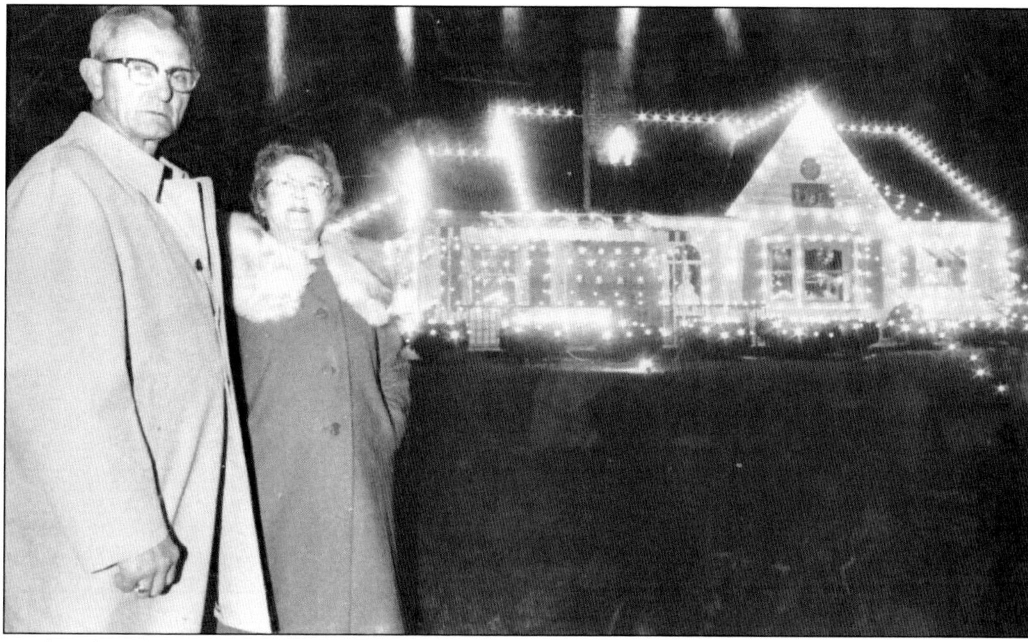

Fred and Mabel Reinhardt stand in front of their home at 6598 Taylor Mill Road decorated for the Christmas holidays in the 1970s. At the time, this was a display worth getting in the car and driving to see. Fred was a builder and developed Mafred Drive in Taylor Mill, named for both of them. (Kenton County Public Library.)

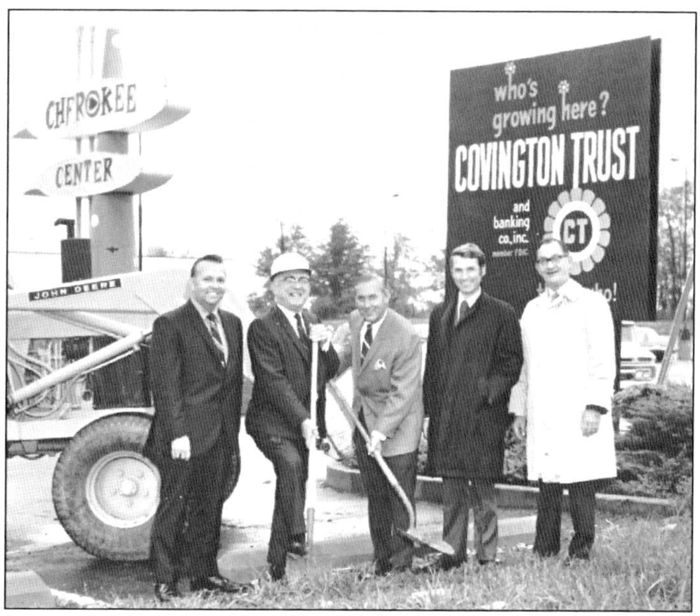

The ground-breaking of Covington Trust Bank in Cherokee Center on Taylor Mill Road was on October 26, 1970. The participants are, from left to right, two unidentified, John Krumpelman, unidentified, and Ed Schmidt. The shopping center, developed in the 1960s, featured a bowling alley and grocery store. The sign on the upper left was a replica of a totem pole. (Kenton County Public Library.)

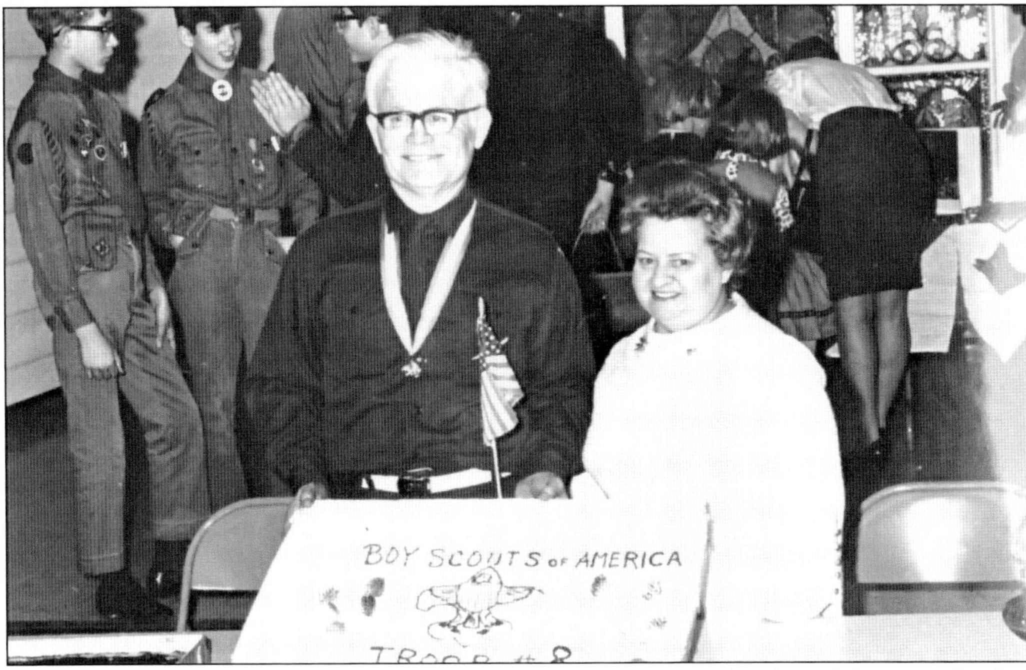

Sterling and Lillian Staggs celebrate at Independence Christian Church in February 1970. Boy Scout Troop No. 8 is celebrating the retirement of scoutmaster Staggs after 16 years of service. Sterling lived from 1912 to 2001. He received the Silver Beaver Award, the highest honor a scoutmaster can receive, and served on the Independence Council for 12 years. Sterling Staggs Park at Madison Pike and Sylvan Drive was named in his honor in 1995 for his civic service. (Kenton County Public Library.)

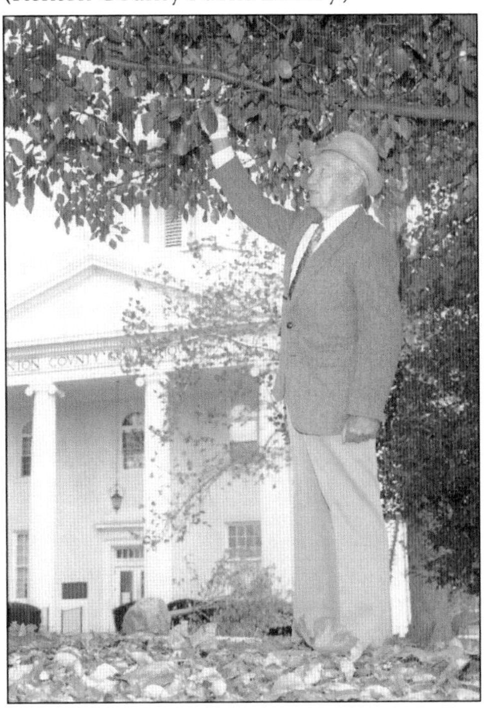

William and Inez Straw lived at 47 McCullum Road, and he was the Kenton County extension agent. He planted 100 ornamental pear trees, and afterward, in 1969, he noticed one did not have any thorns. He developed it into the Aristocrat Pear tree, and it was patented. The name was chosen partly so it would be near the front of alphabetical plant catalogs. In 1989, it was named the official Kenton County tree, and the original discovery tree was moved to the courthouse lawn. He is pictured here in the early 1990s with that tree. He died in July 1995 at the age of 82. Aristocrat Drive is lined with the trees and named for the trees. (Inez Straw.)

Five

A Stroll Downtown

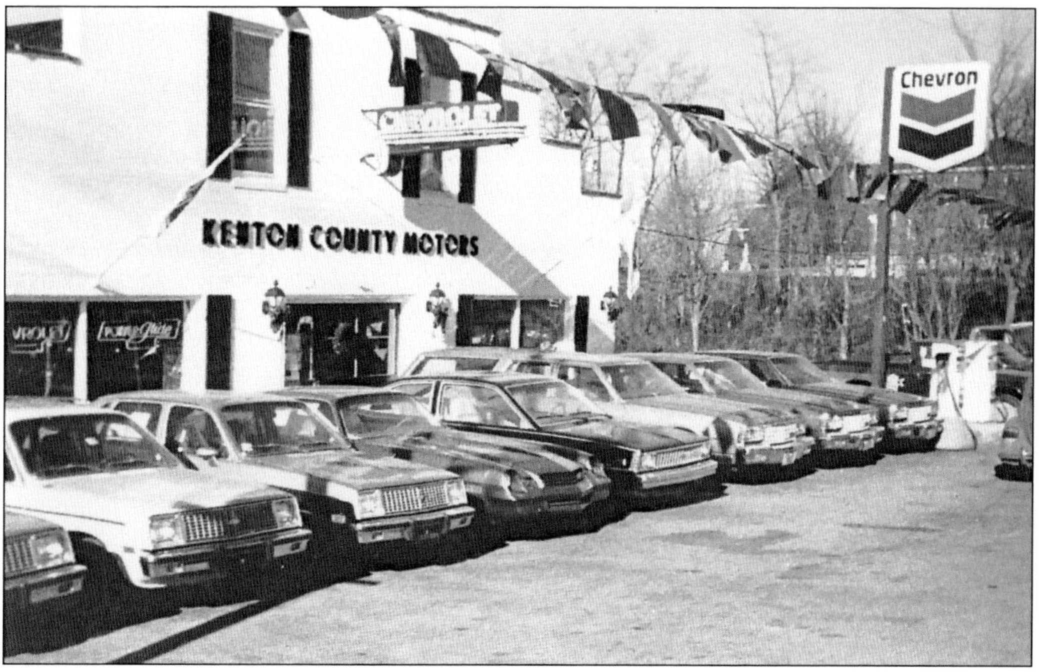

The reader may enjoy this stroll downtown simply by turning the pages or actually strolling the route with book in hand. The stroll begins on the west side of Madison Pike at 5323, proceeds north to Independence Station Road, crosses Madison Pike, and continues on the east side of Madison Pike, south to the place of beginning. Put on some comfortable shoes and enjoy the tour of days gone by, most of which are still visible. A few of the townspeople may stop and say hello. The stroll starts at the Kenton County Motors car dealership, which was owned and operated by John D. Breeden Sr. from 1954 until 1991. After this late 1970s image, the name was changed to Kenton County Chevrolet on this existing building. (Dorothy Breeden.)

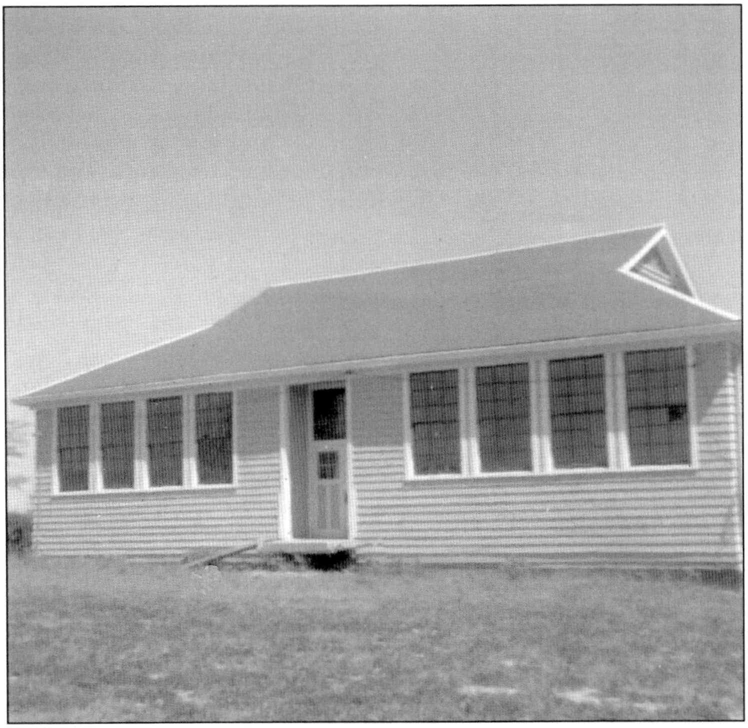

The first St. Cecilia School is shown in May 1965. The school began in the rectory in 1921. This building was dedicated on September 3, 1923. The four room building had two classrooms and two rooms used as a residence for the Sisters. It burned on December 30, 1992, due to an electrical fire. The current school teaches kindergarten through eighth grade. (Eunice Mershon.)

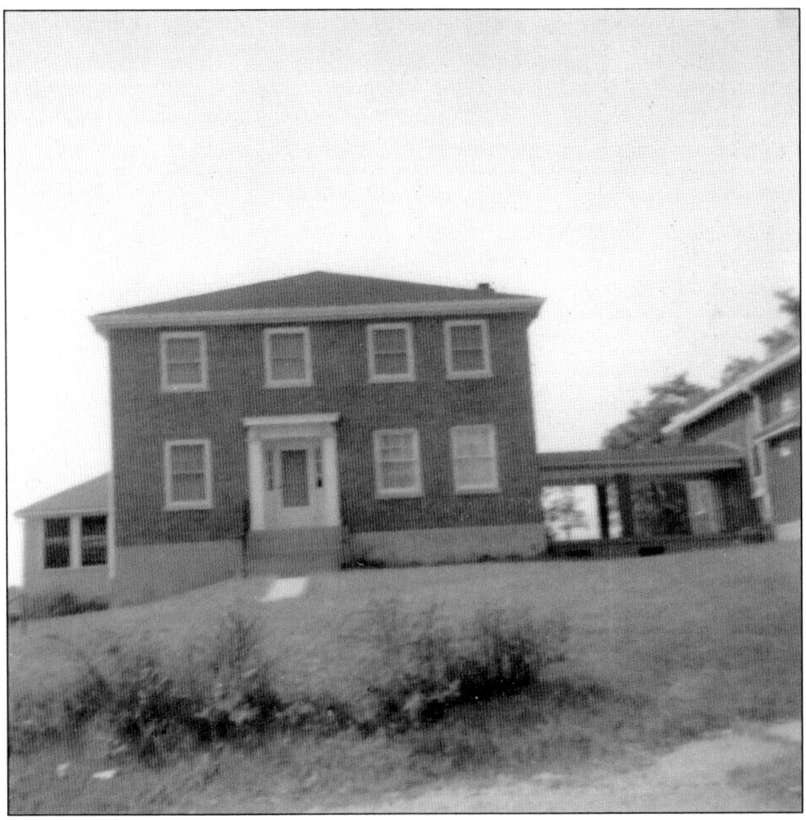

As St. Cecilia School grew, the Sisters moved out of the school building into the existing rectory, and this new rectory was completed in September 1950. The nine-room brick building is still used as the rectory, and it also appears on the cover. This image was taken on October 5, 1957. (Eunice Mershon.)

This St. Cecilia Church building, shown on September 5, 1966, was constructed in 1919 after the previous church burned a few blocks north. An addition was built in 1965. The present church was completed in 1997, and this building was demolished in 2008 for additional parking. (Eunice Mershon.)

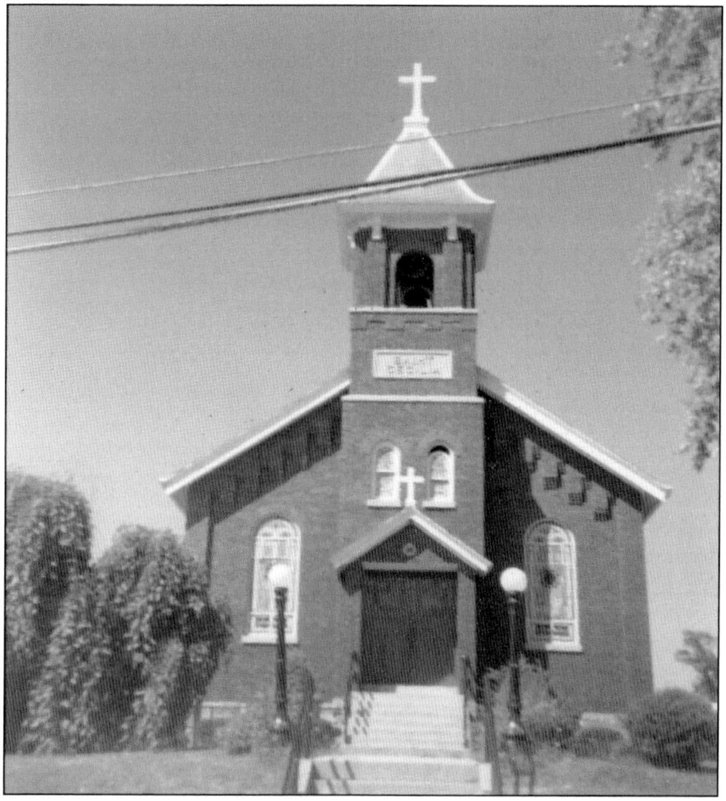

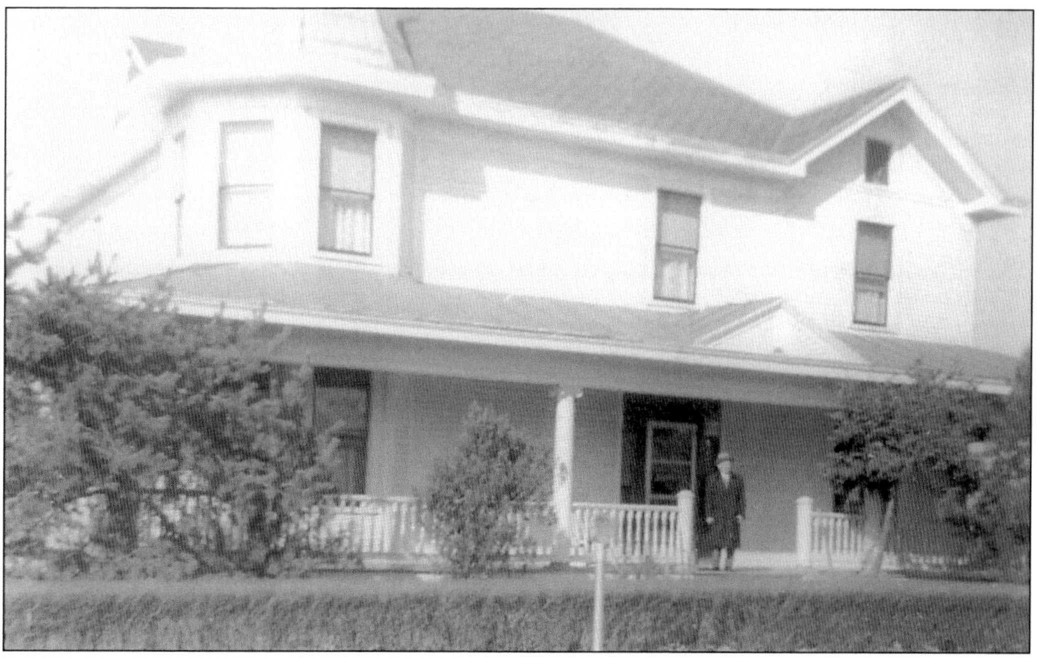

Dr. Fred W. Ray stands in front of his Queen Anne home at 5293 Madison Pike in the 1950s. Dr. Ray had his office in the home, which Kenneth Galloway built for him in 1904 and it still stands today. (Elizabeth Russell.)

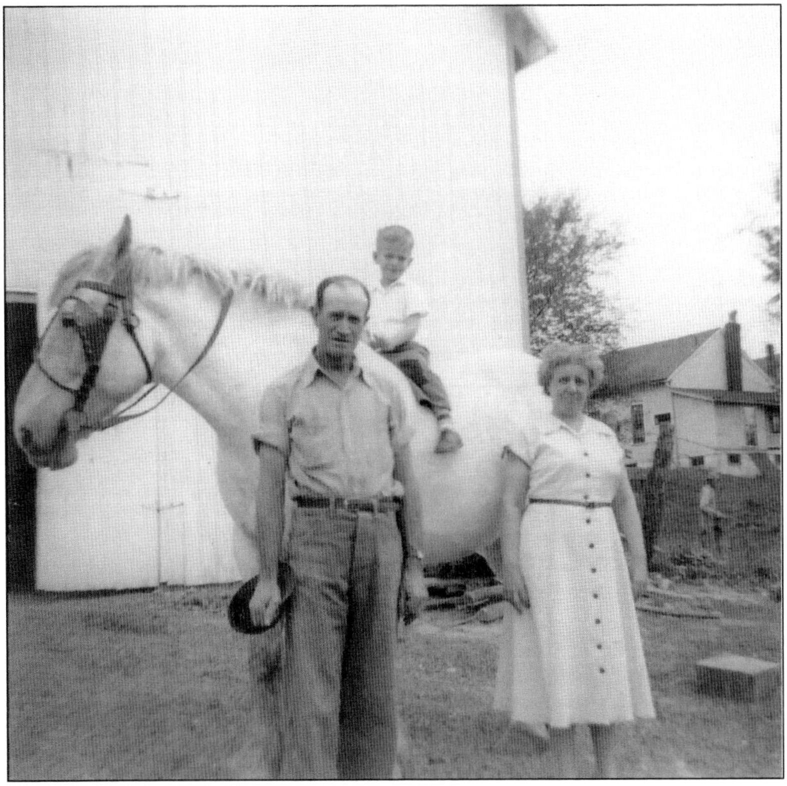

The home at 5293 Madison Pike had a barn behind it, now gone, shown here around 1950. Raymond and Margaret Dickson stand in front of their grandson Tom on the horse. (Elizabeth Russell.)

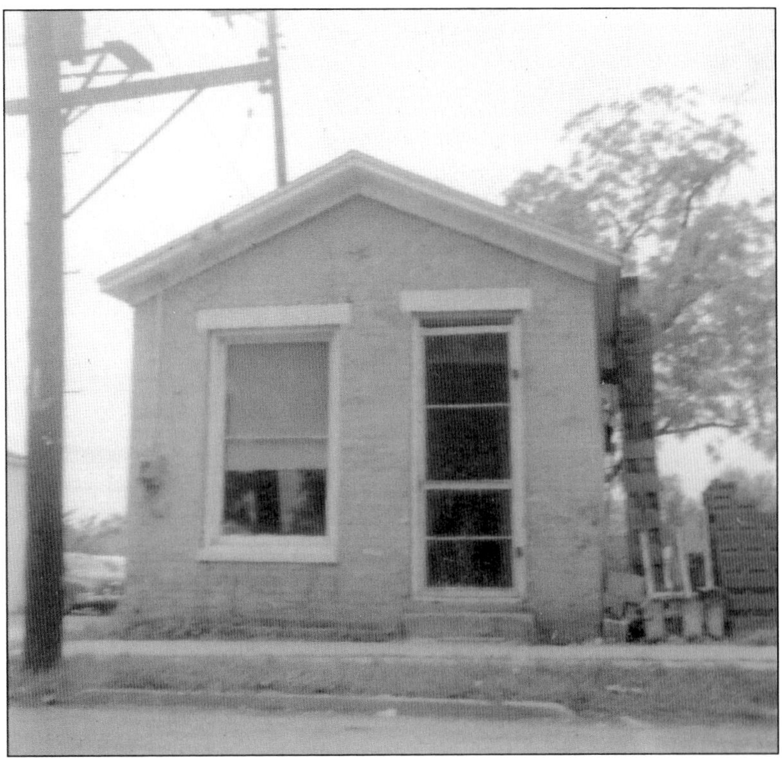

This building was on Madison Pike and north of Independence Road. It was razed for additional parking for Wilson's Department Store, adjacent at 5285 Madison Pike. Dr. J.M. Chambers (pictured on page 11) had his office there, and it was also the post office at one time. This image is from June 25, 1959. (Eunice Mershon.)

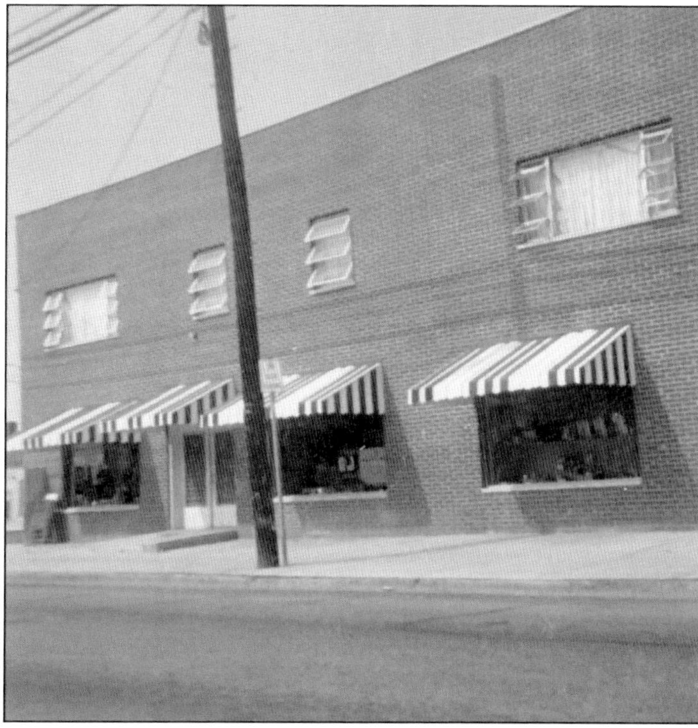

Wilson's Department Store at 5285 Madison Pike is shown on August 27, 1960. It was started and operated by Carrie Schoborg and then the Wilsons. It had just been remodeled within the previous year. A variety of businesses have operated there to this day. (Eunice Mershon.)

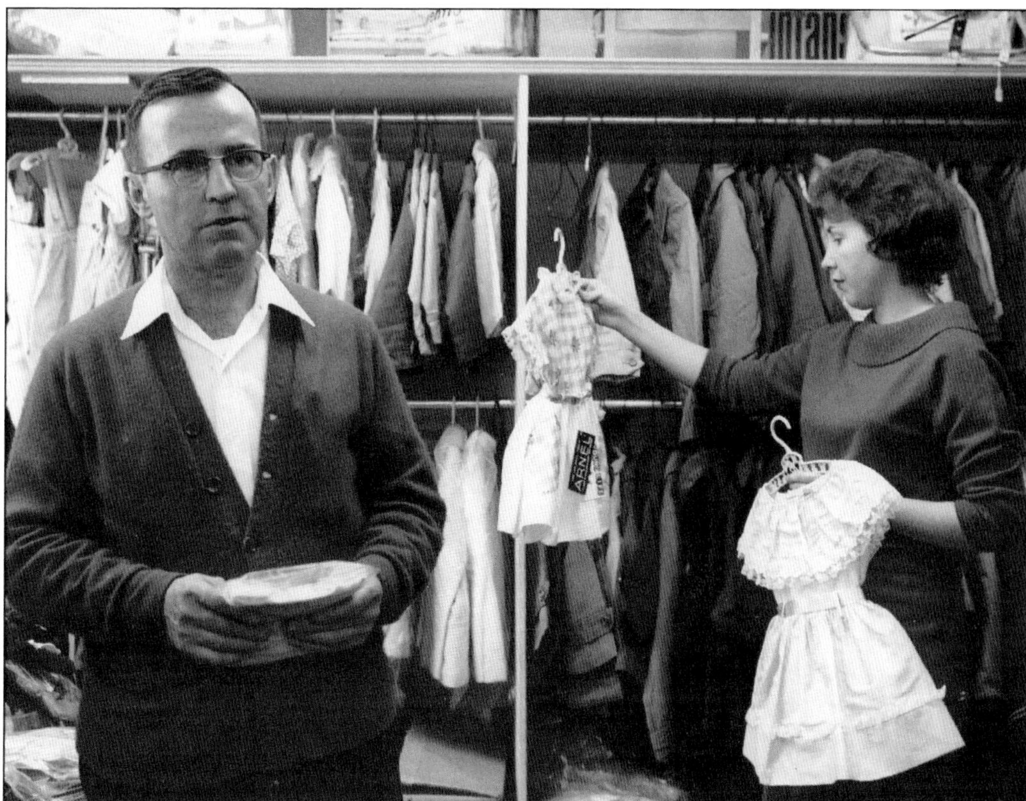

Charles "Chalkie" Wilson and his daughter Jean Wilson Smith check the stock in the children's section of Wilson's Department Store in 1961. A big seller was work clothes, and it had a growing babies' and tots' apparel department. (Brenda Schoborg Hopkins and Jean Wilson Smith.)

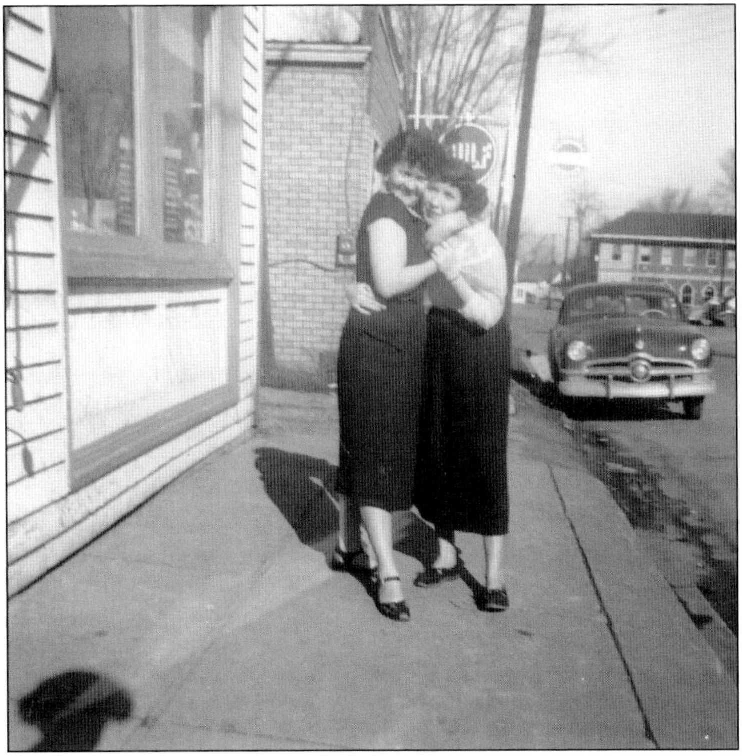

Margaret Wilson, owner of Wilson's Department Store, and her daughter, Mary Ann Wilson, stand in front of Wilson's in the 1940s. The view is to the north towards the next stop on the stroll. (Brenda Schoborg Hopkins and Jean Wilson Smith.)

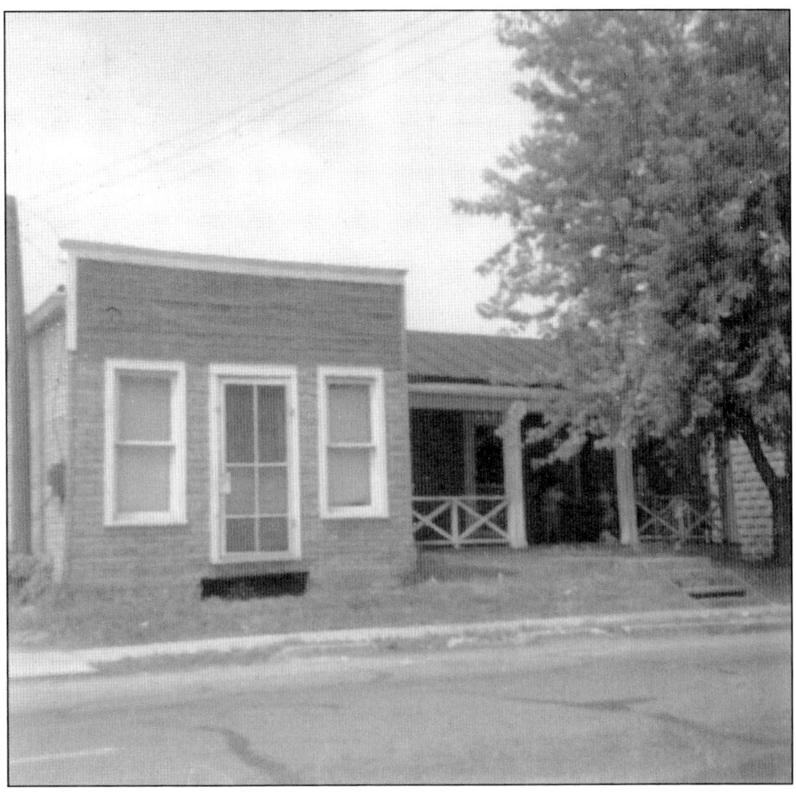

This home at 5279 Madison Pike shown here on August 27, 1960, was torn down for the new post office in 1960. This is reportedly the first home of Dr. Fred Ray before he built his home in 1904. (Eunice Mershon.)

The new post office at 5279 Madison Pike is shown on September 30, 1961, the day it was dedicated. The first postmaster was Bob West. This existing building is used as offices, but it is no longer the post office. (Eunice Mershon.)

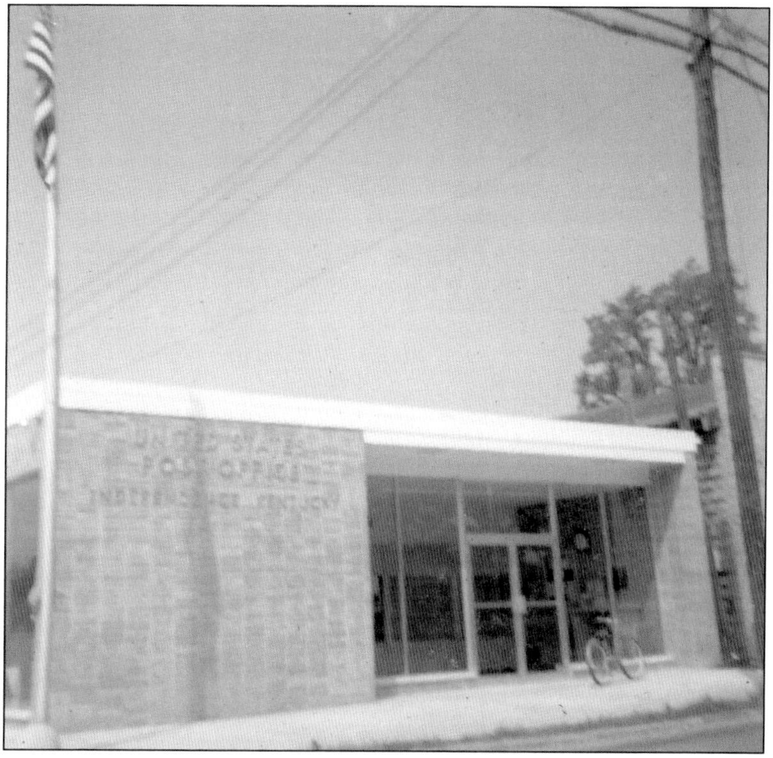

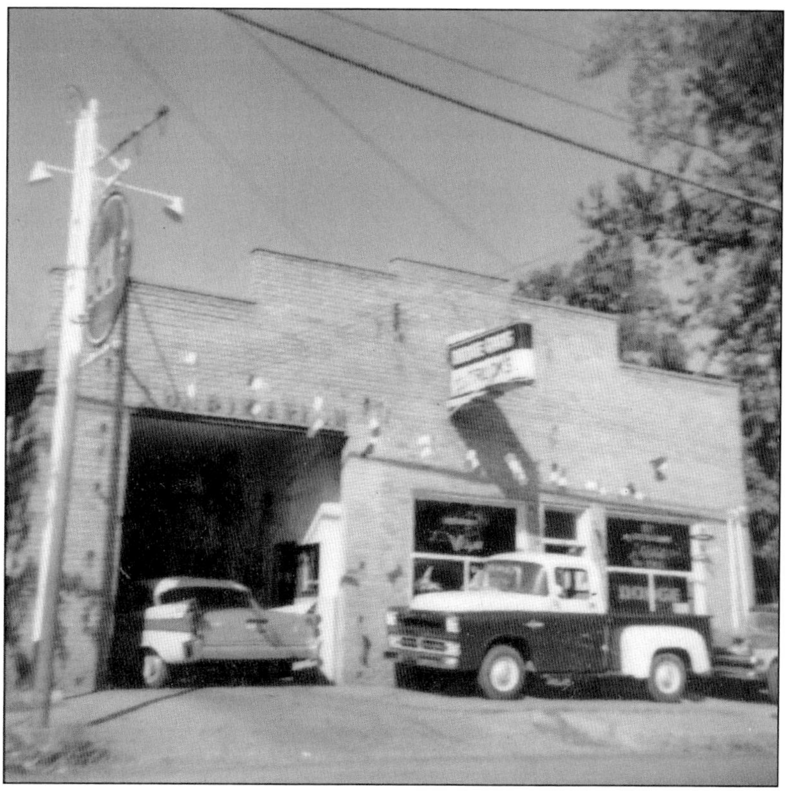

Petit Motors is shown on October 19, 1957, at 5277 Madison Pike. The sign reads "Dodge Cars Trucks." Thereafter, it was a termite company, later Ponzer's Tavern, and now a church. (Eunice Mershon.)

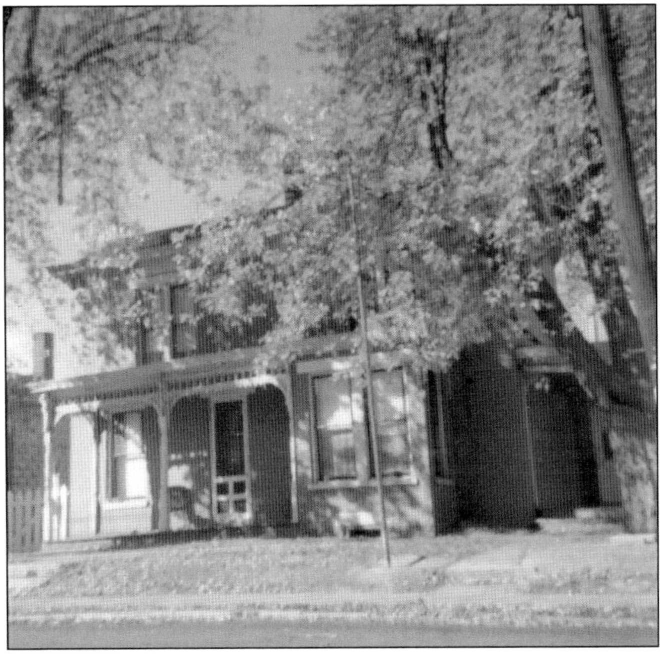

The Fleming family operated a hotel located at 5275 Madison Pike around 1905. Later it was the home of Al Jaeger, who was postmaster and operated a post office in part of the building. It is hard to find a building downtown that has never been the post office. The porch has been removed after this October 19, 1957, image. This existing building has been an insurance agency for several decades. (Eunice Mershon.)

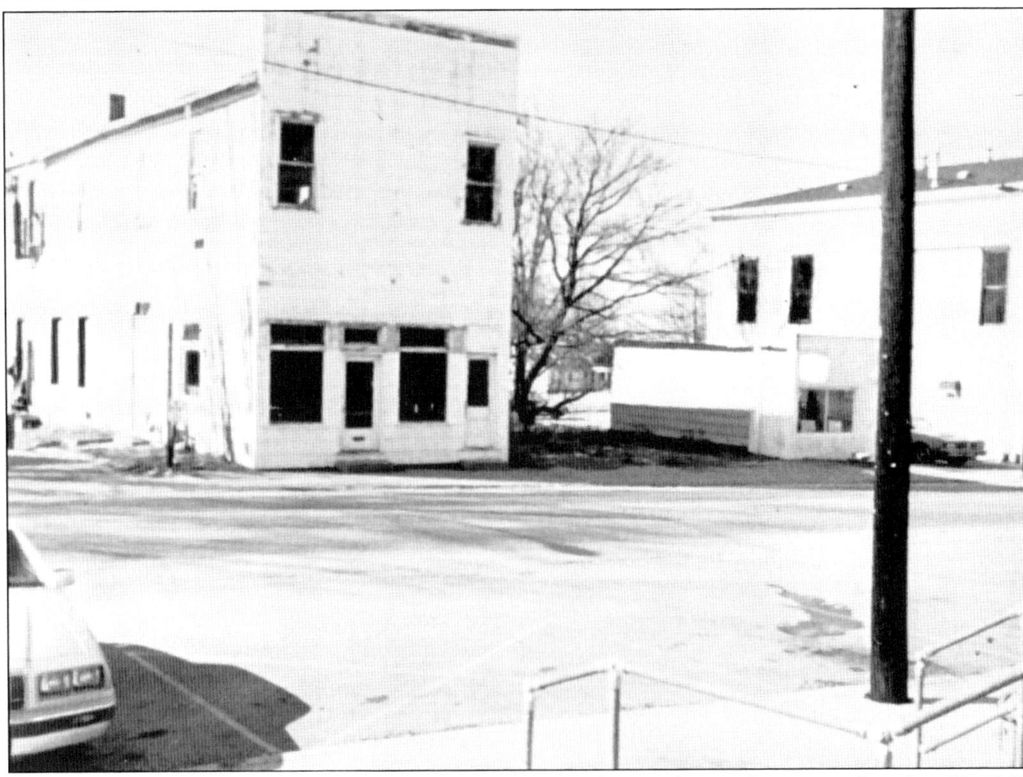

Rel "Buck" Wayman had a real estate office at 5271 Madison Pike, as shown on October 19, 1957. In 1920, it was a one-story building, and a second floor was added for a movie theater later in the 1920s. It was a saloon before Prohibition and then a billiard hall and dry cleaner. It burned in 1988. The railing in the lower right is for the courthouse steps. (Eunice Mershon.)

In this May 30, 1965, image, 5269 Madison Pike is a tavern. It housed a variety of businesses and was built before 1920. The Pepsi sign is hanging out front and a sign says "Tavern" below it. The lower left of the building reads "Sportsman Club." In 1961, it was Chumley's Tavern. The building was razed in the late 1960s. Members of the Moon Brothers Post 275 American Legion stand during this Memorial Day parade. (Eunice Mershon.)

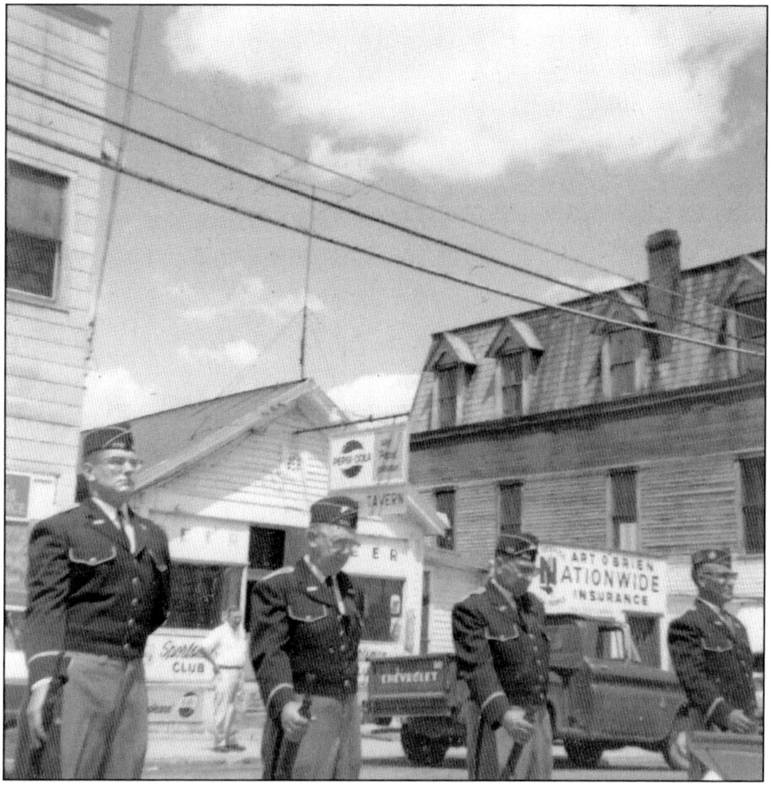

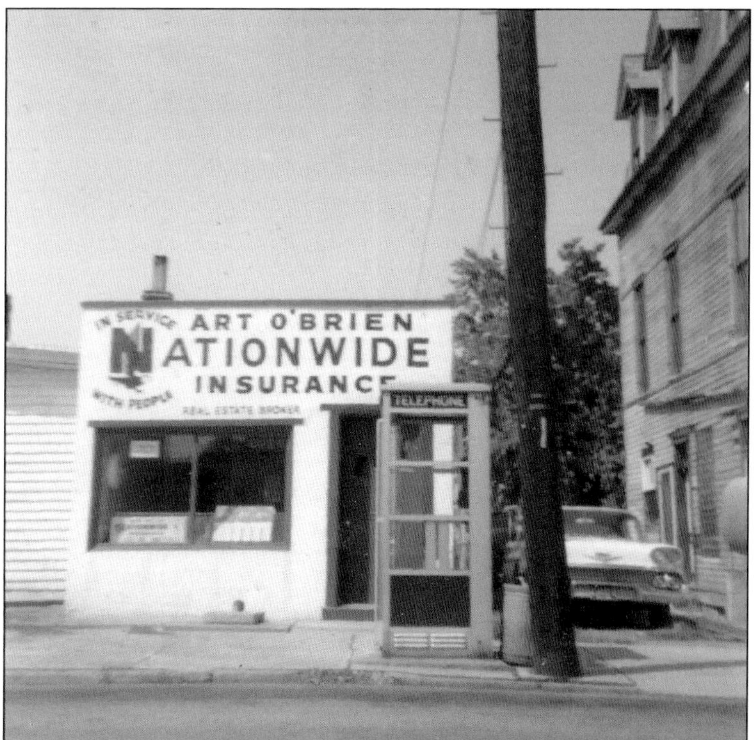

The previous building added on 5267 Madison Pike at some point, and the addition survives, but the original part of the building does not. Art O'Brien operated his insurance office there from 1960 until 1997. He bought the building in 1970. This c. 1966 image shows a public telephone booth in front; they are now almost nonexistent. The building is directly across the street from the courthouse and is now an office. (Eunice Mershon.)

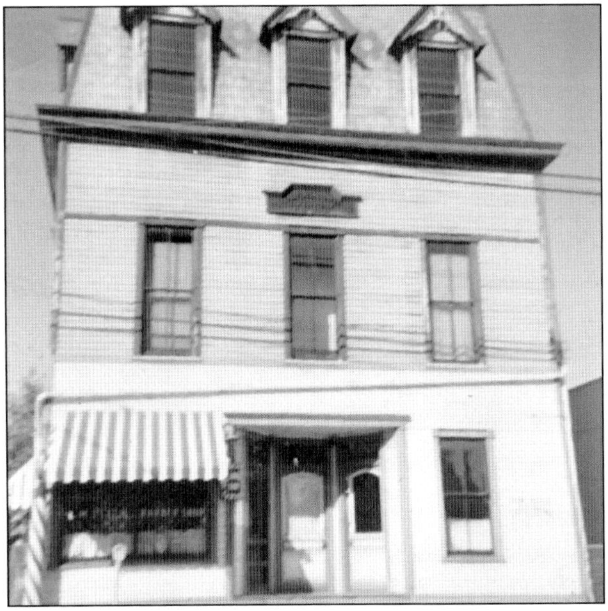

The Odd Fellows hall at 5265 Madison Pike is shown on October 19, 1957. The three-story building with mansard roof had a fire in February 1976, which reduced it to its present two stories (shown on page 41). The first floor usually was occupied by the town barber and other businesses. The second floor was rarely rented. The Daughters of America met for many years on the third floor. A barber pole is visible on the first floor at left. (Eunice Mershon.)

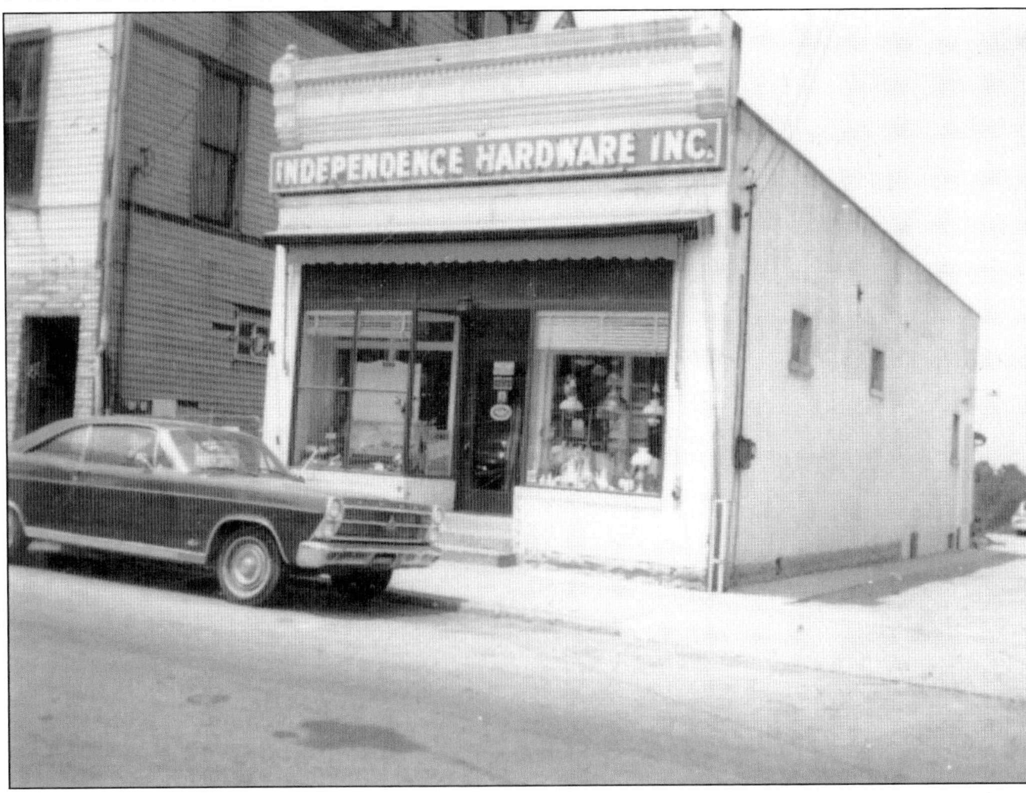

Independence Hardware operated for decades from at least the 1950s to the 1980s at 5263 Madison Pike. It began in 1902 as the home of the Bank of Independence, which opened in 1903. The bank moved across the street in 1920. The business sign hides the sign "Deposit Bank" embedded in the facade in this November 3, 1967, image. With the hardware sign now removed, the original facade sign is visible today. (Jerry Schneider.)

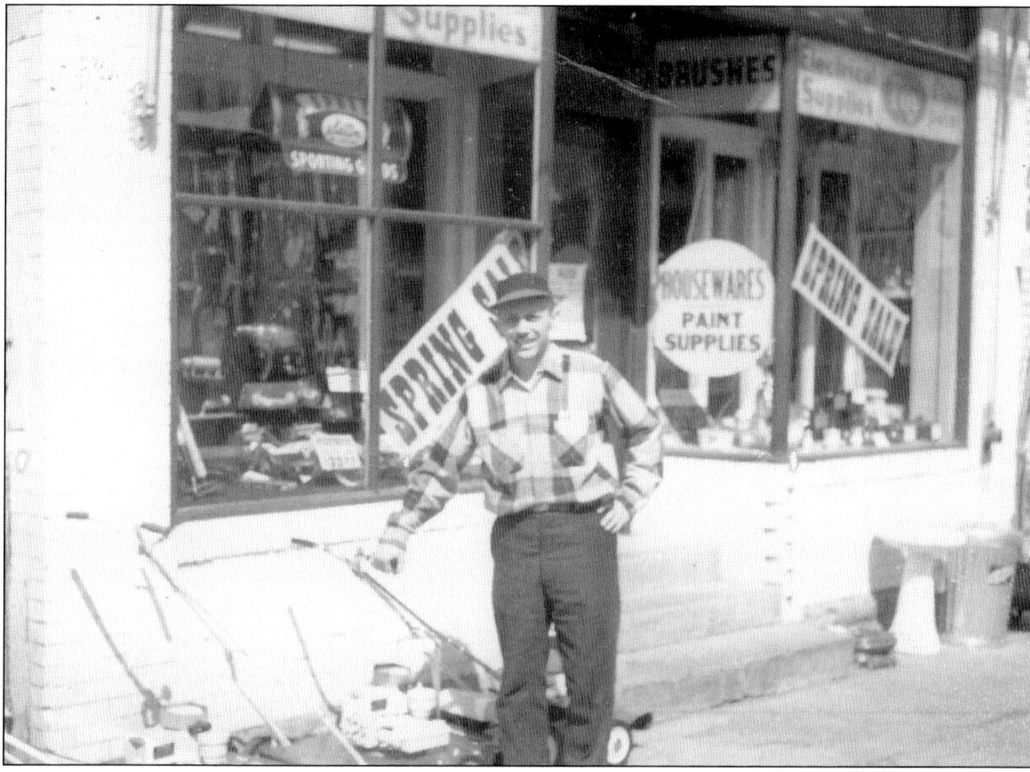

Harold "Hank" Schneider welcomes customers to his Independence Hardware store in the early 1960s. He and wife, Dorothy "Dot," operated the business in the 1950s and 1960s. A customer could find everything needed in this old-time hardware store with Hank and Dot's help, far different from today's big box experience. (Jerry Schneider.)

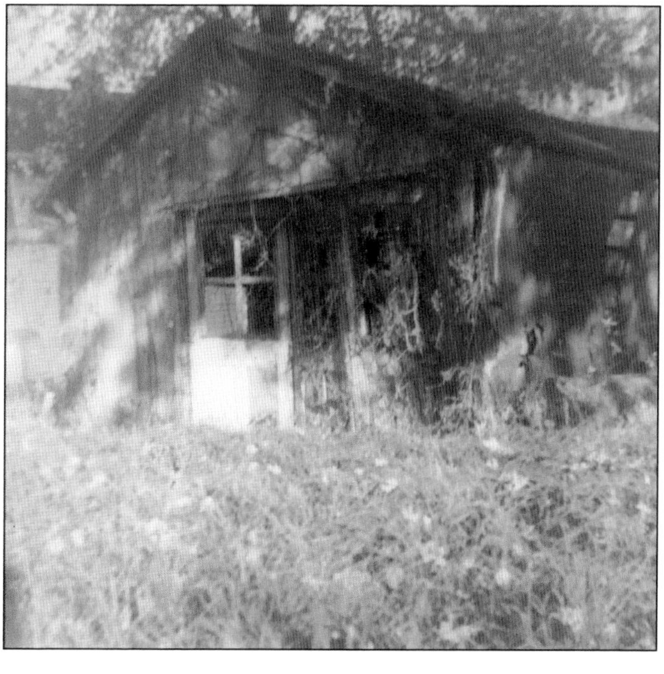

Big Bone Turnpike turns to the left, and a short way down stood an old blacksmith shop on August 24, 1957. At one time it had been operated by Tommy Stephenson. It was torn down not too long after this image was taken. (Eunice Mershon.)

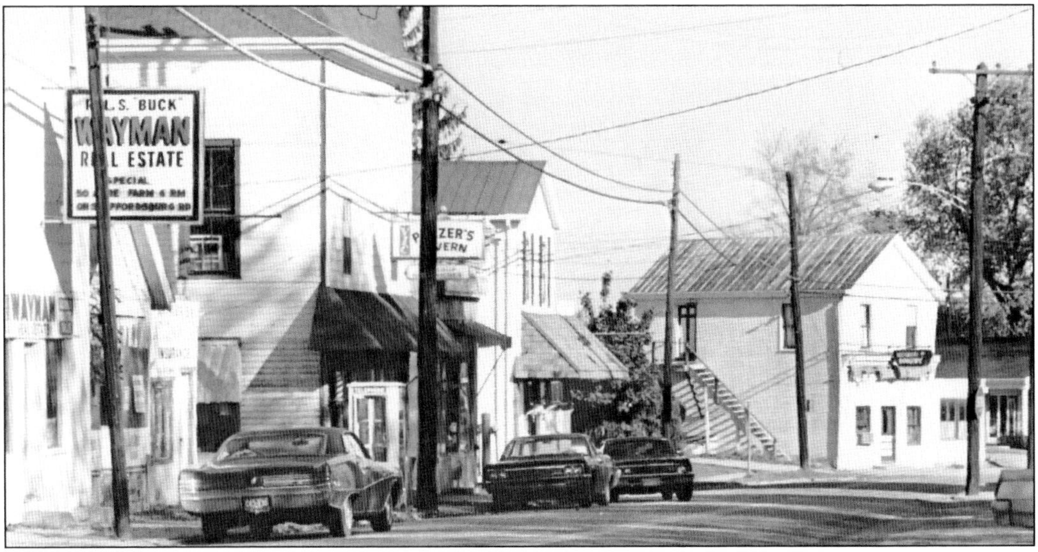

This early-1970s streetscape shows the west side of Madison Pike from the Wayman Real Estate office at 5271 Madison Pike north to the old Schoborg/Galloway store. The Odd Fellows hall is occupied by Vic Ponzer's Tavern in this image. (Kenton County Public Library.)

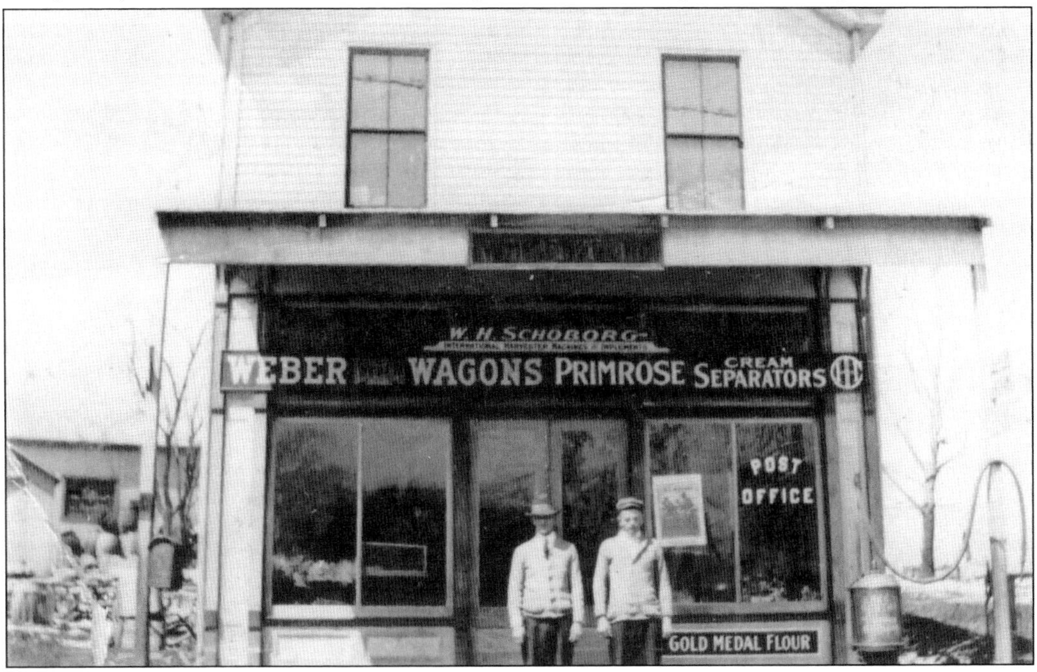

W.H. Schoborg's store, pictured around 1920 at approximately 5251 Madison Pike, was the post office at this time, which shortly thereafter moved to the old bank/future hardware store at 5263 Madison Pike. Under "W.H. Schoborg," the sign reads "International Harvester Machines and Implements." A cream separator was a canister that stood about three feet tall on legs, and the farmer poured the fresh milk in it. Gravity separated the lighter cream to the top and the farmer drained the milk from the bottom and then the cream. This was a much-used device necessary for Kenton County's large dairy business at that time. The building was demolished. (Karen Fisk Koch.)

Rounding the bend with the grocery on the left, on the right is a house owned by the Durr family at probably 5247 Madison Pike. A bank was later constructed on the site, which housed the Independence city offices from approximately 1995 until 2004. Standing in front of the new Bank of Independence in the 1930s are, from left to right, Charlie Williams, Joe Warren, and unidentified. The sign above them reads "No parking this side of street." Gasoline was available beside the store; the circular sign reads "Gulf." (M. W. Jackson.)

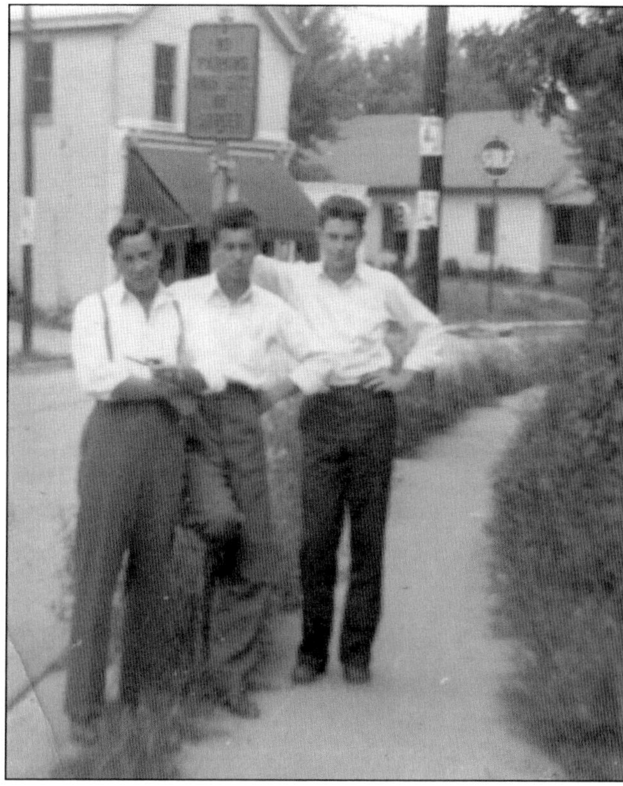

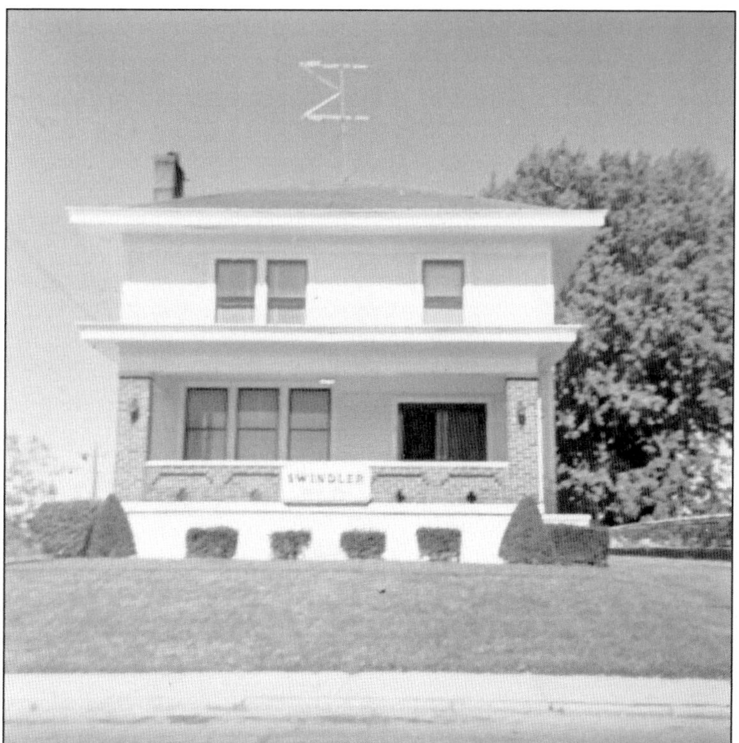

Swindler Funeral Home at 5245 Madison Pike is the site of the original St. Cecilia Church, which burned in 1919. Subsequently, Galloway constructed a house on the site for the Bannister sisters, and in 1937, T.M. and Viola Swindler purchased the house and converted it to a funeral home. The first manager was Charlie Dorsey, and after his death, he was succeeded by Frank LeMaster. The funeral home shown in this 1966 image is still family-operated and is believed to be the oldest family business in downtown Independence today. (Eunice Mershon.)

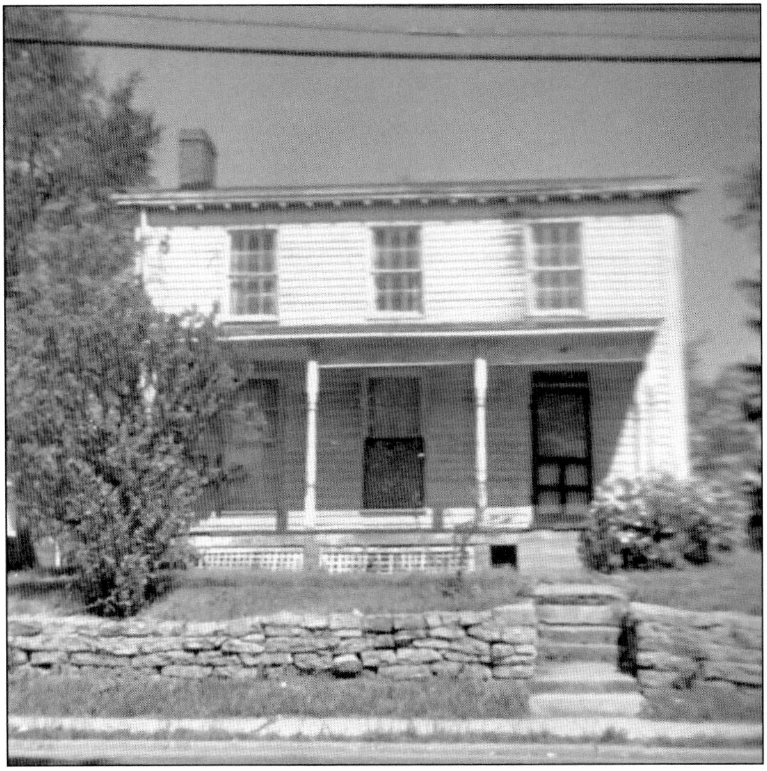

Fult Williams and then his daughter Alice Jane Williams owned this home at 5243 Madison Pike. It was razed for a parking lot for the adjacent funeral home. This image is from around 1966. (Eunice Mershon.)

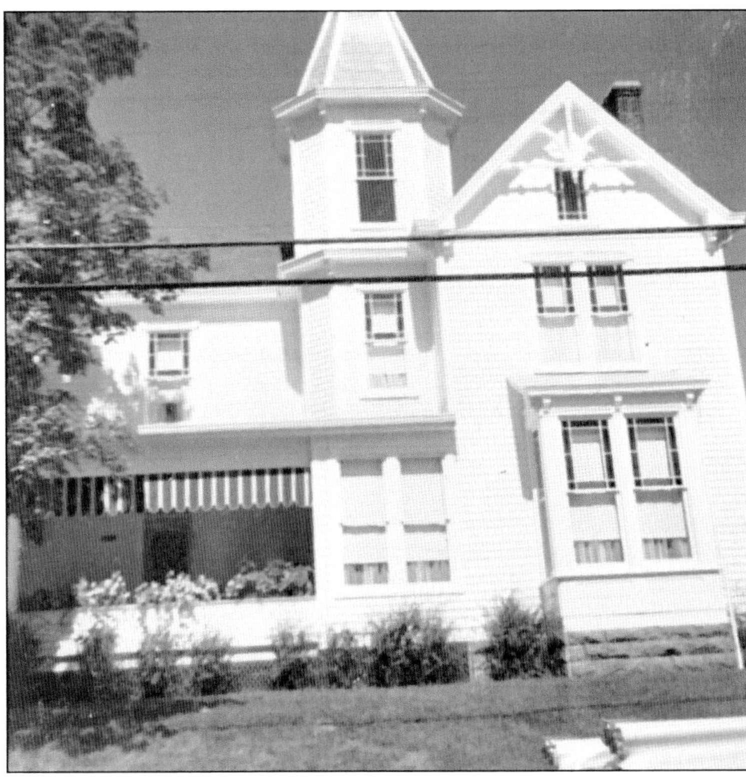

The c. 1887 Queen Anne Metcalf-Stephens House at 5241 Madison Pike is the only building in Independence listed on the National Register of Historic Places. It has not changed significantly from this 1966 image. It has been lovingly restored inside, with original woodwork and stained-glass windows retained. (Eunice Mershon.)

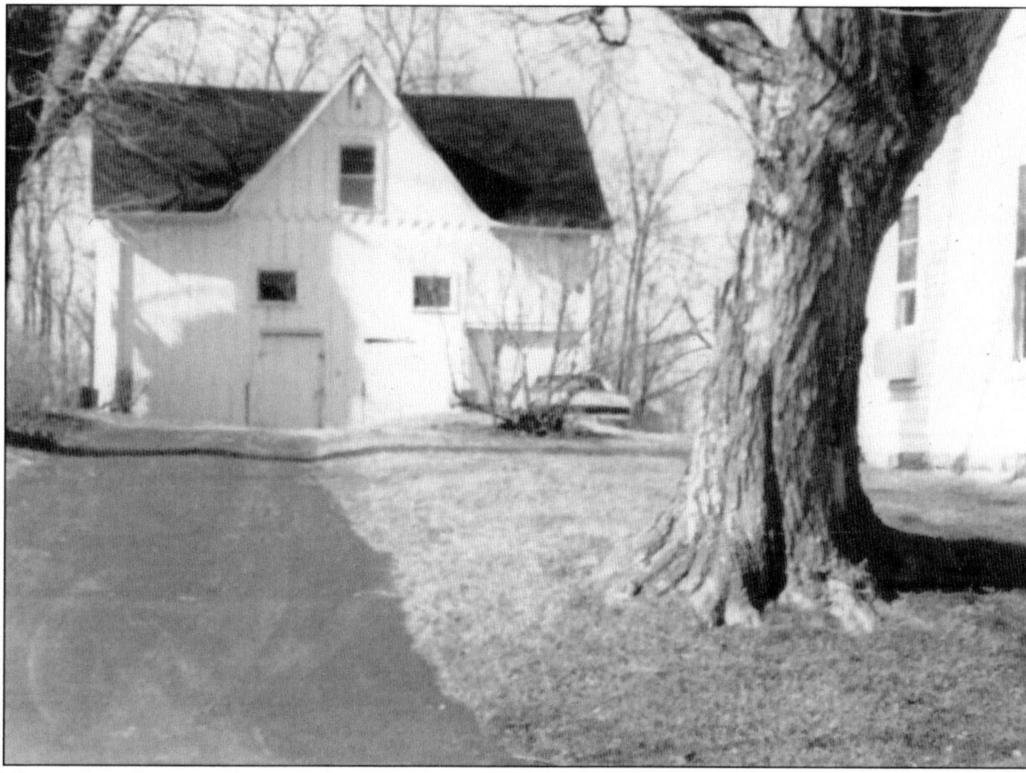

The carriage house to the rear of 5241 Madison Pike was razed in 2005, when it became unsalvageable. The early owners would house their horses and buggies and later their automobiles in it. It is shown in 1989. (Eunice Mershon.)

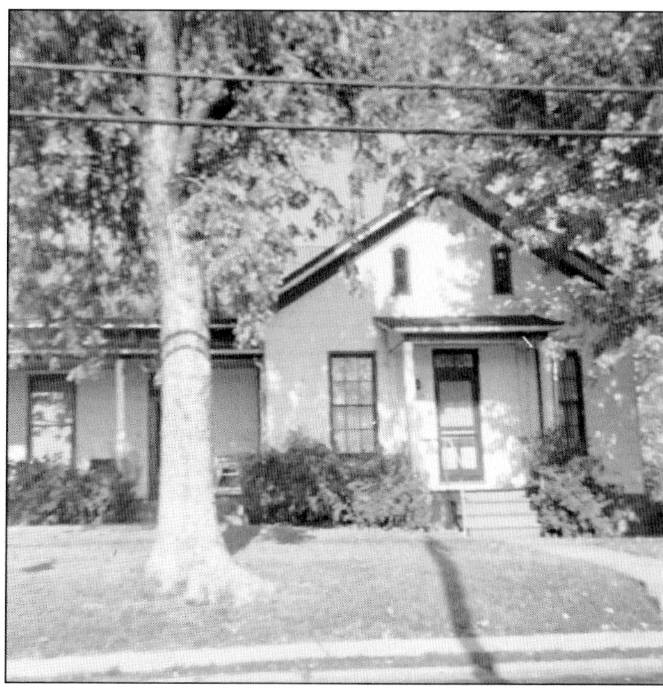

This historic home at 5235 Madison Pike in 1894 was a school started by George W. and Mary Dunlap. Later, C.V. Lucy and his mother ran it until Independence School was opened in 1912. Lena Mills lived there for many years. It has changed little from The 1897 *Catalogue of the Independence High School* picture (page 109) in this 1965 image. (Eunice Mershon.)

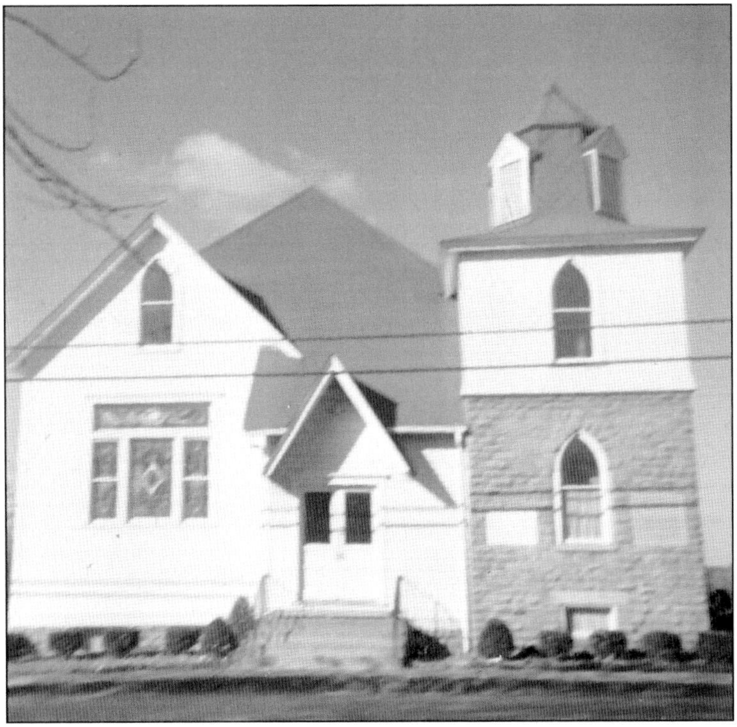

Independence Christian Church, shown here in 1966, is at 5221 Madison Pike. This church was razed and the present building dedicated in 1968. The church began as a Presbyterian church around 1900, but as interest waned, it became Independence Christian Church in 1910. (Eunice Mershon.)

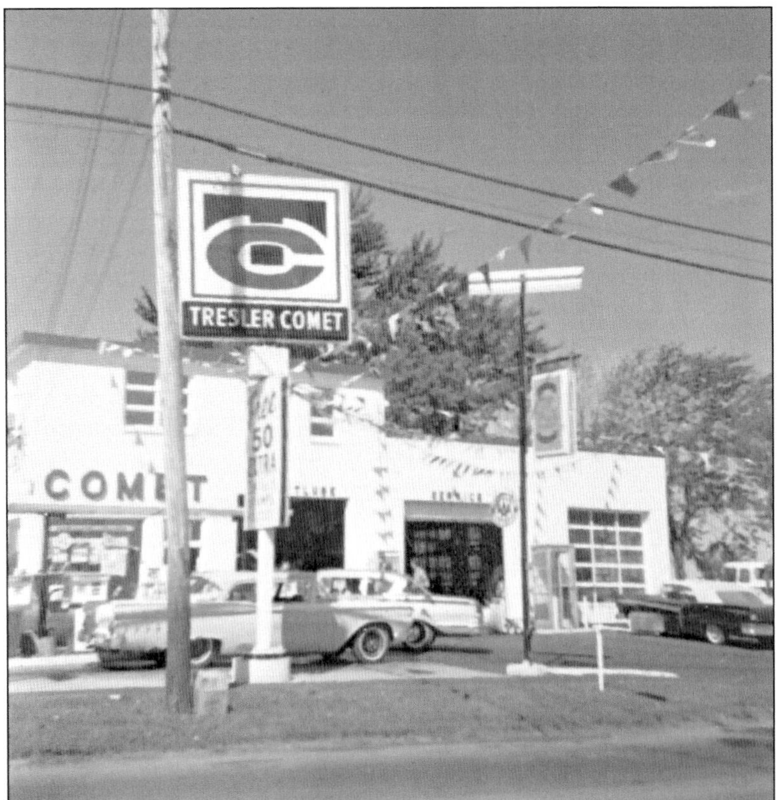

Chapman's service station at 5213 Madison Pike, shown on September 5, 1966, had four gas pumps and was a Shell dealer before it became a Tresler Comet station. Don Chapman ran it for many years. The sign over the left bay reads "Service." It is an automotive business today. (Eunice Mershon.)

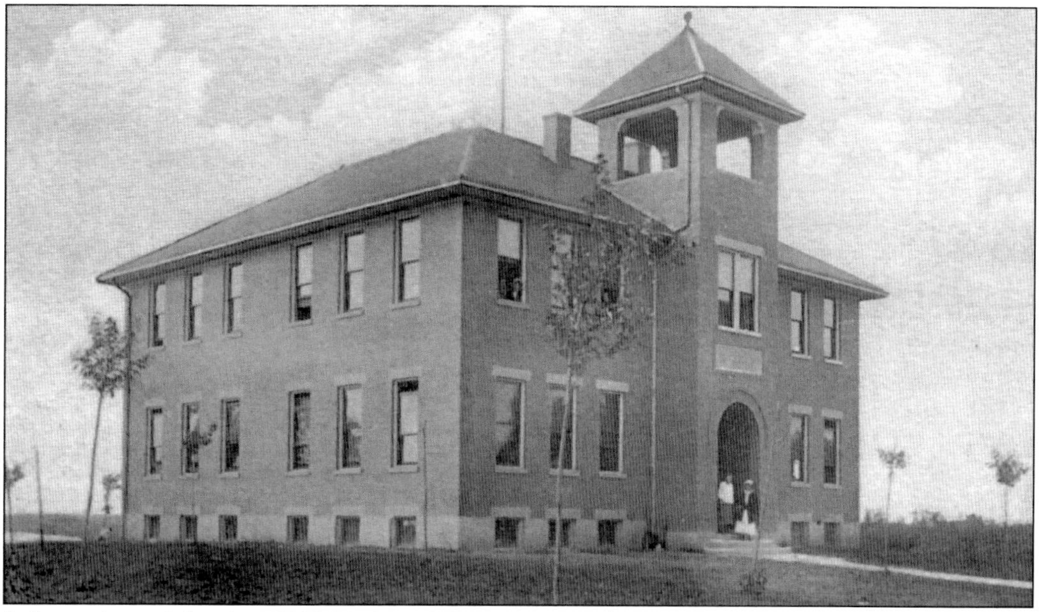

Independence School, at 5209 Madison Pike, was opened in 1912. This postcard image was taken soon after it opened. The last graduating class was in 1937, and then the high school moved to Simon Kenton High School. It continued to be an elementary school until 1954. It has seen a variety of uses since then with various businesses and was a florist for a while. Today it is used as apartments. (Jerry Schneider.)

Crossing Independence Station Road at the corner with Madison Pike is Criswell's service station, owned by Joe Criswell. In this October 19, 1957, image, the pumps, one dispensing regular and the other ethyl gasoline, are ready for a customer. The building at 5195 Madison Pike was remodeled into an office some time later and is a store today. (Eunice Mershon.)

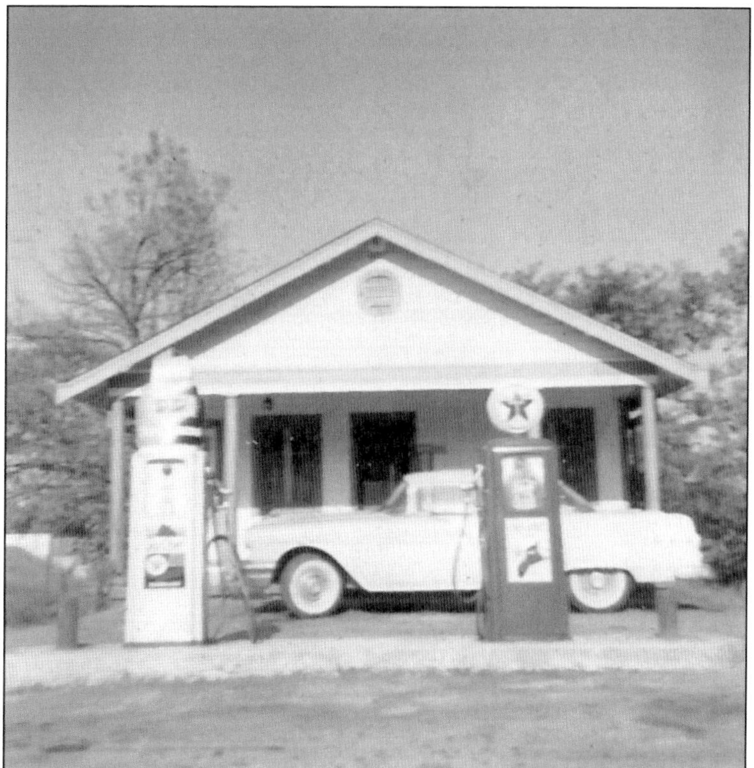

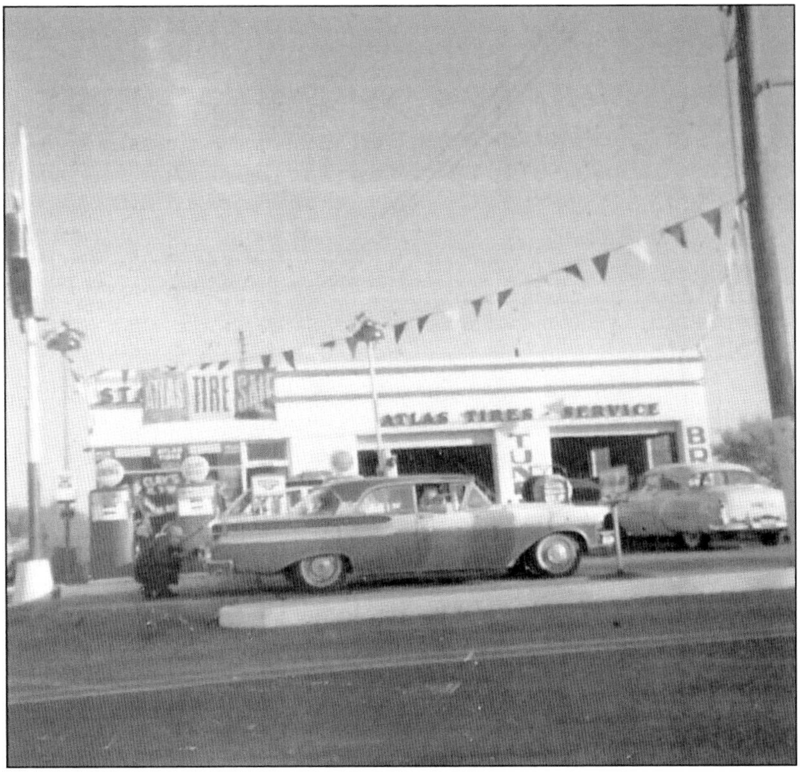

Crossing to the east side of Madison Pike and beginning the return trip south, Schadler's Standard Oil station at 5200 Madison Pike, is pictured around 1966. The sign above the two bays reads "Atlas Tires—Service." The usual two gas pumps are to the left. More bays were later added on the south side of the building, and it remains in use today, several owners after George Schadler. (Eunice Mershon.)

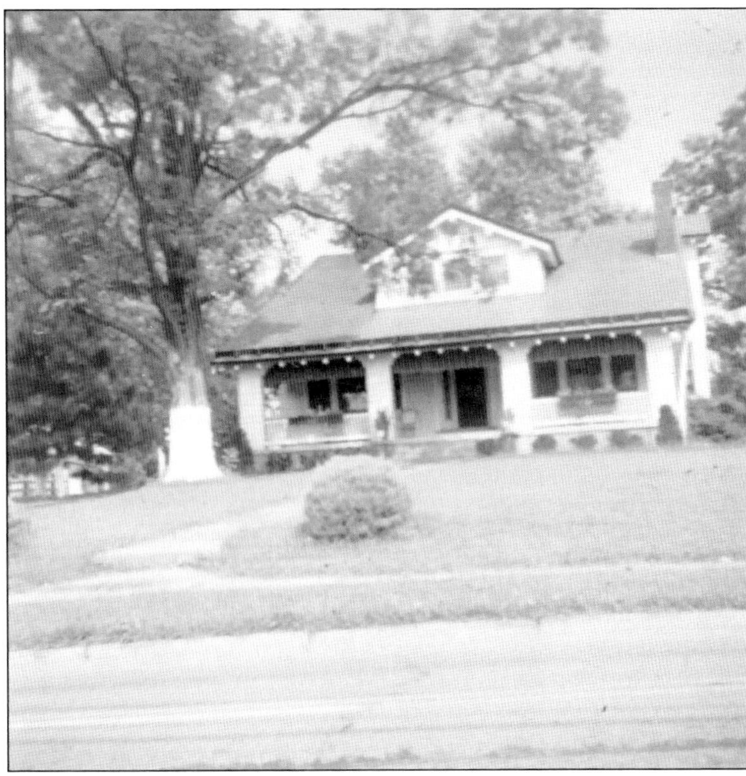

Northcutt Brothers (who built the new courthouse in 1912) built this home at 5220 Madison Pike in 1907 for Dr. Tilford T. Metcalf. He bought the large acreage from a Mr. Oxley. Dr. Metcalf had a row of windows built in the basement so he would have enough light to conduct autopsies. He died in 1914, and his widow, Annabel, sold the house to Sandford Roberts in 1944. The Roberts family operated a dairy, and today it is the only working farm on the stroll. This image was taken on August 24, 1957. (Eunice Mershon.)

Independence Baptist Church moved south to Nicholson, and Grace Baptist, its current owner, opened at 5228 Madison Pike about the time this image was taken in June 1965. The church was built in 1927. (Eunice Mershon.)

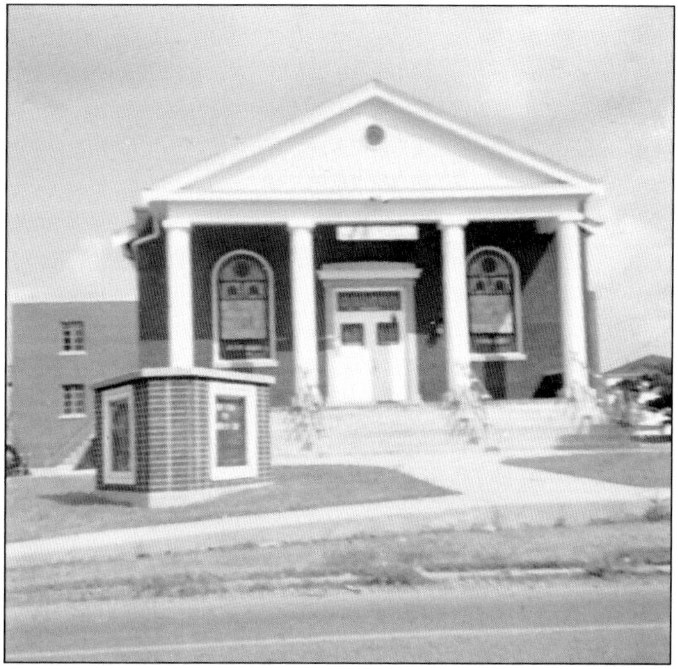

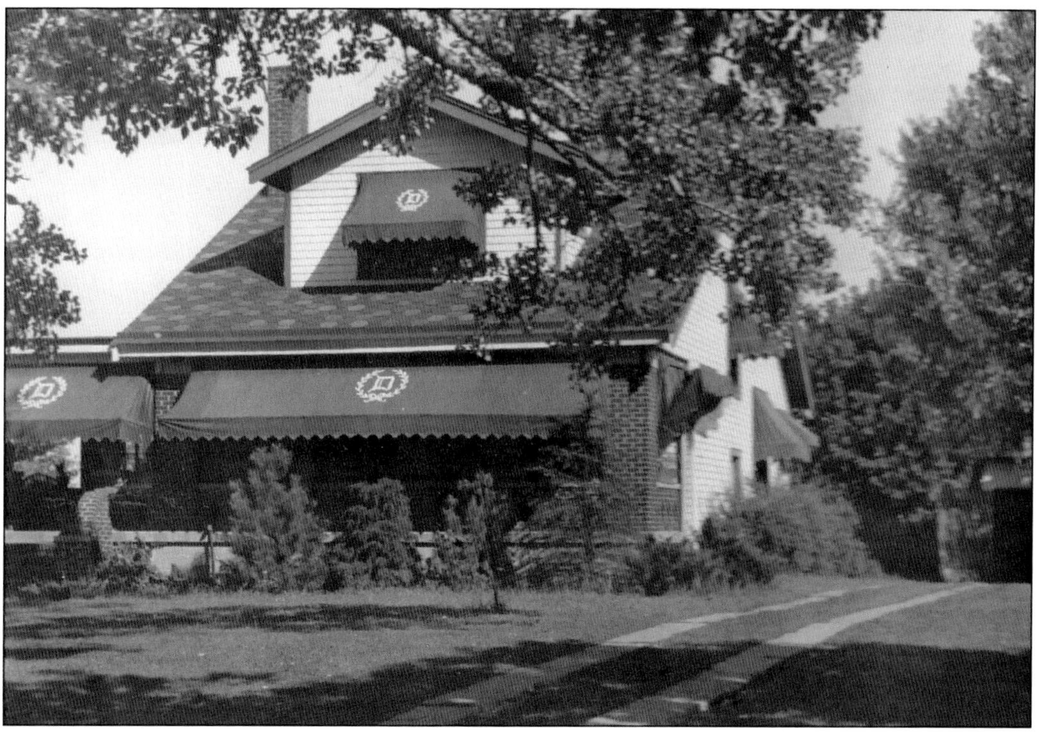

Dr. Franklin Daugherty and his wife, Virginia Hogrefe Daugherty, lived and had his medical office at 5232 Madison Pike in this 1940s image. He started practicing medicine in 1925, and his son—with the same name—also practiced medicine in Independence. Later, Marion Schadler moved there, where he still lives today, and he served as mayor from 1974 to 1990. (Senator Katie Kratz Stine.)

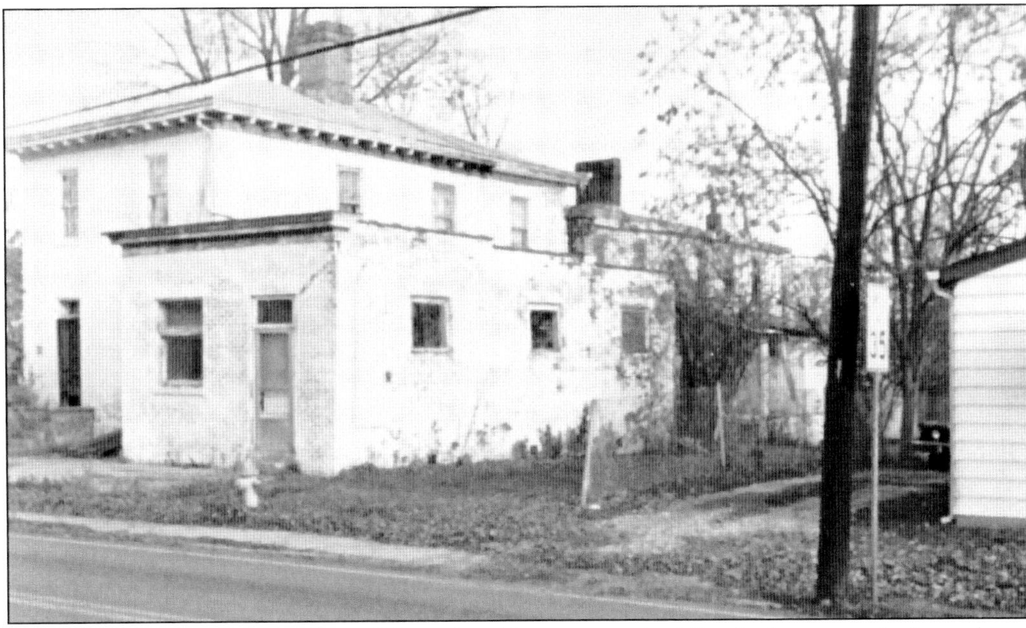

The Oxley House at 5234 Madison Pike is the oldest existing building in downtown Independence. An addition to the c. 1847 house on the south side is shown in this November 1988 image. The addition was removed to restore the house to its original condition. It is now a museum, open by appointment. (Eunice Mershon.)

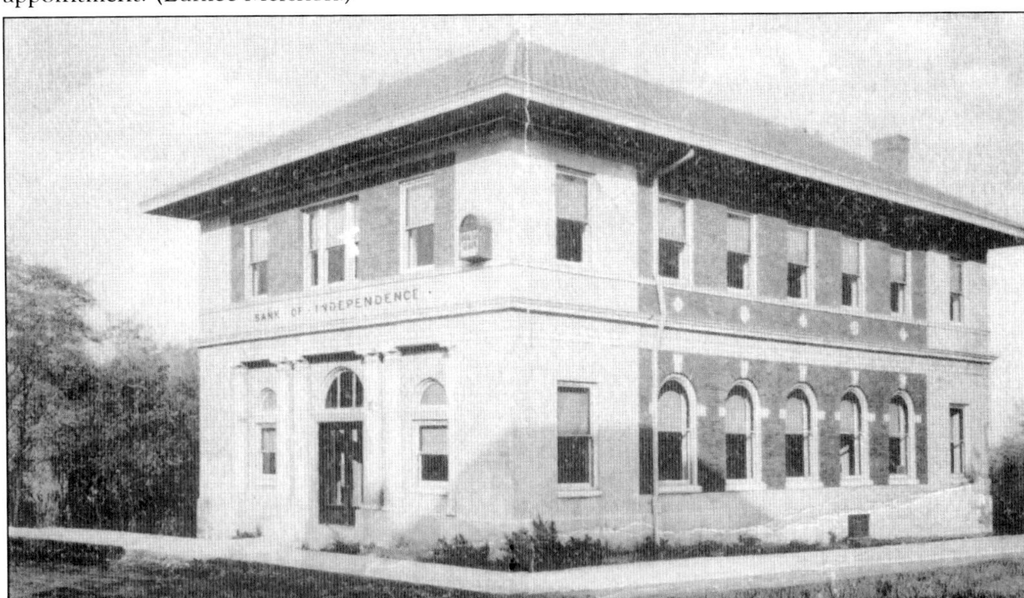

The Bank of Independence opened for business in 1903 across the street, and when it outgrew that building, it constructed this one in 1920 at 5263 Madison Pike at the intersection with McCullum Road. The building is practically unchanged since this postcard image taken in the early 1920s. Various businesses have operated on the second floor, but the first floor has continuously operated as a bank to this day. Around 1971, the Bank of Independence merged with Peoples Liberty Bank, which has merged several more times thereafter. (Jerry Schneider.)

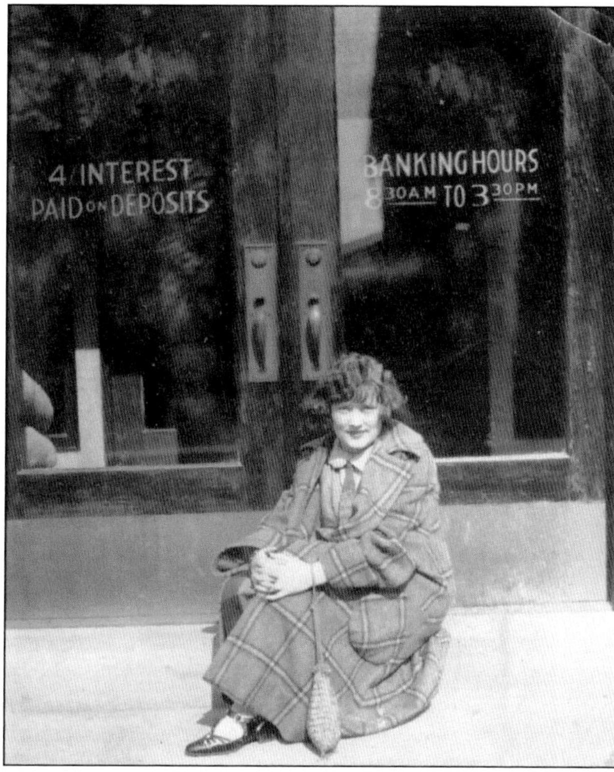

Sitting on the front step of the Bank of Independence in the 1920s is Hazel Stone. "Banker's hours" referred to the relatively few hours a bank was open compared to the long workday of a farmer. Balancing the books took a long time without the technology of today, so a bank had to close early to have enough time to balance the day's business. Banker's hours were 8:30 a.m. to 3:30 p.m. at that time. (Peggy Powers Baum.)

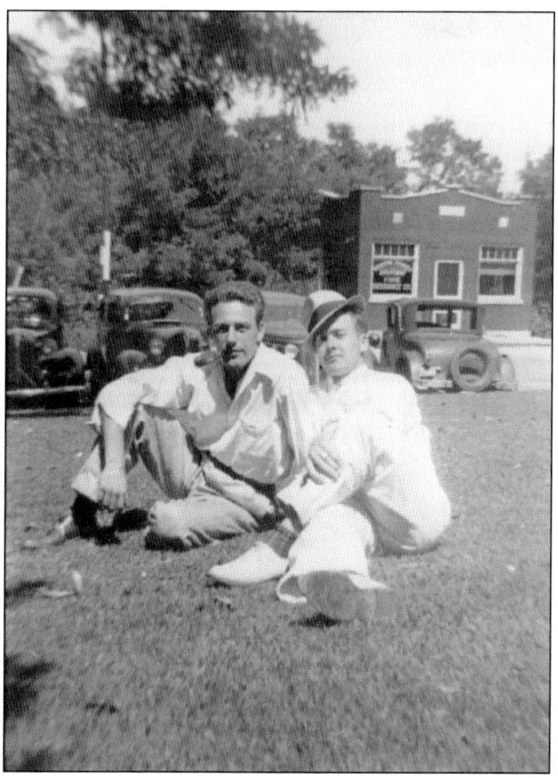

Lloyd Baldwin (left) and Howard Clinkenbeard rest on the courthouse lawn in the 1930s. Behind them, just behind the bank, is Kenton County Fire Assessment Company at 8 McCullum Road. The company has been doing business for over 100 years and is still in that brick building today. Baldwin was a radio announcer for WCKY and the moderator for the *It's Academic* television show. (M.W. Jackson.)

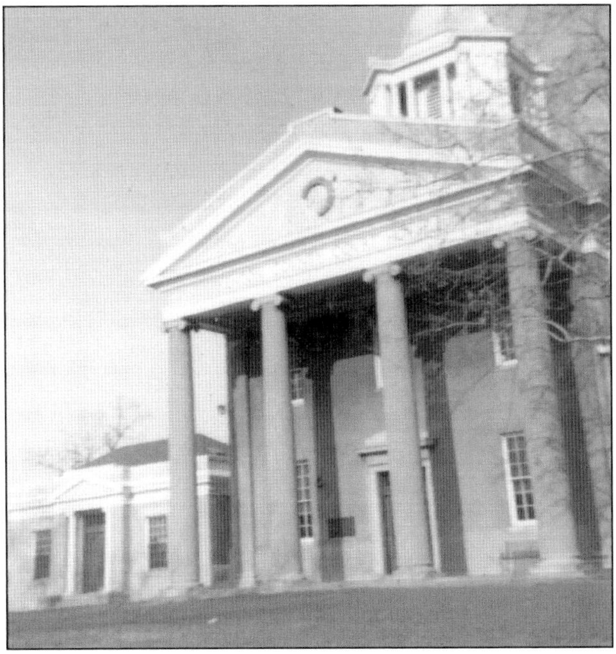

The Kenton County Courthouse, at 5272 Madison Pike, stands watch over the center of town, here shown on April 18, 1958, before it was painted white in 1964. It was constructed in 1912, replacing the courthouse built in the early 1840s. Various veterans' memorials have graced the northwest corner of the square, and one is there today. The official Kenton County tree, the Aristocrat Pear, is planted on the south side of the lawn. The courthouse is open for weekday business to the public. County land records from 1840 to the present are kept in the clerk's office. The Kenton County Fiscal Court alternates its meetings between the Independence and Covington courthouses. (Eunice Mershon.)

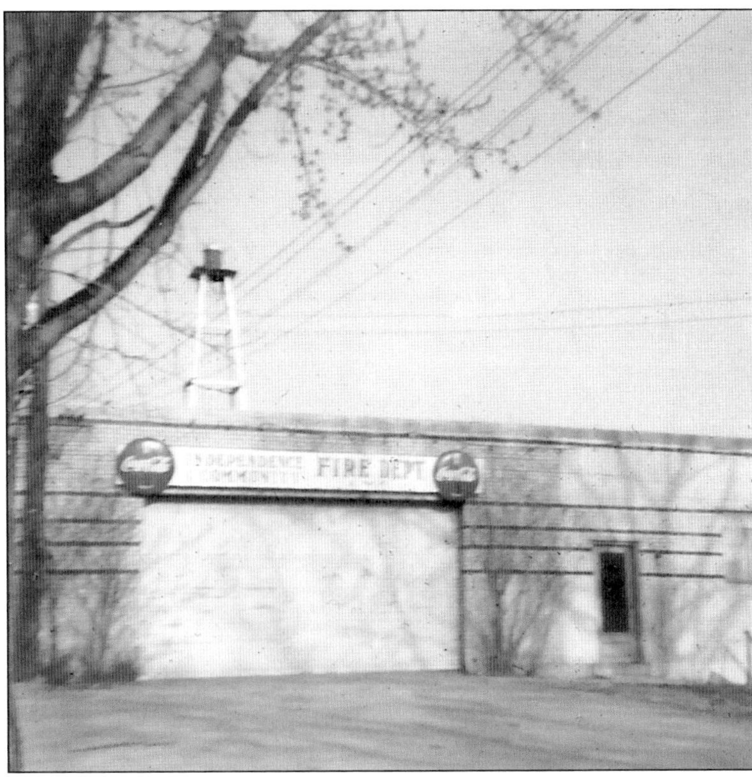

Next door to the courthouse at 5278 Madison Pike was the Independence & Community Fire Department, shown on April 18, 1958. The old Kenton County jail stood here from the 1800s until at least 1920. In 1939, the fire house was built, and used until the new one was built in 1999. It is used now by the county. Firemen's picnics were held every summer on the grounds and behind the courthouse. They were the primary fundraisers for the department and a great place to get a fish sandwich. (Eunice Mershon.)

Standing out in front of her restaurant next door to the fire house at 5284 Madison Pike is Zella Frazier around 1937. These signs of the times reveal much about days gone by. Lunch was only a quarter, and the ladies did not have to worry about being bothered by the men of the day, because they had their own tables! The streetscape in front of the courthouse is visible with the Bank of Independence in the left background. The sign also makes a cameo in the 1937 Independence homemade film that has circulated around town. Zella and her husband, William, owned the building from 1937 to 1946. (M.W. Jackson.)

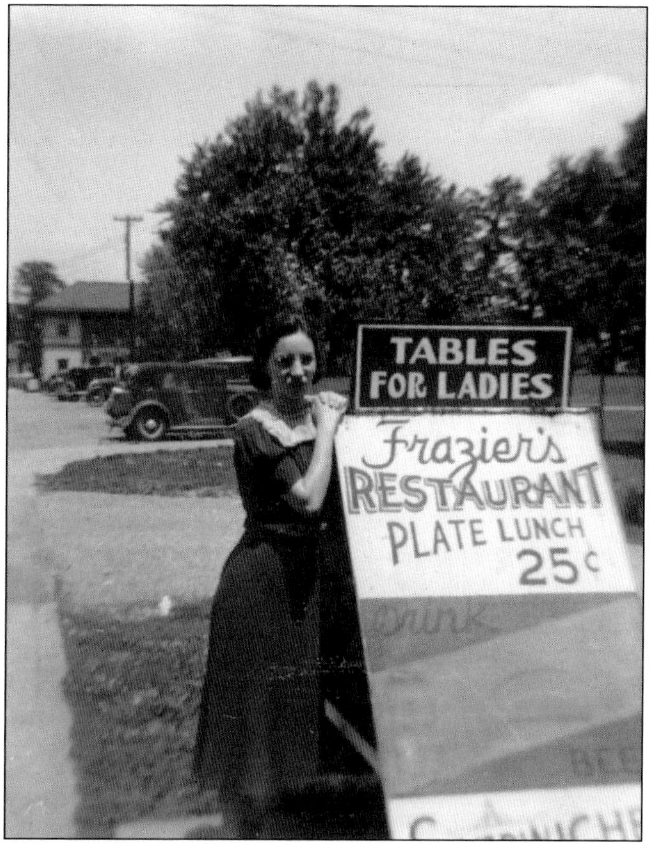

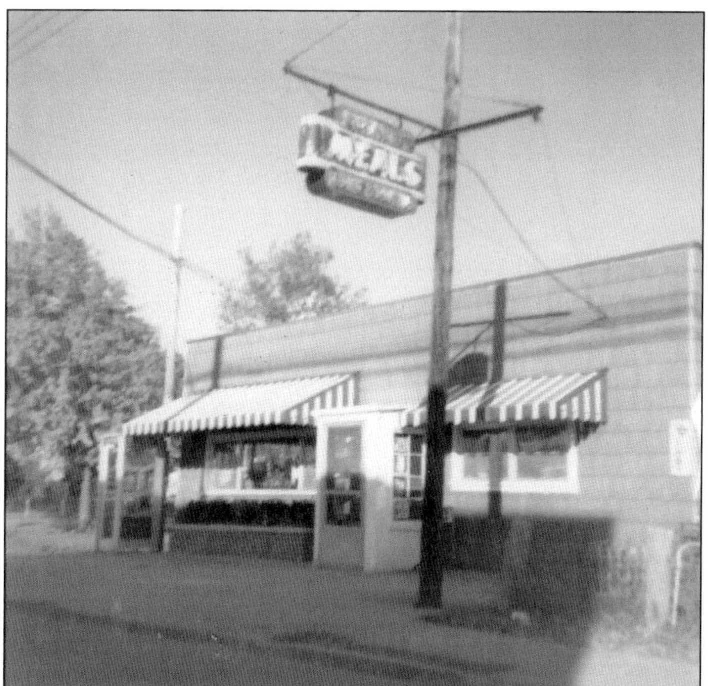

After Frazier's Restaurant, Stewart's was operating in this October 15, 1966, image of 5284 Madison Pike. A fire damaged the building earlier in the 1960s, and a variety of businesses have operated there over the years to the present day. (Eunice Mershon.)

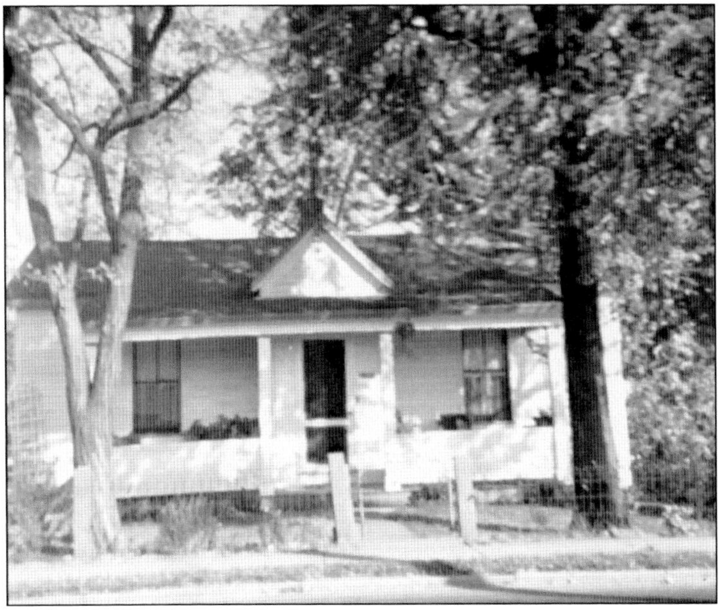

This home at 5286 Madison Pike housed the first telephone exchange in 1907. It was a "sleeping post," with no calls at night. Most customers were on a 10-party line, and the generator was hand-cranked for connections. It is still used as a home, as it was in this 1966 image. (Eunice Mershon.)

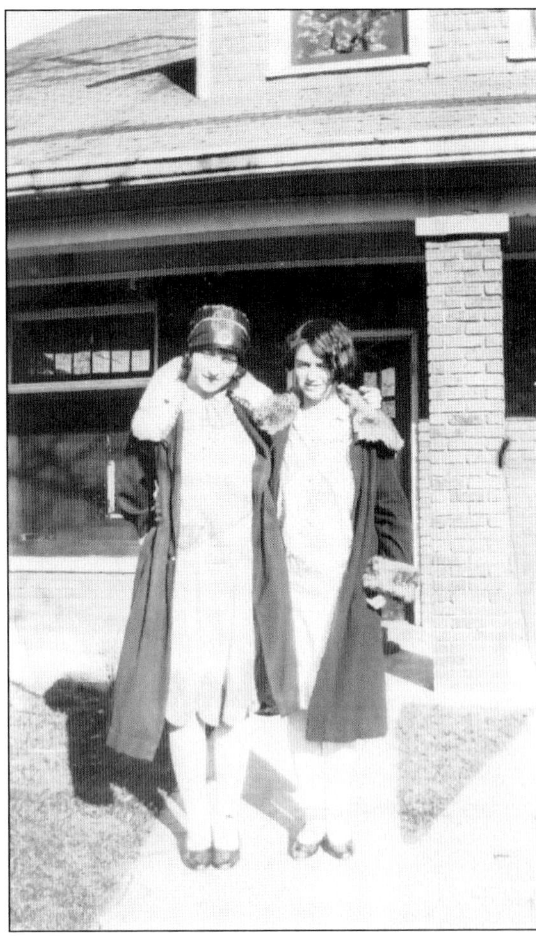

Zelma Beard and Margie Mills (Powers) pose in front of the Beard home at 5292 Madison Pike in the 1920s. The home was later used for the offices of the City of Independence. It has been torn down, and now a new office building has been built. (Peggy Powers Baum.)

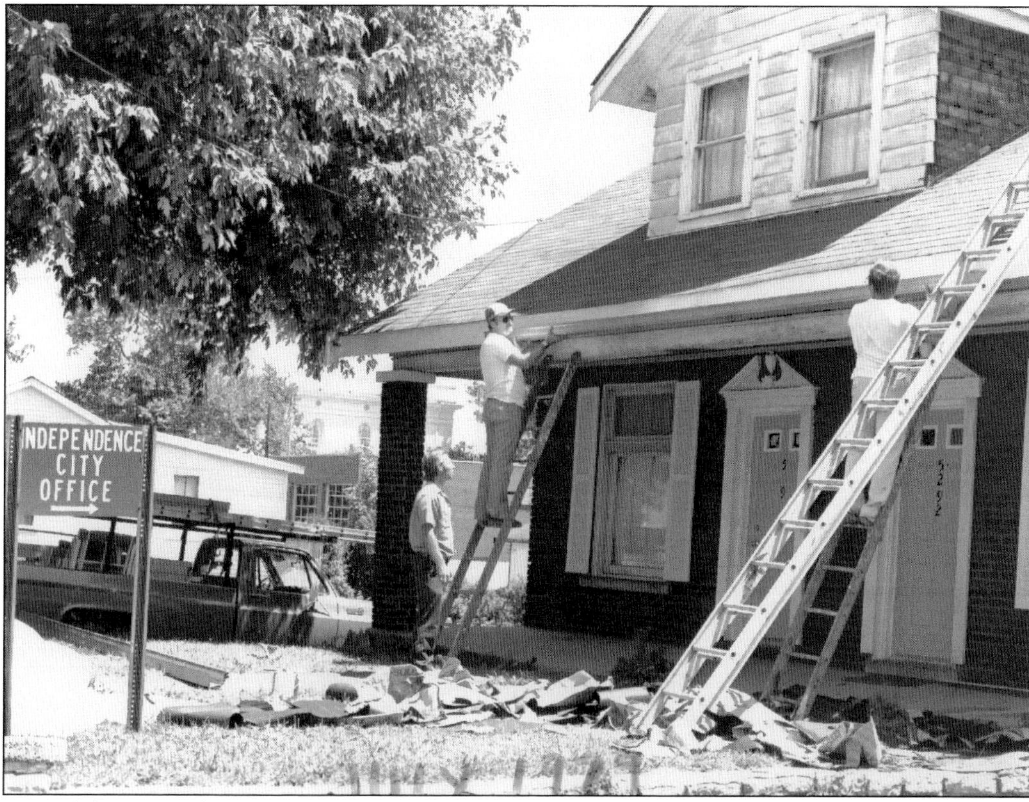

Remodeling is under way at the new Independence City office at 5292 Madison Pike in this July 1979 photograph. It was the first time the city had its own office building, and it was used by the city until approximately 1995. (City of Independence.)

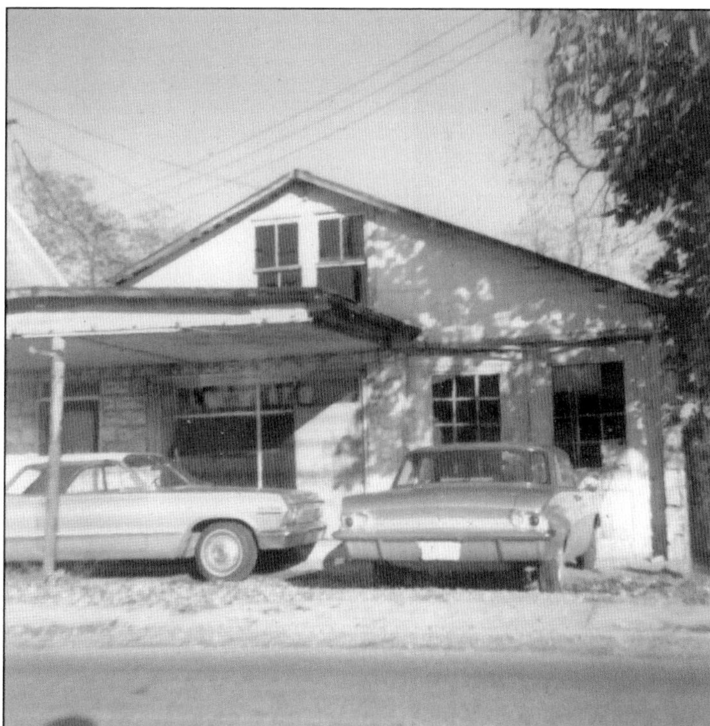

Just south and across from 5293 Madison Pike on the east side of the street was a garage that sold gasoline and was also a residence. Dr. Fred Ray, then Dick Colclough, and then Larry Rounds owned it. It was empty at the time of this October 15, 1966, image. It has been torn down for new office construction. (Eunice Mershon.)

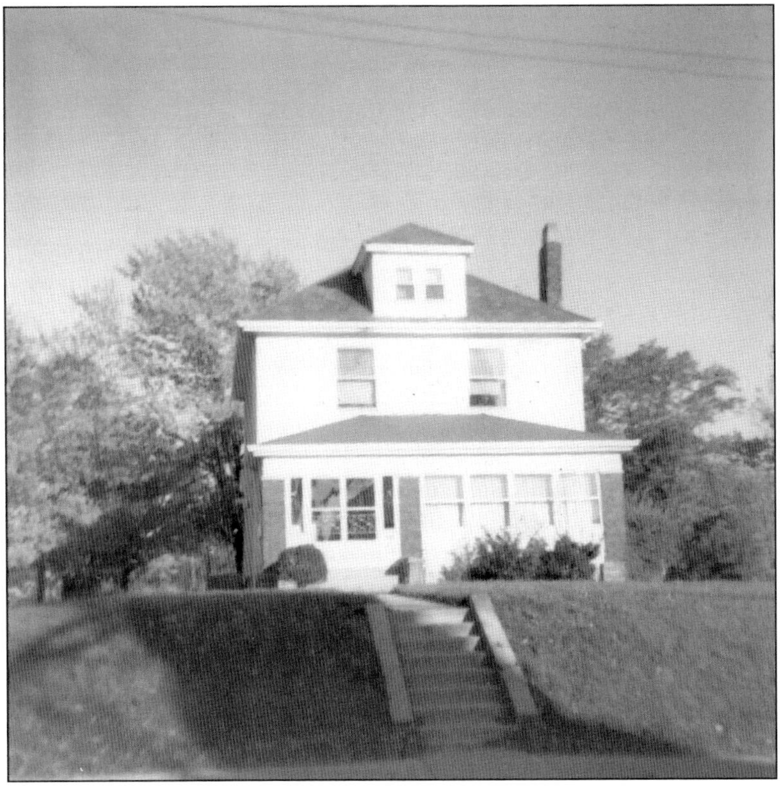

The former home of Dr. Charles Petty is at 5310 Madison Pike, shown on October 15, 1966. Dr. Petty began practicing in 1895 and moved to Independence in 1898. He recalled wearing out a buggy every two years. At age 90, he was "semiretired." It is still a residence. (Eunice Mershon.)

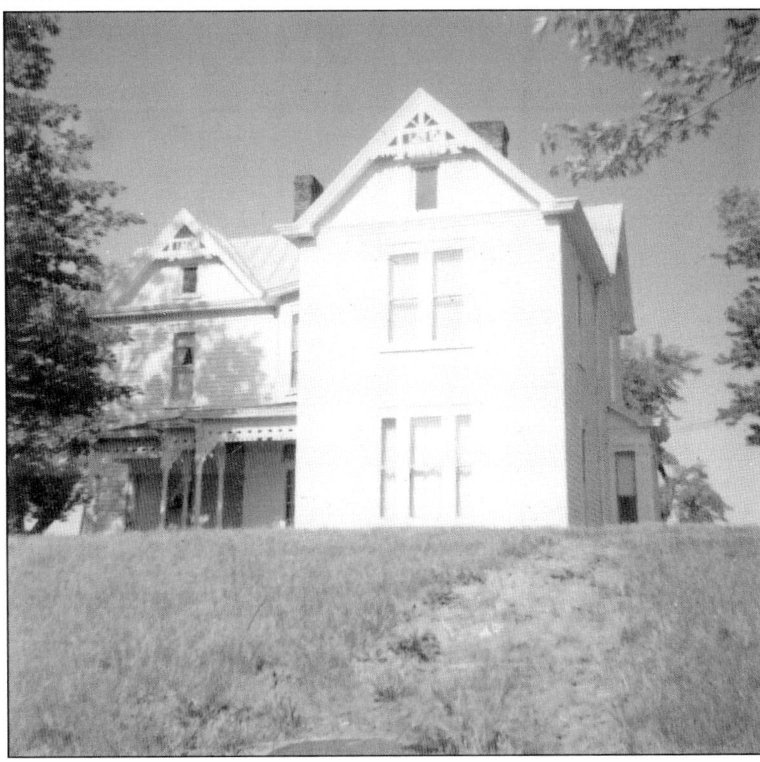

The stroll concludes at Hartland subdivision. The home of Roy Tomlin on Madison Pike is shown on May 30, 1965. This large farm abutted the cemetery on the farm's south side. It was previously the home of Dr. Loomis. It was burned by the fire department in 1998 to make way for Hartland subdivision. (Eunice Mershon.)

Six

CHURCHES AND SCHOOLS

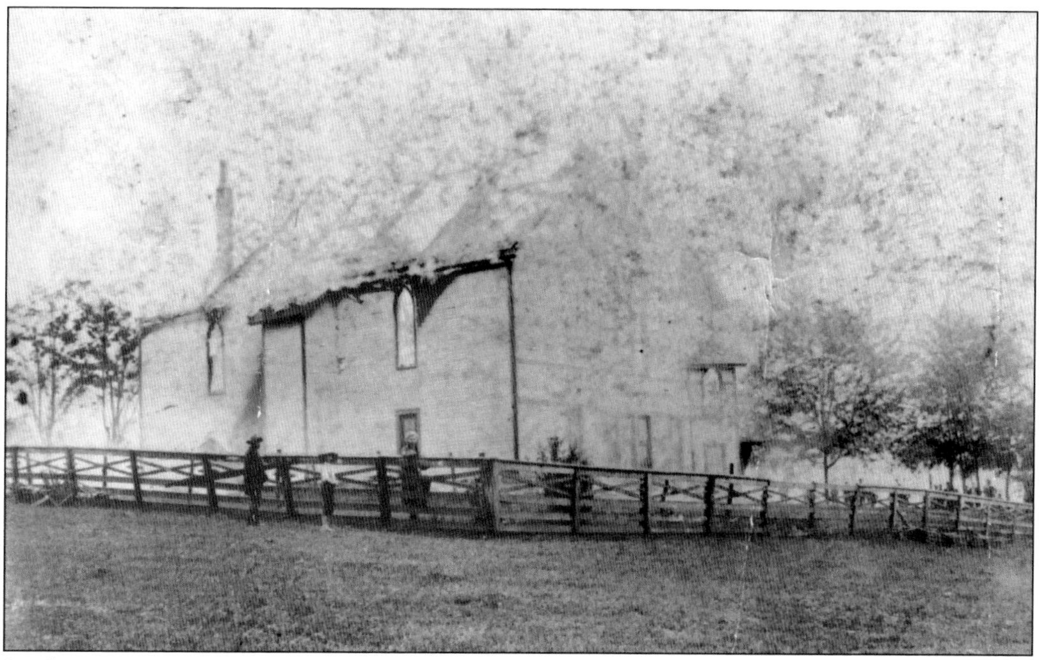

Presbyterian minister George W. Dunlap began preaching and generated sufficient interest for a Union Church to be erected in 1884. Various denominations took turns using the common church. It seated 600 people. Unfortunately, on May 25, 1895, lightning struck the church, and it caught fire. Samuel Folmer saw the smoke and grabbed his camera. The only picture known of it shows it on fire, with the roof already gone and the rafters exposed. Spectators are on the left and right along the fence. Some chairs are piled along the fence, probably saved when the fire was discovered. It burned to the ground and nothing was ever built there. It was on the north side of the driveway of 5220 Madison Pike. The current owner reports that pieces of the church are found when the ground is disturbed. (Jerry Schneider.)

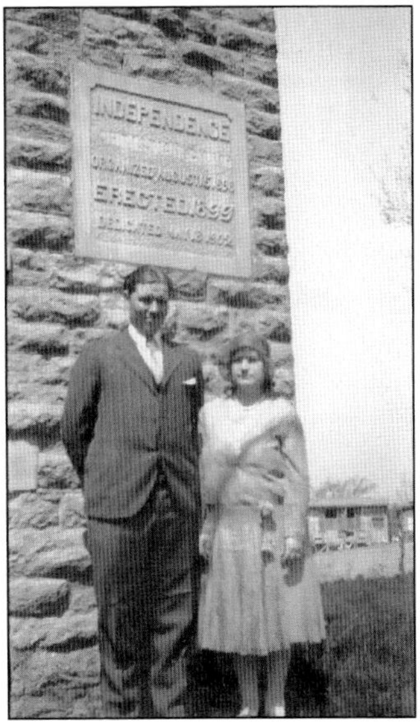

Stanley and Katie Gibson stand in front of Independence Christian Church in 1930. The church building was torn down in 1967 for the current building. This building, erected in 1899, began as a Presbyterian church and became Independence Christian in 1910. After the fire of Union Church, this successor church was built across the street. (Bob and Thelma Gibson.)

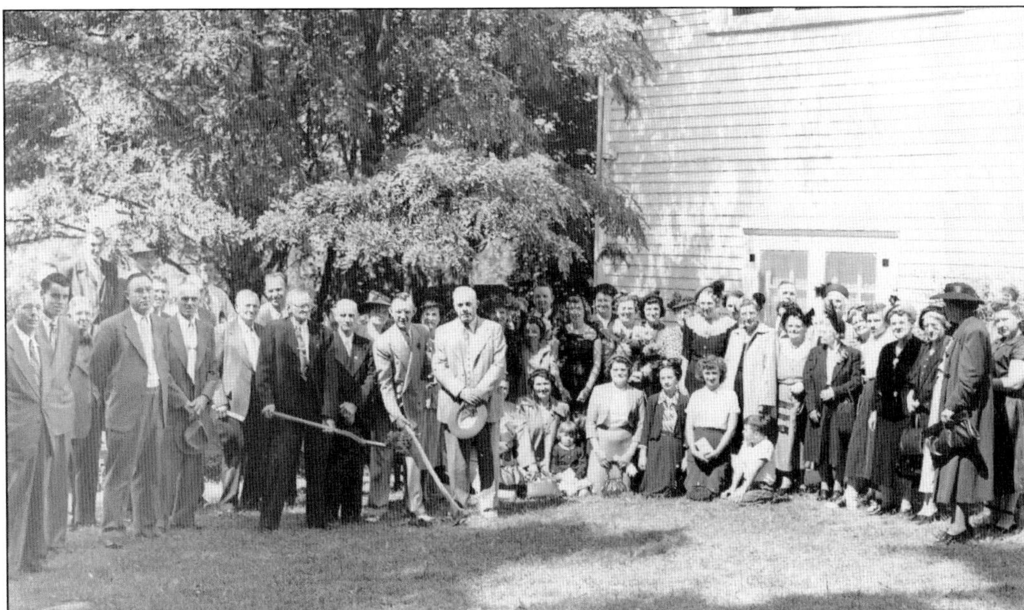

At this Independence Christian Church ground-breaking ceremony in the 1950s for a church addition, are, from left to right, (first row) Mr. Chambers, Howard Williams, Mr. Bagby, Earl Williams, Randall Wagner behind, Ralph Ervin, Mr. Sanders, Mike Wagner with shovel, Floyd Armstrong, Rev. Arthur Tipton, S.A. Roberts with hat in hand, three unidentified, the four ladies kneeling together are Helen Mann, Ruby Armstrong, Ursula Lee, and unidentified; (second row) Norman Ervin, Kenny Rummel, unidentified to lady in hat behind pastor, who is Clara Flerage, unidentified to lady with arm showing at corner of building, who is Addie Tipton, Ethel Williams, two unidentified, Mae Wayman, Mrs. Chambers, Auline Ervin, Virginia Maners, unidentified, Les Fraser, Patsy Wagner, Mrs. Armstrong, Mrs. Sanders, Mrs. Gibson behind her, Mrs. Mann, Doris Williams, Rose Roberts, Helen Fraser (who passed the historic tintype on page 11 and her history files, which were a resource for this book, to Dorothy Schneider), Sadie Wagner, and Mrs. Rummel. (Randall Wagner.)

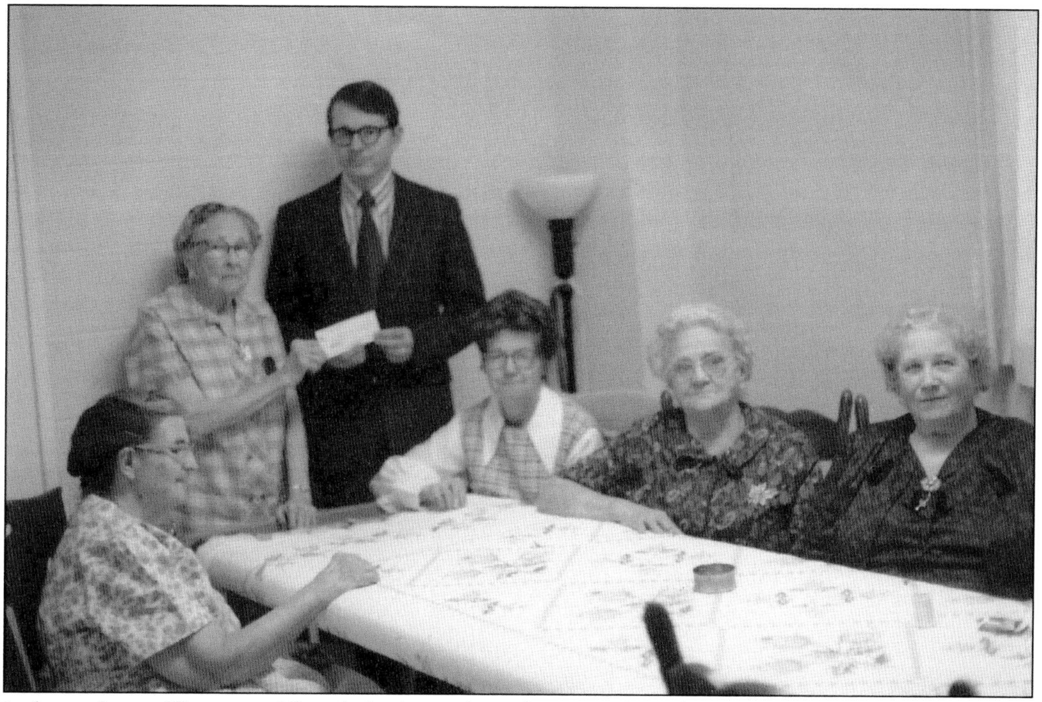

Independence Christian Church had a quilting bee in 1972. Shown from left to right are Mary Esther Stephens, Hallie Wagner, Pastor Maurice Johnson, Bettie Wayman, Lena Mills, and Elsie Hiteman. (Bob and Thelma Gibson.)

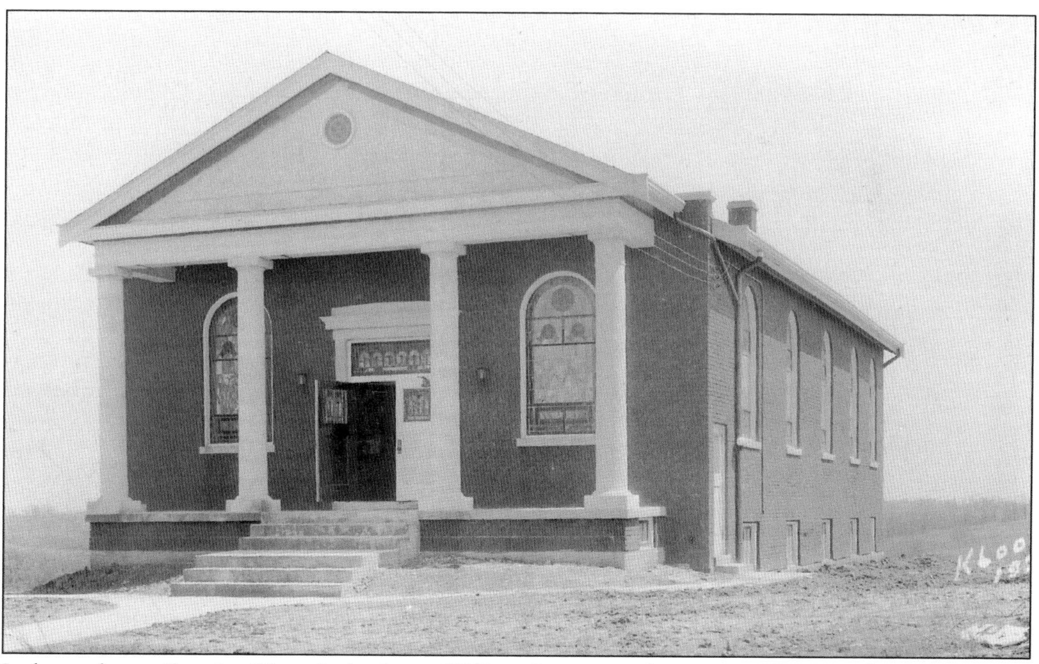

Independence Baptist Church, built in 1927, is shown in this postcard image from the 1930s. The church moved to a new building in Nicholson in 1965, and Grace Baptist began and still ministers in the building at 5228 Madison Pike. (Bob and Thelma Gibson.)

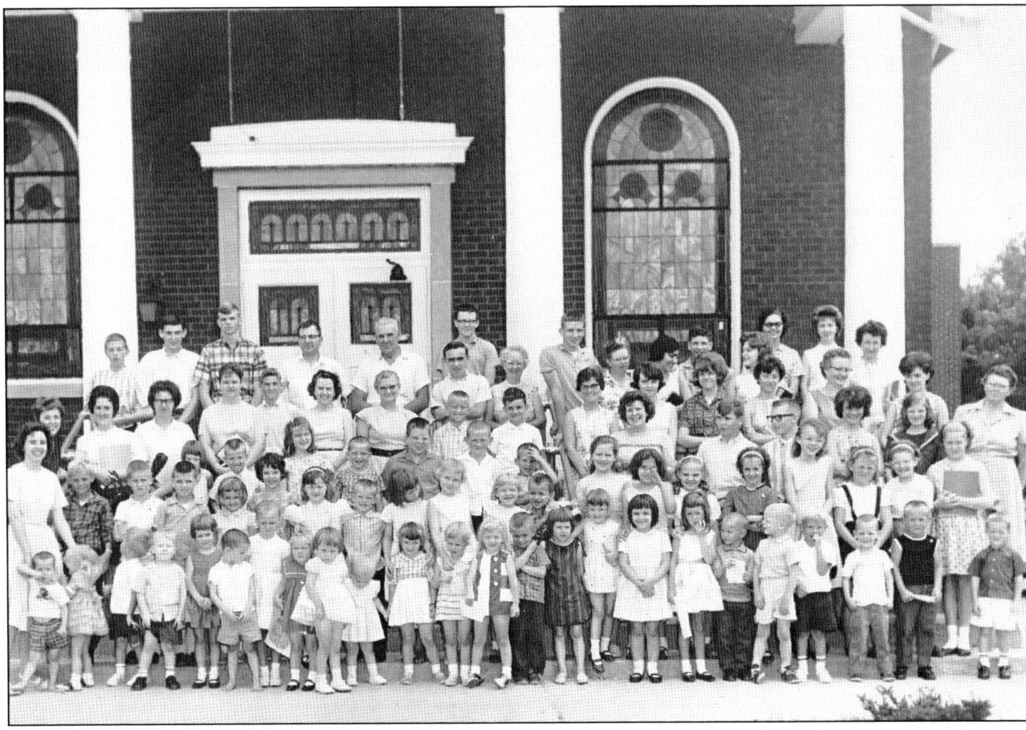

Near the beginning of Grace Baptist Church's ministry, the vacation Bible school poses in front of the church in June 1965. They are, from left to right, (first row) Aleda Smallwood, three unidentified children, Rick Webb, eighth from left Melanie Simpson, and Debra Kerr (author); (second row) eighth from left Lori Simpson; (third row) third from left Beverly Blanton, four unidentified, Mrs. Kureger, Don Schadler, Jim Kerr, two unidentified children, and Mrs. Douglas; (fourth row) three unidentified, Ruth Deck, Chuck Tolliver, Inez Straw, Mrs. Cook, two unidentified, Marian Tolliver, three unidentified, Mrs. Ashcraft, and Pat Markins; (fifth row) Tom Kerr, Mike Tolliver, Dave Schadler, Pastor Kureger, Mr. Deushman, Greg McMillan, Mary Rector, Billy Blanton, Rosella Schadler, Brenda Cook, Bobby Blanton, Karen Meier, unidentified, JoAnn Kerr, and Betty Blanton. (Aleda Smallwood.)

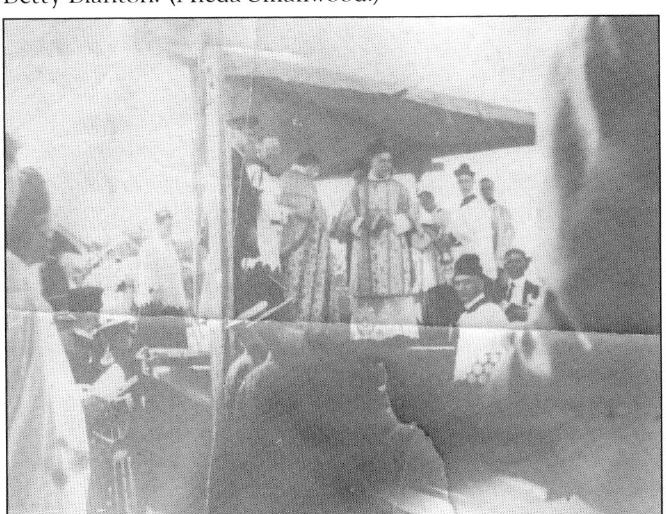

After the first church burned in 1919, St. Cecilia wasted no time in constructing a new church at 5313 Madison Pike. This image captures the laying of the cornerstone on July 27, 1919. A procession began at the courthouse and marched to the grounds for the ceremony. The Right Reverend Bishop Ferdinand Brossart officiated, and high mass was offered. (Karen Fisk Koch.)

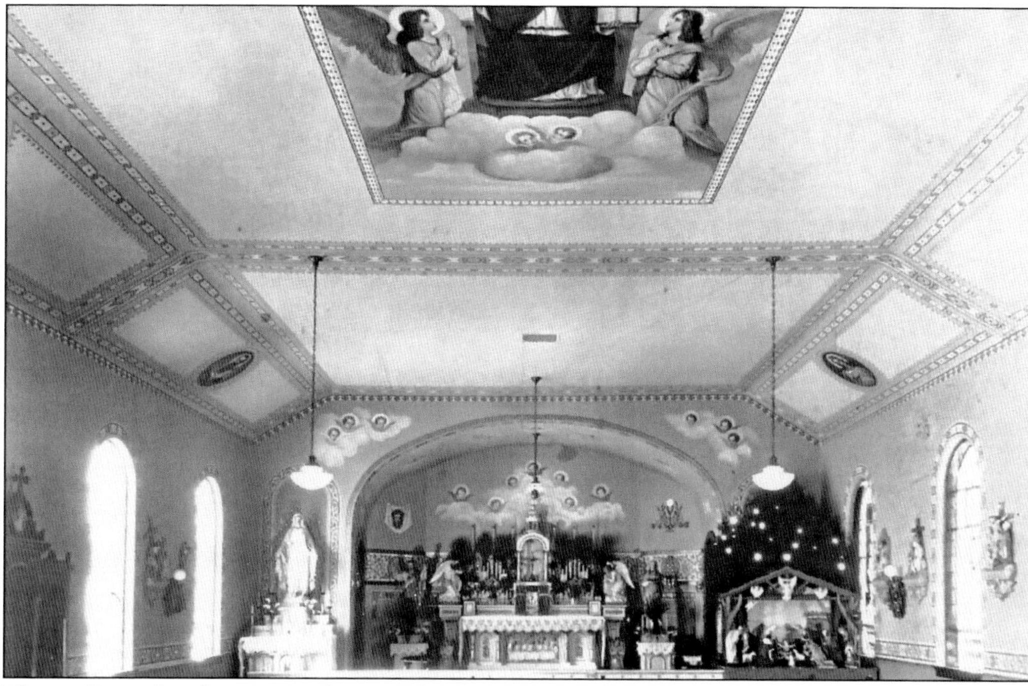

The walls and ceiling were plain in the 1919 St. Cecilia Church until 1927, when Theodore Brasch painted these beautiful murals, shown in the 1930s. This accomplished artist trained in Europe. Various relics from this church were saved and are still used in the present church. (Mary Lou Schoborg Kaub.)

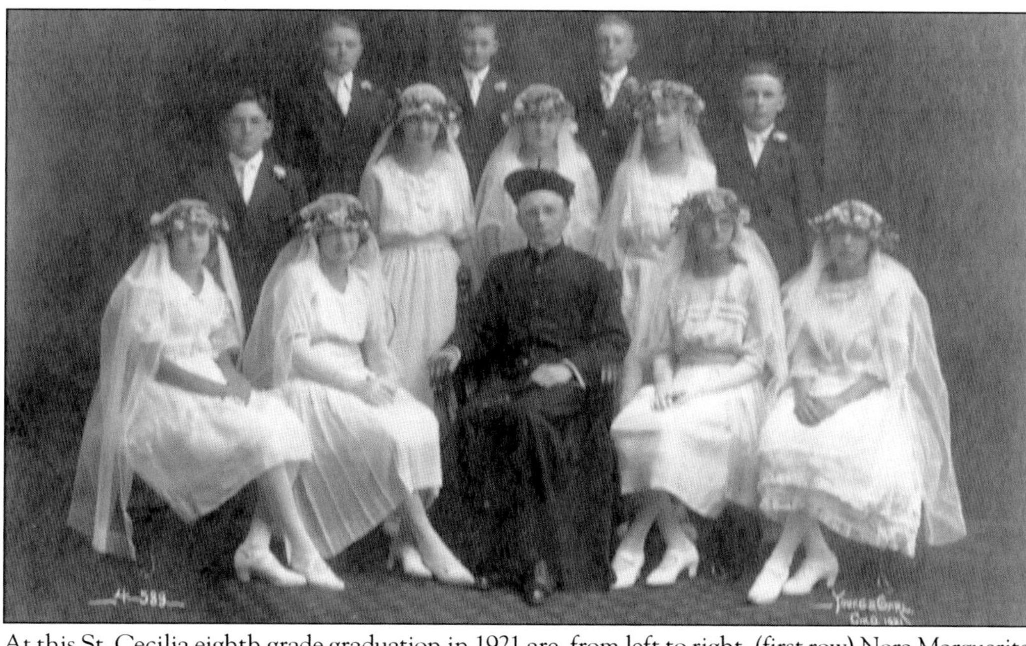

At this St. Cecilia eighth grade graduation in 1921 are, from left to right, (first row) Nora Marguerite Mills, Margaret Gadker, Fr. Henry Herringhaus, Eleanor Herzog, and Mary Ellen Canty; (second row) Stanley Hergott, Irene McGraf, Mary Carroll, Hilda Blau, and Charles Wilson; (third row) Herman Schoborg, Willie Gadker, and Raymond Blau. (Mary Lou Schoborg Kaub.)

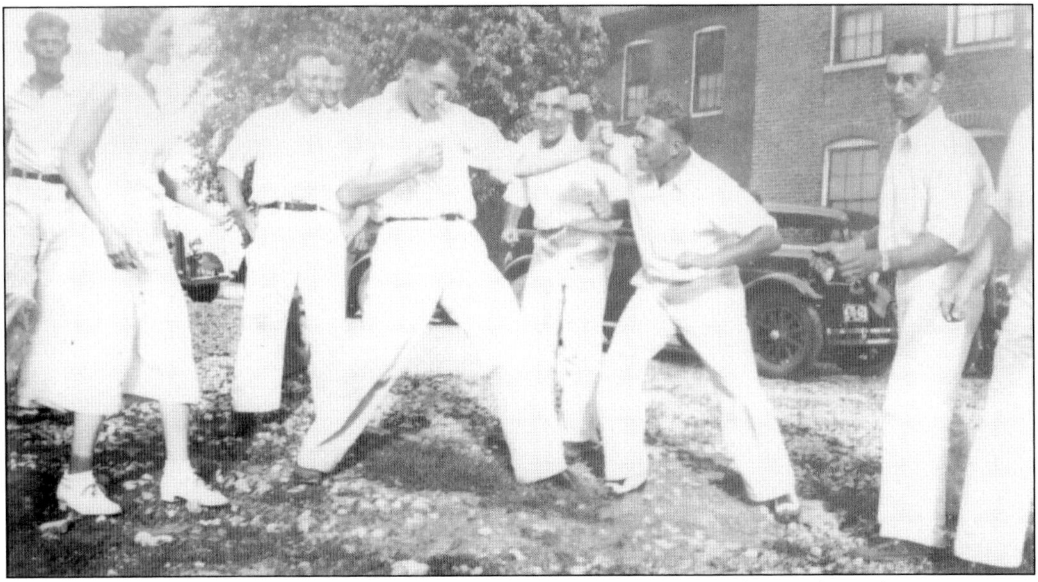

Enjoying a playful sparring match are boxers Ambrose Powers on the left and Stanley Hergott on the right. C. Kaub is the spectator on the far right. They are part of the St. Cecilia Social Club in the 1930s. (Peggy Powers Baum.)

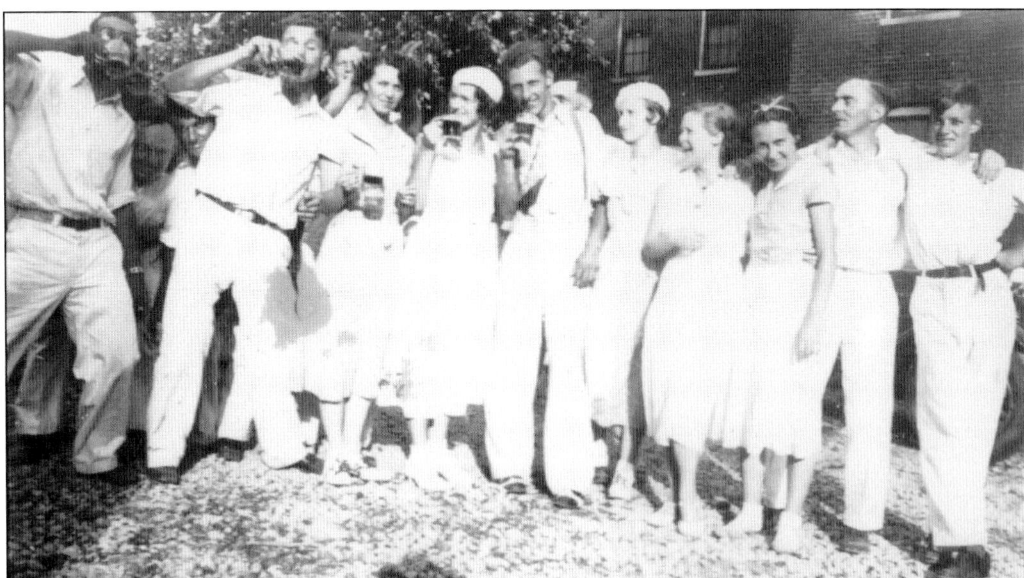

This is another photograph of the St. Cecilia Social Club in the 1930s. This group really seems to enjoy each other and have a good time. The story of St. Cecilia Church is one of steady growth throughout its history since its founding in 1880. (Peggy Powers Baum.)

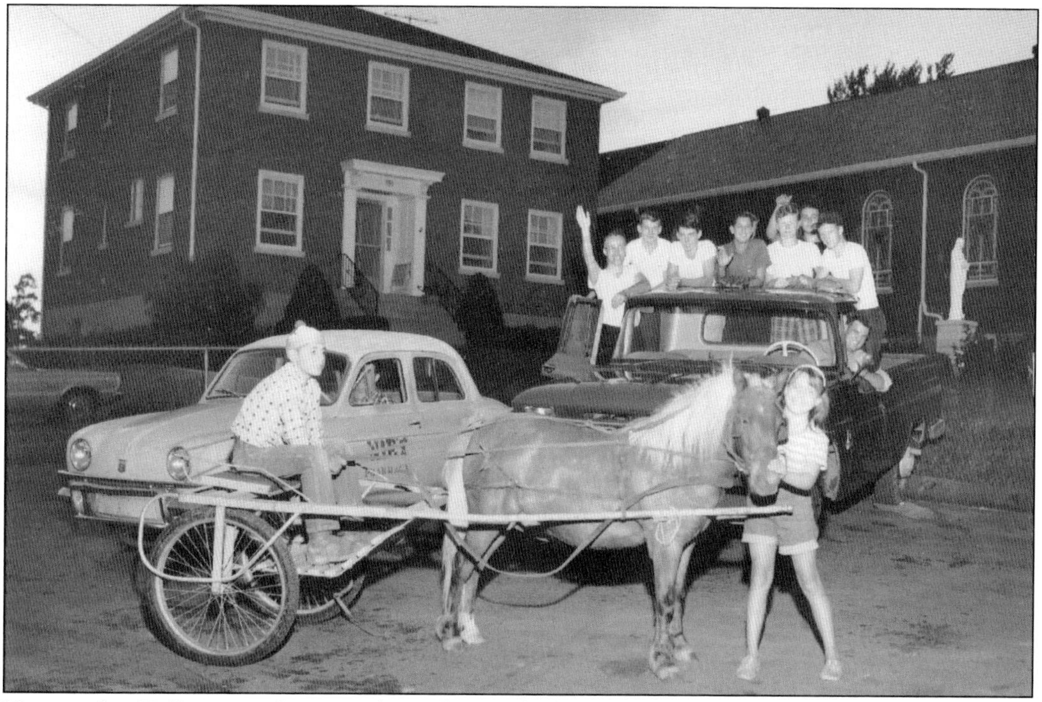

Here is the 1963 cover photograph. It shows all the elements that make Independence what it is: faith—the church; family—the siblings with the horse; friends—the group in the truck; farming—if there's a pony, there's a farm somewhere; family business—the businessman in the car; and fun—everyone is having a good time. (Mary Lou Schoborg Kaub.)

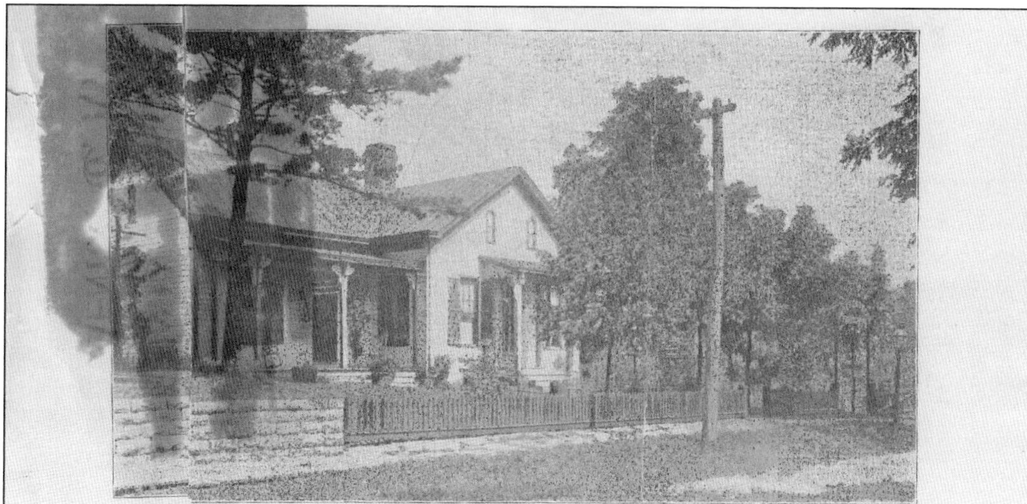

INDEPENDENCE HIGH SCHOOL.

In February 1894, George W. Dunlap and his wife, Mary, started a private high school at 5235 Madison Pike. He was particularly interested in Latin. In their 1897 *Catalogue of the Independence High School*, they list the teachers, subjects taught and cost of study. In this front page from that catalog, the school building is pictured. Courses of study for all four high school years were offered. Note the archway on the right, which reads "Independence High School." (Barbara Giles Gabbard.)

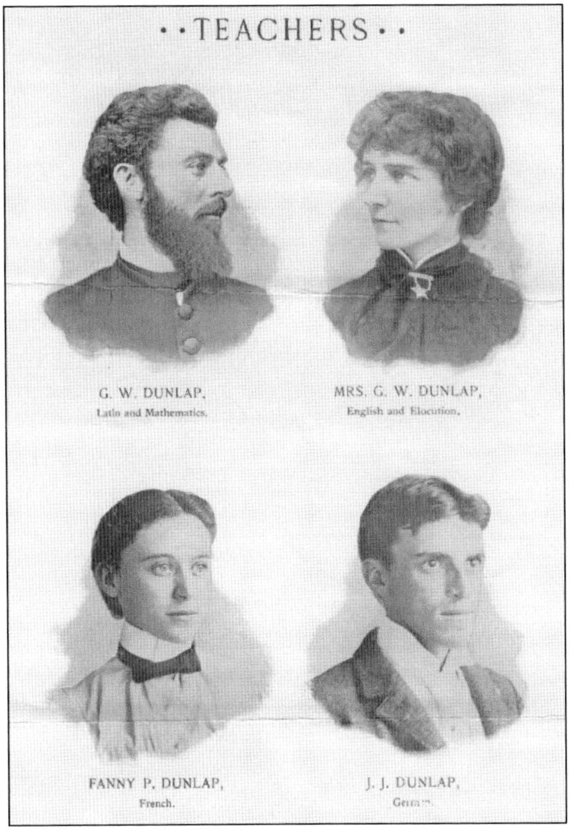

In another page from the catalog, the teachers of Independence High School are pictured. A difference of opinion on proper teaching methods is not new. Speaking about mathematics, the catalog states, "We believe mental solutions as a separate lesson have been neglected of late years, and we require daily recitations in that branch." George W. Dunlap was also a Presbyterian minister and started Union Church. (Barbara Giles Gabbard.)

TERMS.

Board, per week	$3.00
" Monday to Friday	2.00
Tuition, per month	3.00
Matriculation Fee (to buy supplementary reading)	.50
Stall Rent, per month	.25
Elocution, per month	.50
Vocal Culture, per month	1.00

Only members of Elocution Class will be eligible to contend for prizes in oratorical and declamatory contests.

For further information regarding the school apply in person or by letter to the undersigned.

G. W. DUNLAP,
Independence, Ky.

Engraved and Printed by
AMERICAN PROCESS ENGRAVING CO.,
Cincinnati, Ohio.

The terms for studying at the private Independence High School are given in this page from their 1897 catalog. In 1897, horses were the mode of transportation, so students had to board their horses for 25¢ a month. If student lived a distance away, they had to board at the school, because it was not practical to travel several miles a day. The first term began September 6, 1897, and closed December 24. The second term ended April 22, 1898. Schools closed for the summer so the children could help on the farm. (Barbara Giles Gabbard.)

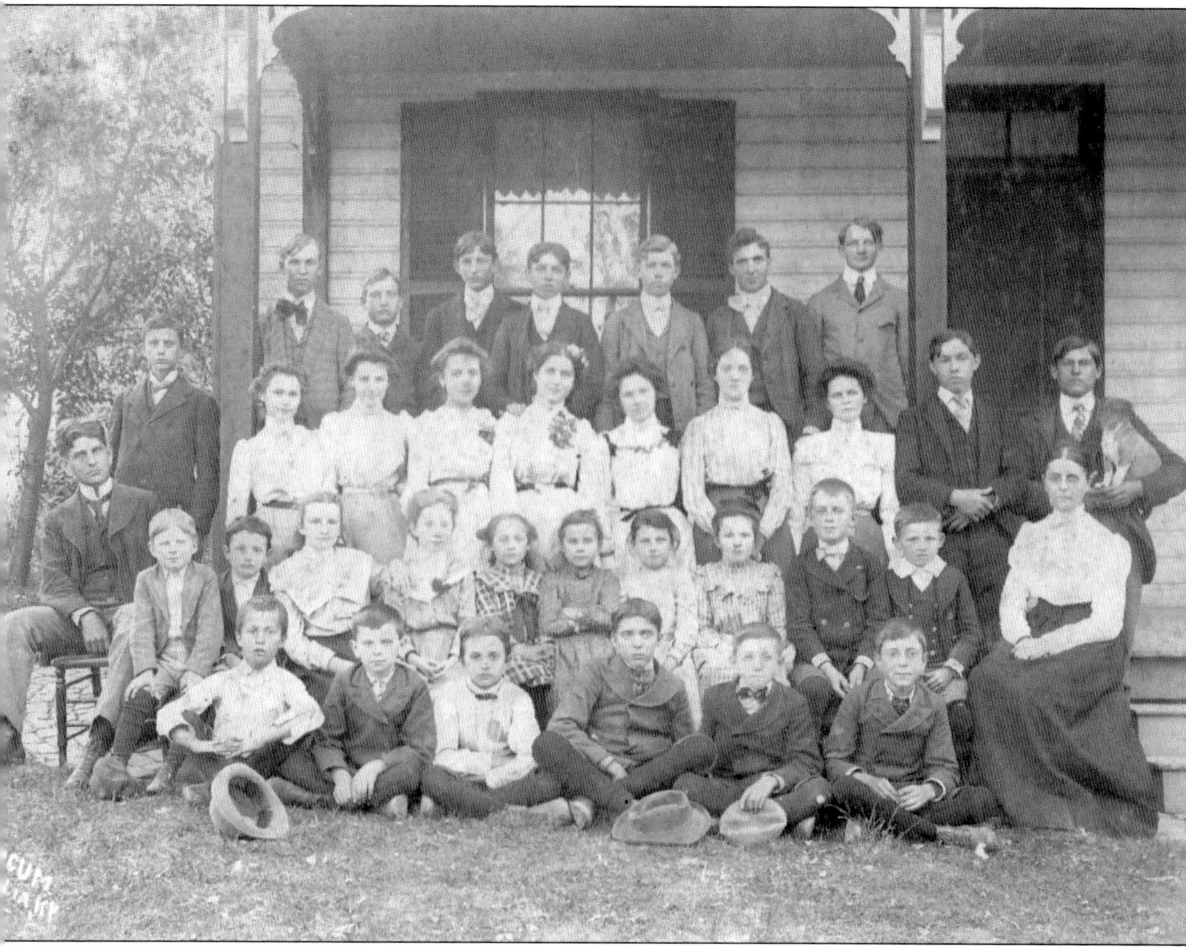

In 1898, Charles V. Lucy and his mother, Nina, bought the Dunlap school. In this rare image from 1906–1907, the entire school poses outside the building with the all the names inscribed on the back of the photograph. The only omissions are those too faded to read. From left to right, they are (first row) M.C. Northcutt, Oscar Rankin, Robert Morgan, Willie Jaeger, Clifford Wilson, and Charlie Jones; (second row) teacher Charles V. Lucy, Robert Hume, Vemont Rankin, Margie Williams, Nellie Metcalf, Sallie Terry, Lillian Northcutt, Ollia? Fleming, Ruth Stephens, Philip Hume, Neil Loomis, and principal Nina Lucy; (third row) Joe Northcutt, Edna Mendenhall, Addie Rankin, Margie Rant, ? Martin, Millie Stephens, Bessie Adams, ? Northcutt, Cleveland Mills, and Sidney Northcutt; (fourth row) John Klette, Dan Terry, William Ragan, Atwood Culbertson, Eugene ?, Ralph Luck, and Denver Pelly. The boys politely took off their hats and laid them in front. (Karen Fisk Koch.)

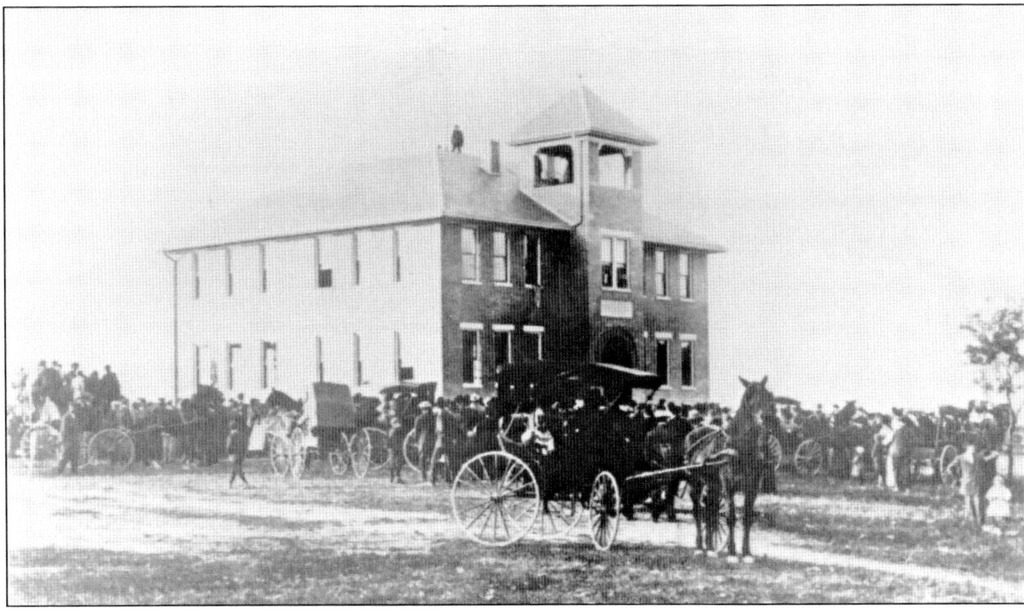

A 1908 law set up county school boards, and the Kenton County School Board took over the Lucy school in February 1910. A new school was erected at 5209 Madison Pike. The school for all grades opened in fall 1912, and when the new courthouse was dedicated on October 21, 1912, the board took advantage of the large crowd in town that day to dedicate the school also. This image shows the dedication in progress. The first graduate in the new building was Eunice Bird in 1913, a class of one. (Kenton County Public Library.)

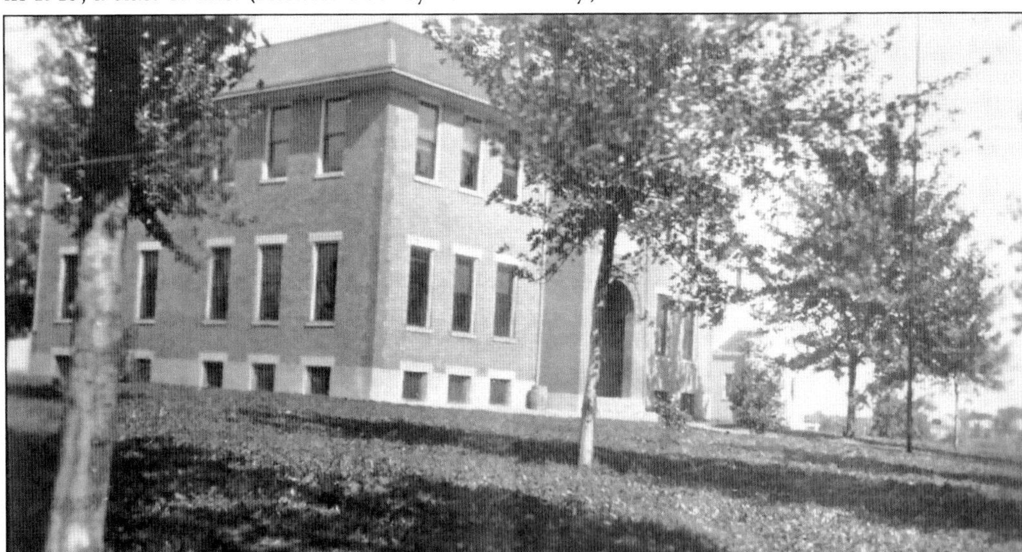

In this postcard image of Independence School a few years later, around 1920, some trees are growing. Charles Lucy closed his private school in town to become the first principal from 1912 to 1918. In 1916, grades one through eight were in four classrooms on the first floor, with each teacher handling two grades. The second floor housed the high school in two rooms with two teachers. The remaining equivalent of two classrooms was used as an auditorium. (Kenton County Public Library.)

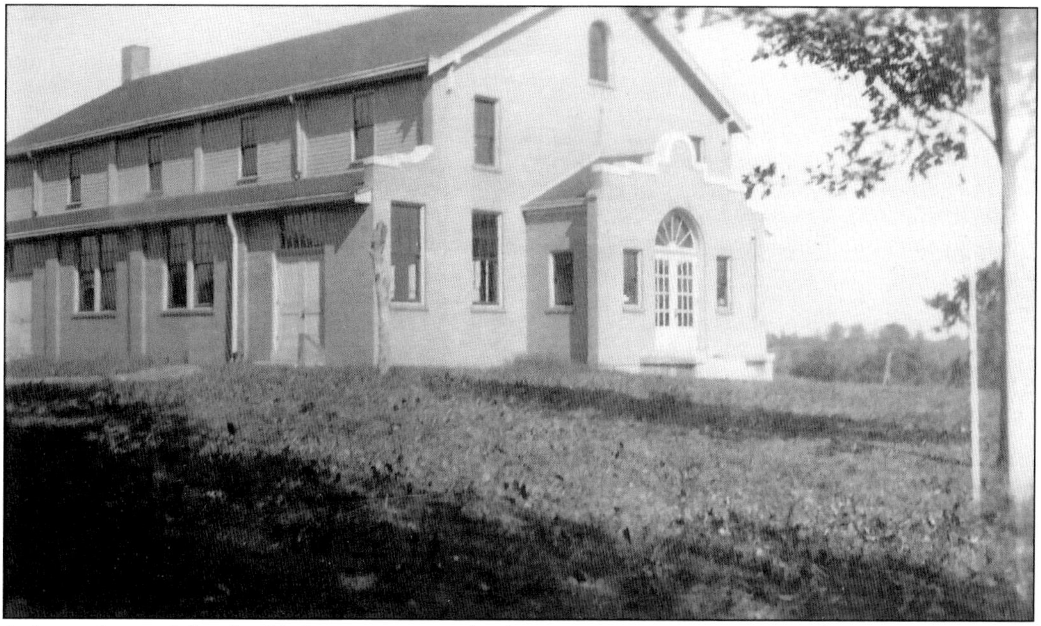

Independence School added a gymnasium/auditorium in 1924 at a cost of $12,000. It is shown here in the 1940s. In 1928, a six-room frame building was erected in the rear of the school. The gymnasium/auditorium was demolished to make room for a service station and is a strip shopping center today. (Bob and Thelma Gibson.)

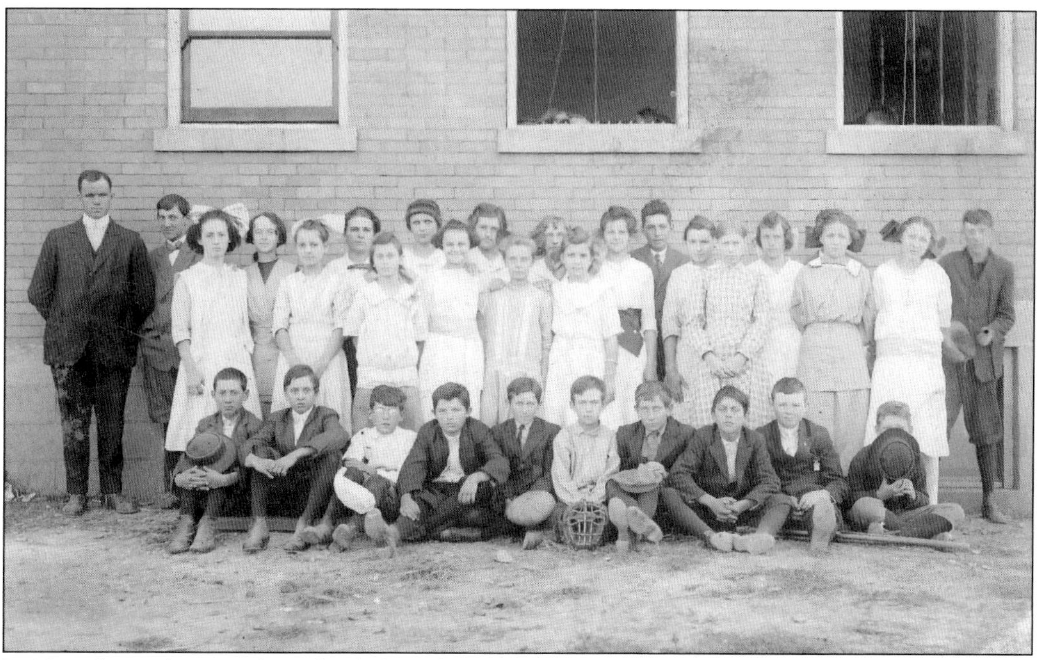

In 1914, the sixth, seventh, and eighth grade classes pose outside Independence School. The teacher, C. Rich, is on the left. At least five of the girls have large bows in their hair, and the boy in first row at right apparently did not want to be in the photograph. (Bob and Thelma Gibson.)

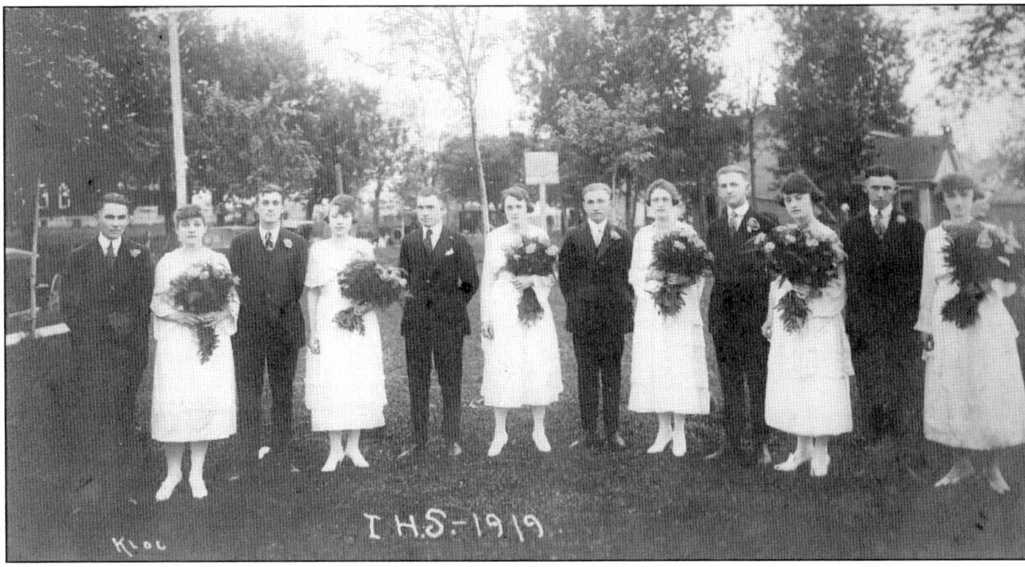

The Independence High School graduating class of 1919 is, from left to right, Vernon Wade, Virginia Hogrefe, Regina Kinman, Minnie Kinman, Milton Hall, Frances Stephenson, Goebel Armstrong, Ethel Stephens, John W. Shaw, Stella Stephenson, Lloyd Bird, and Amy Shaw. (J.B. Losey.)

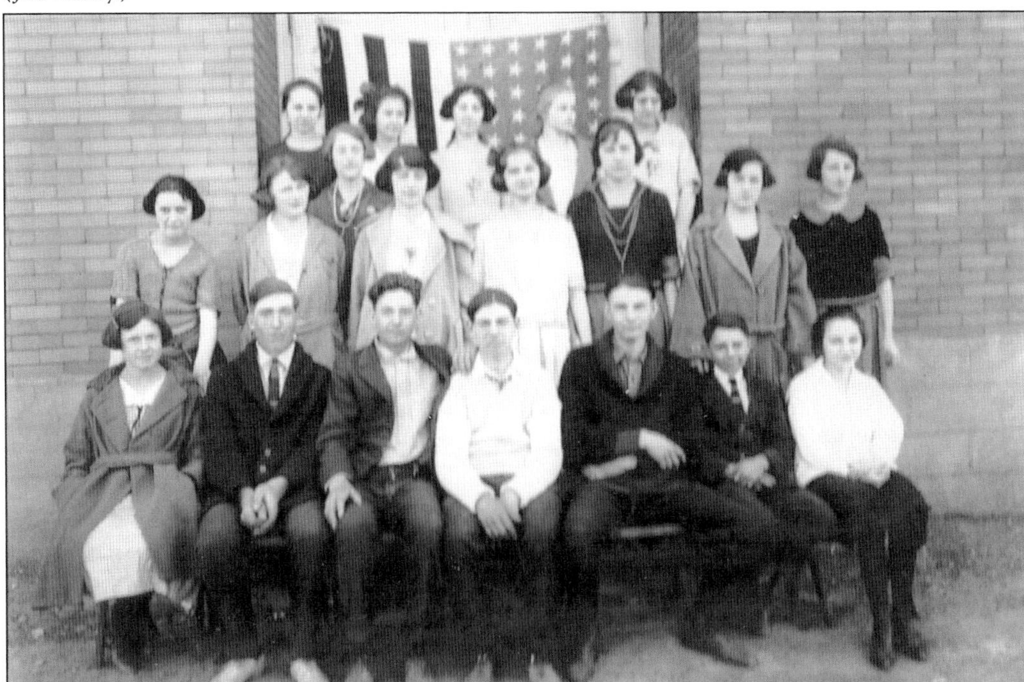

The freshman class of 1922 at Independence High School is, from left to right, (first row) ? Williams, Alton Petty, ? Menefee, Howard Osborne, Elton House, Orie Wayman, and Violet Hergott; (second row) Margie Mills, two unidentified, Ena Petty, Zelma Beard, ? Long, Katherine Goodrich, and Claire Maddox; (third row) Edith Gearheart, ? Menefee, Margaret Gearheart, Katherine Afterkirk, and Julia Folmer. (Peggy Powers Baum.)

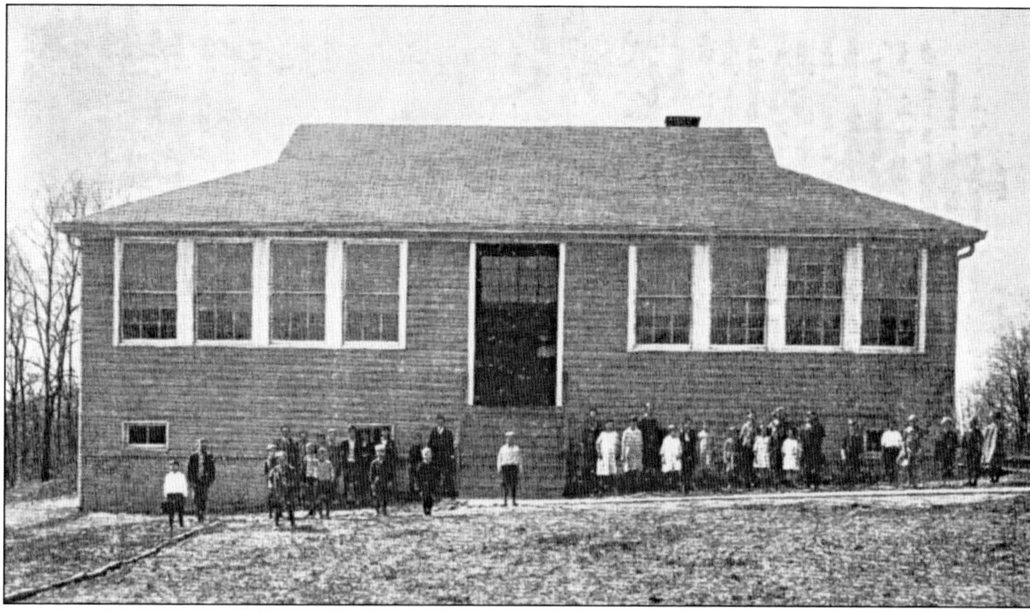

In 1921, Father Heringhaus of St. Cecilia Church felt a parochial school was needed. Not all were in agreement, so he offered the rectory for classroom space as a trial and lived with a church family. The trial was a success, and all supported a new building. This first school building was dedicated on September 3, 1923, and opened with 48 students. This postcard image is from the 1920s. (Mary Lou Schoborg Kaub.)

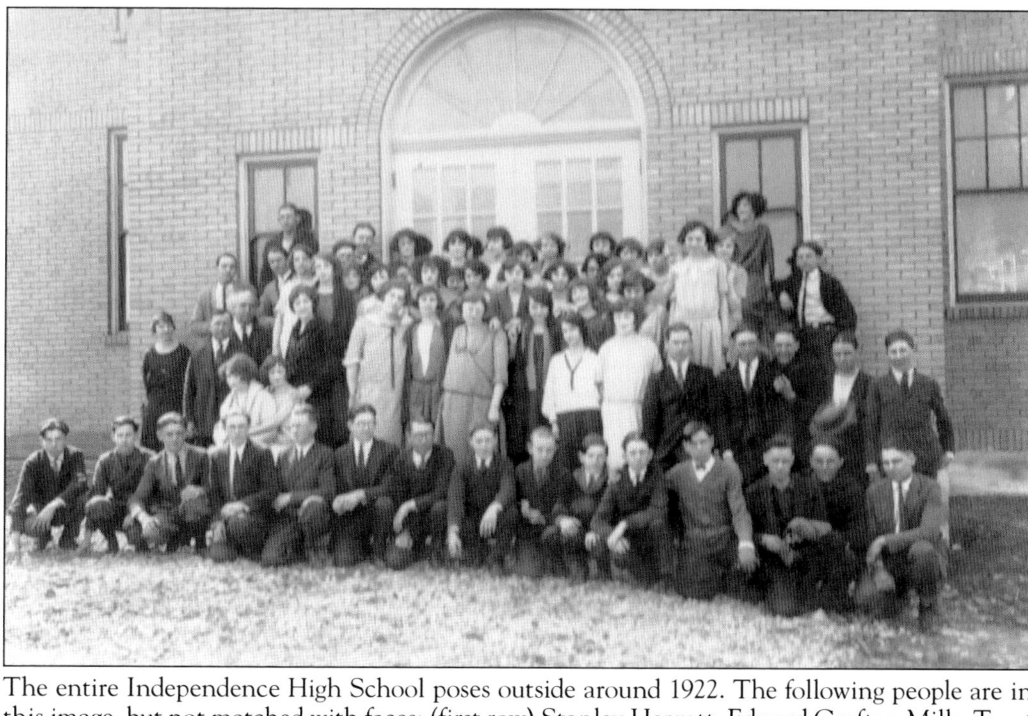

The entire Independence High School poses outside around 1922. The following people are in this image, but not matched with faces: (first row) Stanley Hergott, Edward Grafton Mills, Trent Pickett, and George Forman; (second row) Helen Stone; (third row) Russell England. (Peggy Powers Baum.)

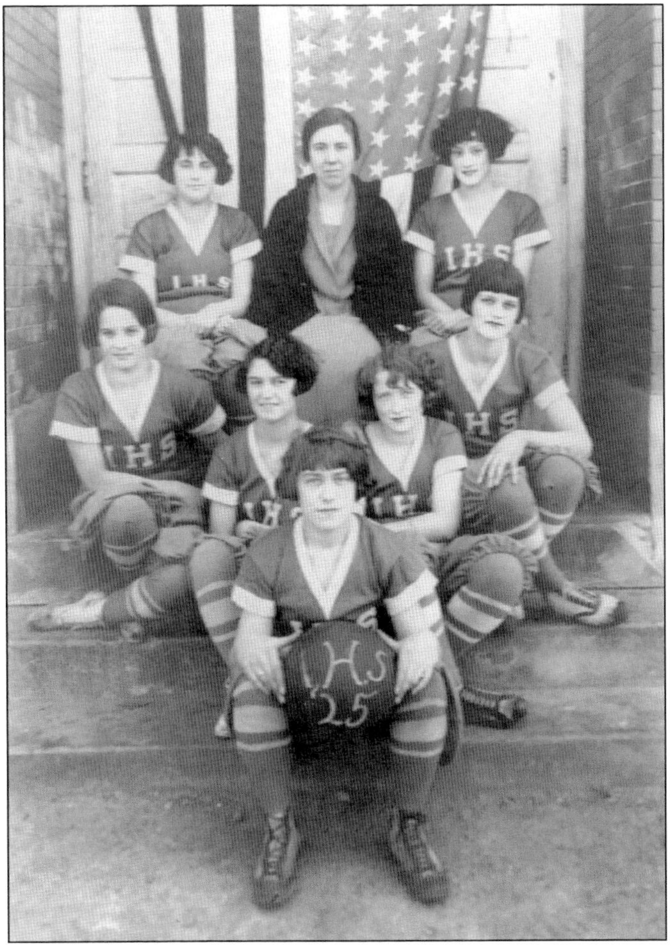

The 1925 girls' basketball team poses on the steps of Independence High School. They are, from left to right, (first row) Jenny Wilson with basketball; (second row) Margie Mills and Helen Stone; (third row) Margaret Flerlage and Marie Schwall; (fourth row) Nellie Carter, coach Elma Taylor, and Marjorie Carlisle. (Peggy Powers Baum.)

The entire Independence High School graduating class of 1926 is, from left to right, Margaret Gearhart, Ena Petty, Edith Gearhart, Margaret Wompson, Julia Folmer, Katherine Goodrich, Claire Maddox, Viola Hergott, and Margie Mills. One boy reportedly showed up the first day of school, saw he was the only boy, and never came back. Casting of the school plays was problematic for the all-girl class. (Peggy Powers Baum.)

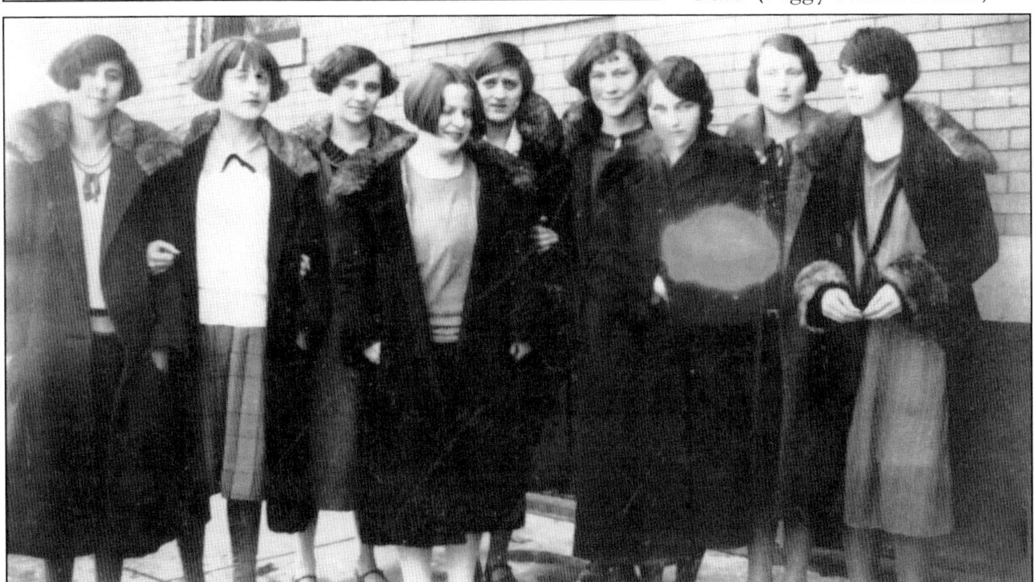

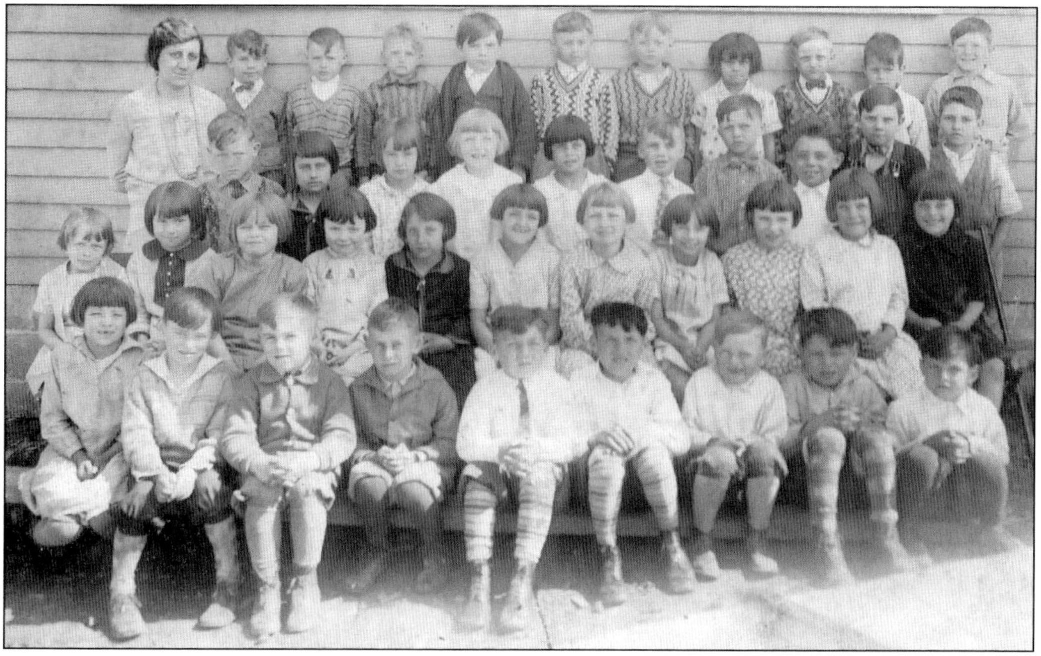

The third-grade class of Independence School in 1929–1930 poses outside the school. All are unidentified except (first row) Wayne Richardson and Chester Ballinger (second and third from left); (second row) Eleanor Losey and Virginia Ervin (seventh and ninth from left). (J.B. Losey.)

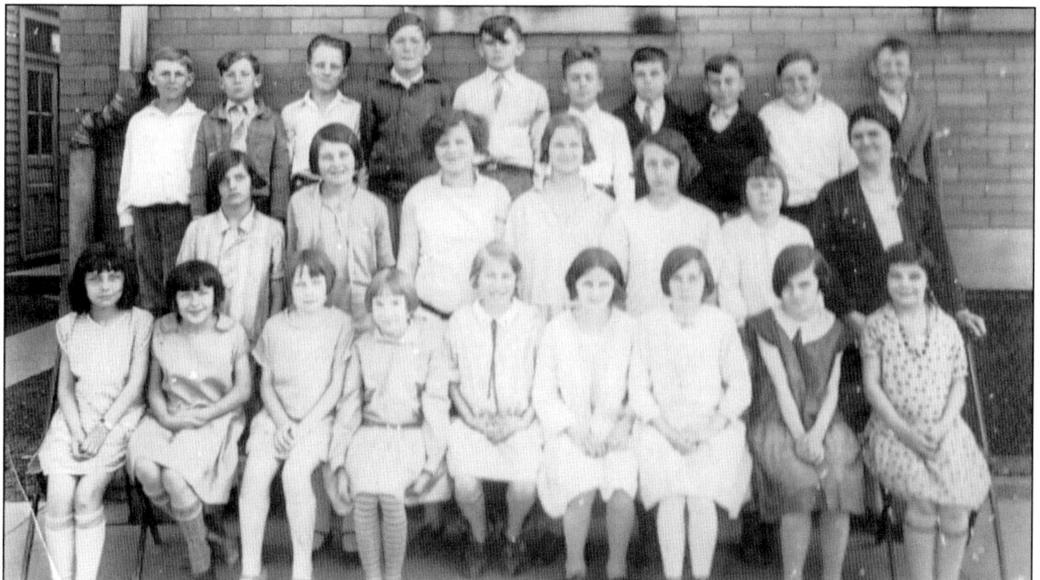

The fifth-grade class of Independence School poses on May 3, 1929. They are, from left to right, (first row) Mary Emma Goddard, Dorothy Vallandingham, Virginia Coleman, Mary E. Pruett, Cecil Mae Stephens, Ruby Parker, Sylvia Williams, Evelyn Richardson, and Mildred Wayman; (second row) Eleanor Rankin, Ruth Tomlin, Mildred Branner, Kave Armstrong, Sarah Lanberg, Hilda Williams, and teacher Lena Mills; (third row) Harold England, Lee Smith, Warren Dorman, Johnnie North, Edwin R?, Howard Clinkenbeard, James Masters, Charles Petty, Fenton Hiles, and Rich Glenn. (Virginia Coleman Watson.)

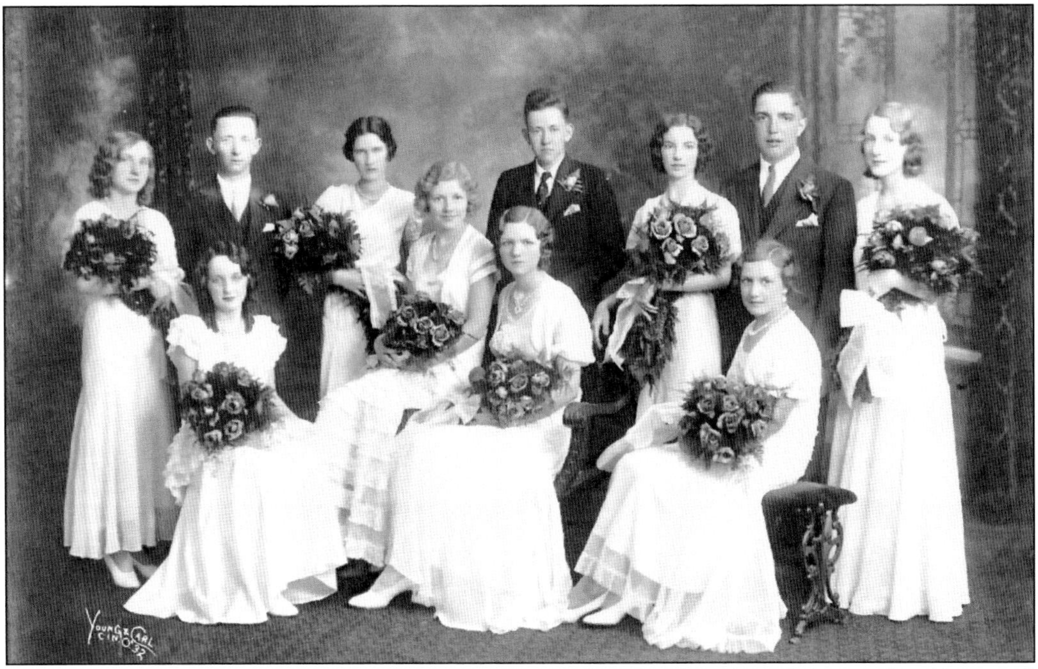

The graduating class of 1932 from Independence High School is, from left to right, (first row) Shirlie Williams, Anna Mae Schlapp, Mary Fisk, and Lillian Sowder; (second row) Virginia Pruett, Shirley Moffett, Lenora Hoffman, Gordon Moore, Letha Richardson, William Soden, and Norma Burnside. (Virginia Pruett Moffett.)

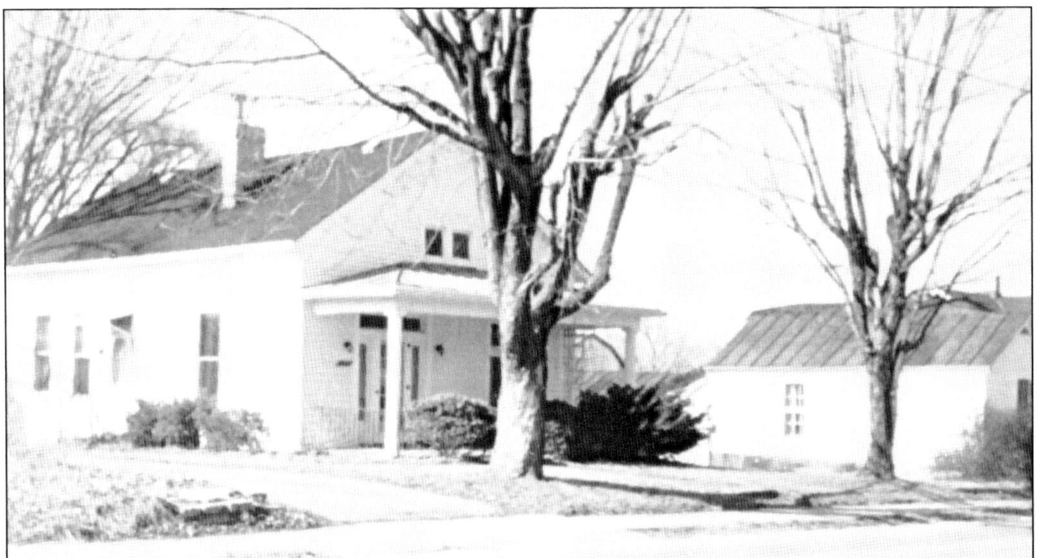

This building was used as a school for African Americans and was located on the west side of Madison Pike. It was later owned by Dr. Fred Ray, and Dorothy Goshorn lived there in the 1940s. Bob and Elizabeth Russell lived there later. It was demolished for expansion of the new St. Cecilia Church in the 1990s and is shown in 1988. (Eunice Mershon.)

Jean Moss, left, and Billie Banfield, both 14, stand in front of Simon Kenton in 1939. The new school was dedicated on September 5, 1937, with an initial enrollment of 496 students. The school at 11132 Madison Pike was built as a Depression-era public works program along with Dixie Heights High School. The school taught the seventh through the 12th grades initially. (Eunice Mershon.)

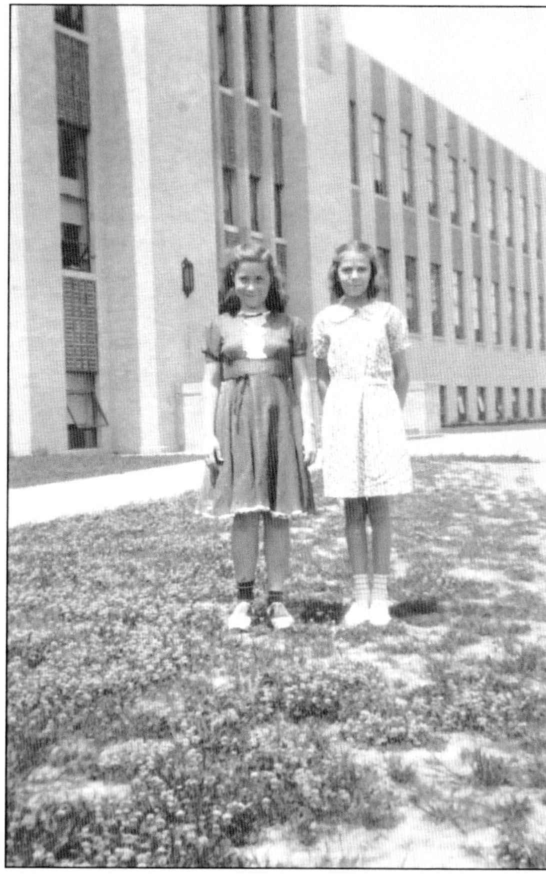

Simon Kenton High School students pose in front of the school in 1940. They are, from left to right, Dorothy Moore, Harold Rector, and Minnie Daugherty. (Senator Katie Kratz Stine.)

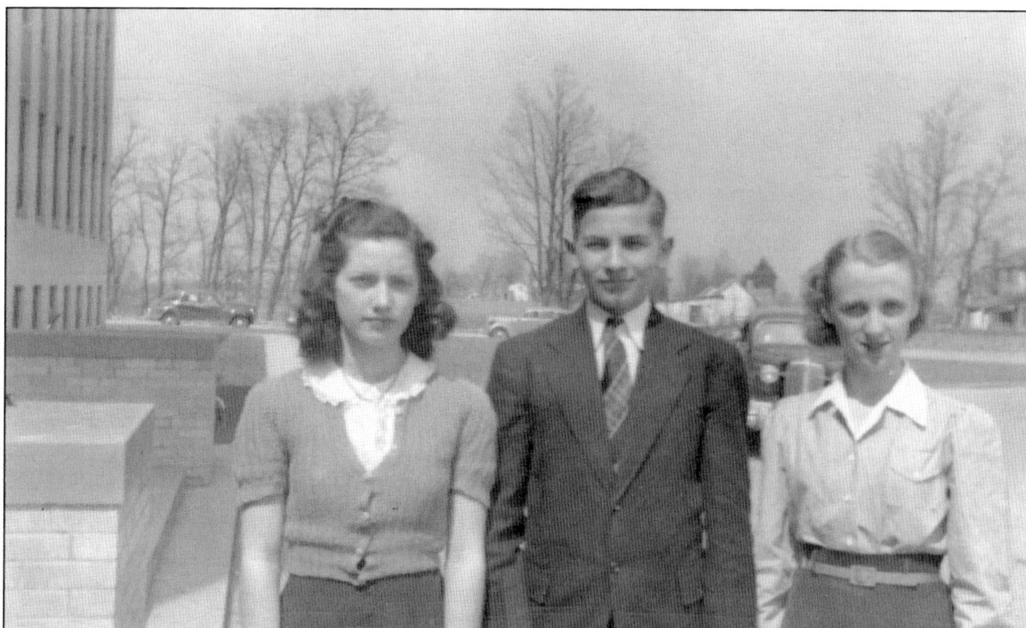

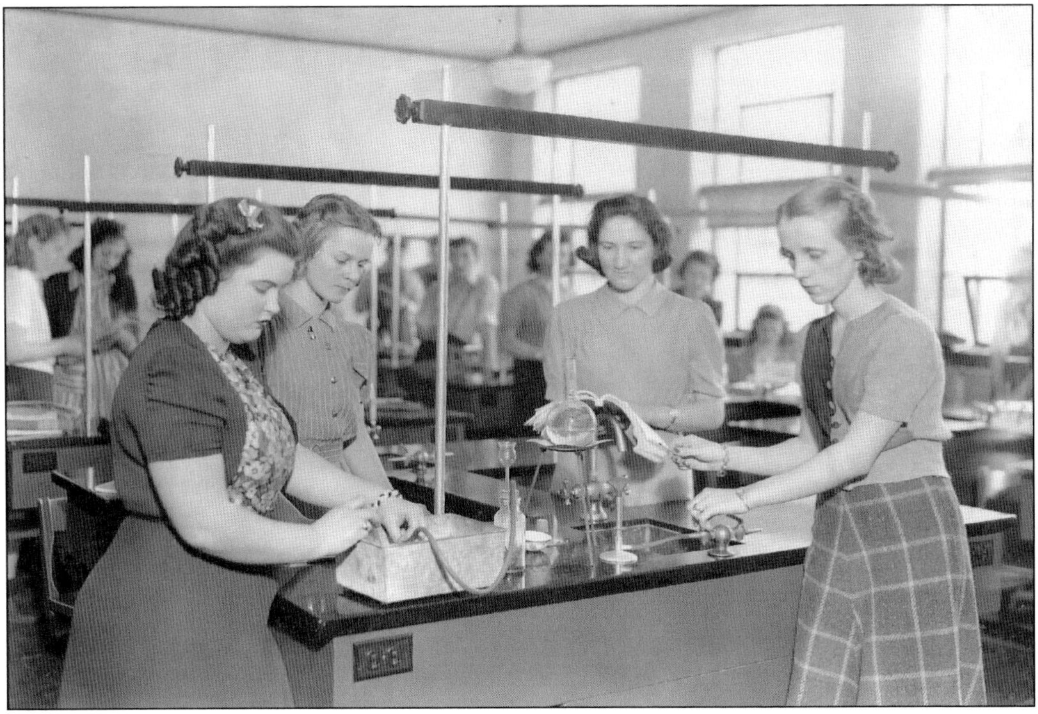

In 1940, these Simon Kenton students are busy at work in the chemistry lab; from left to right are Jenny Hillard, Naomi Menefee, Olga Zanella, and Minnie V. Daugherty. Mr. Hall was the chemistry teacher. (Senator Katie Kratz Stine.)

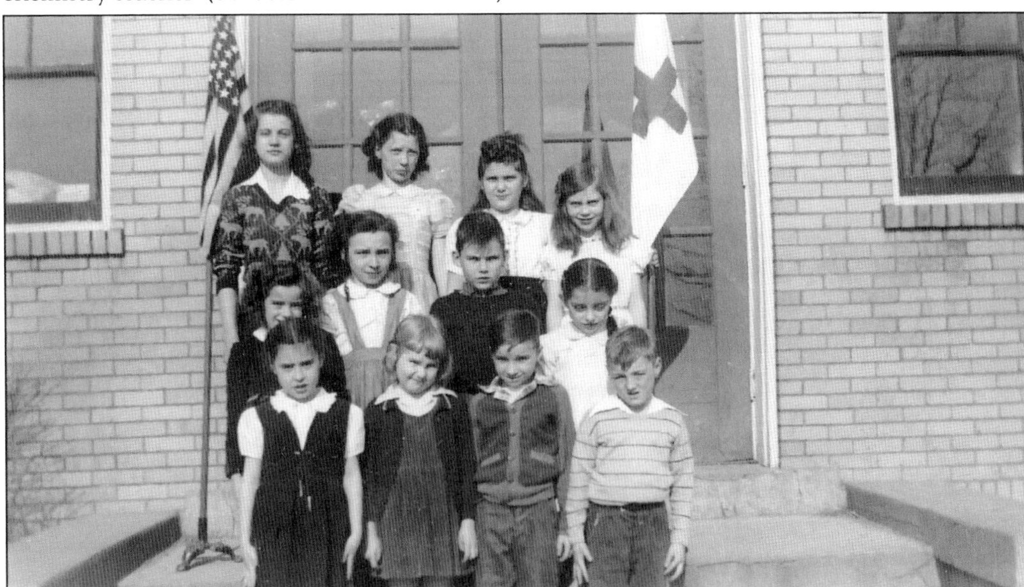

At Independence School in April 1946, the students with the highest grade that month posed for a congratulatory picture. They are, from left to right, (first row) Donna Lancaster, Shirley Collins, Lee Giles, and John Butler; (second row) Edwina Miller, Shirley Hunt, Larry Richardson, and Wanda Barnes; (third row) Polly Warren, Joan Carlisle, Betty Gaskins, and Dale Webster. (Barbara Giles Gabbard.)

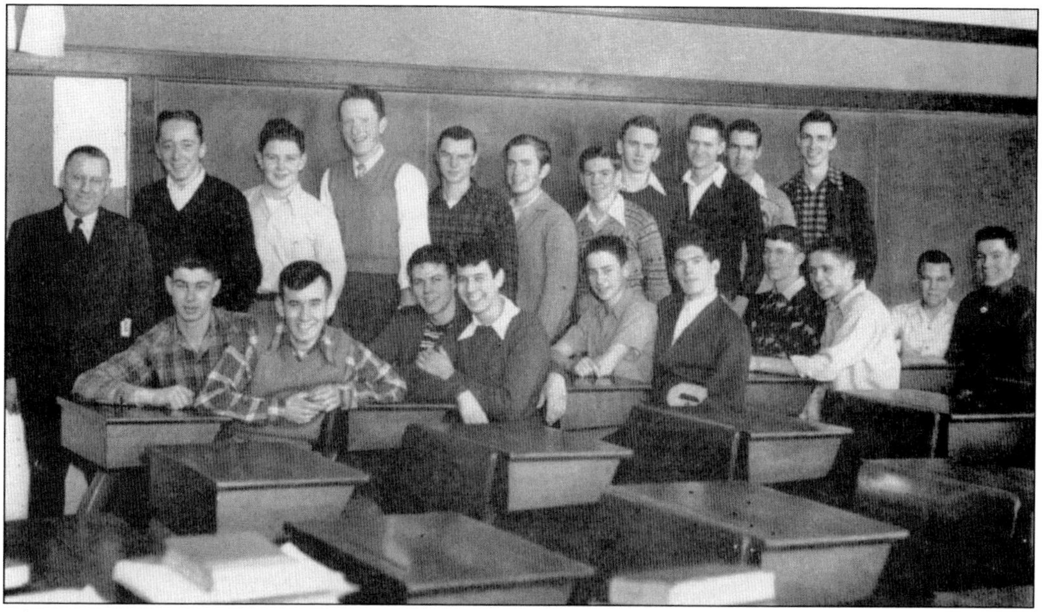

The 1947–1948 Senior Hi Y Club at Simon Kenton was for boys interested in Christian standards and living. They are, from left to right, (first row) Russ England, Carl Dryden, Jerry Mundy, Don Duncan, Frank LeMaster, Tom Kerr, Ray Finnell, Charlie Dorsey, Wayne Hicks, and Roy Rector; (second row) Dr. Paul Clark, John Reed, Richard Dorsey, Claude Taylor, Marvin Menefee, Ray Farmer, Wayne England, Paul Jackson, Ben Harney, Donald Keeney, and Malvin Cobb. (Glenna Lancaster Bridges.)

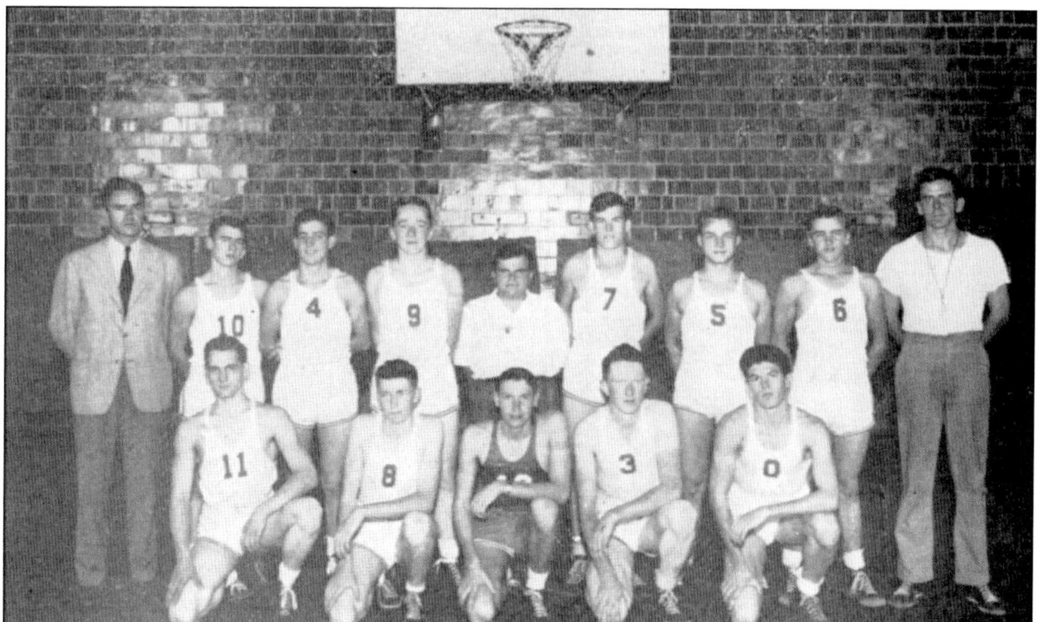

Simon Kenton's basketball team in 1947 was, from left to right, (first row) Franklin Daugherty, Ray Finnell, Earl Napier, Claude Taylor, and Tom Kerr; (second row) Coach Faulkner, Alan Herold, Eugene Barnett, Johnny Reed, Oscar Brewer, Herschel Campbell, Donald Myers, Robert Armstrong, and Coach Swim. (Glenna Lancaster Bridges.)

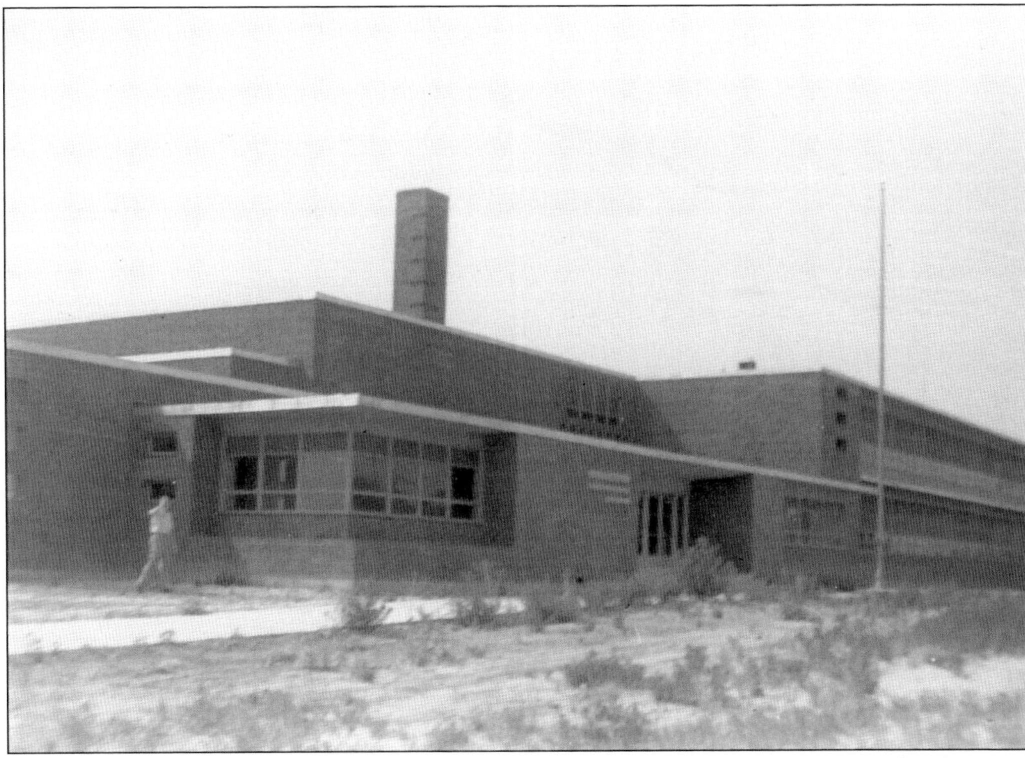

Kenton Elementary School is just completed in this 1951 image. The 20-room school opened with 650 students and 22 teachers and cost $480,000. Even after it opened, Independence School continued to operate until 1954. It is at 11246 Madison Pike, next door and south of Simon Kenton. (Bob and Thelma Gibson.)

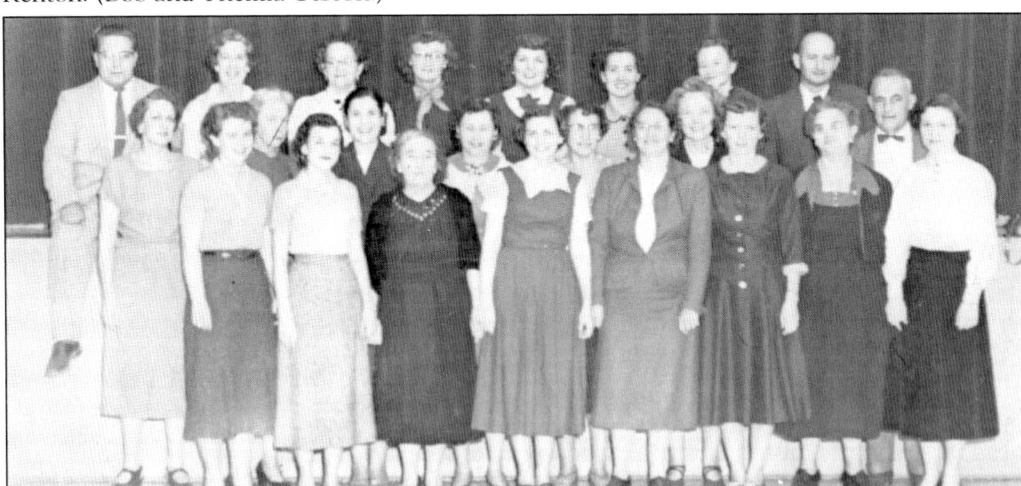

The Kenton Elementary teachers for the 1955–1956 school year are, from left to right, (first row) Wanda Jo White, Genopal Cole, Sayda Clore, Ida Mae Mullins, Bertha Beckett, Hazel Jones, Lena J. Mills, and Lucy Williams; (second row) Minerva Rigg, Mary Jane Cooper, Margaret Shropshire, Mayme Folmer, Katharina Antrobus, Ruth Mason, and F.D. Caton; (third row) Harold Earle, Alice J. Williams, Margaret Baird, Mary B. Bates, Mildred Popp, Jean Reed, Mary Jo Draper, and Wayne Bailey. (Marrilyn Mershon Hamilton.)

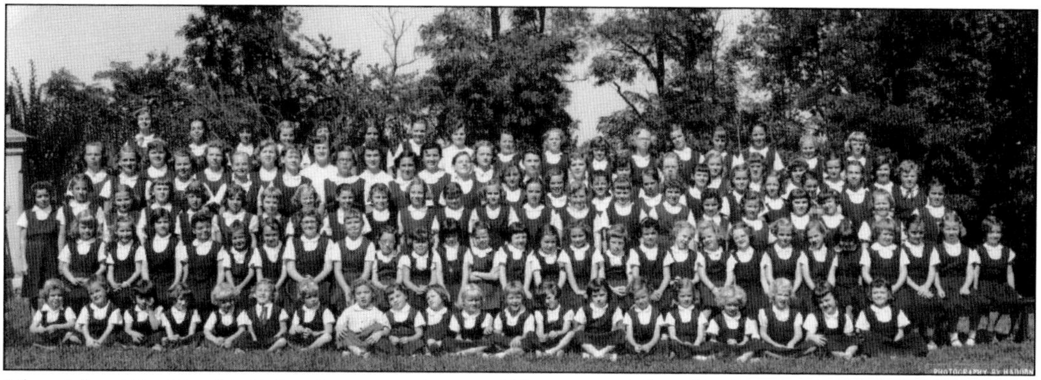

The girls of St. Cecilia School pose in this c. 1957 image. After the four-room school was built in 1923, a one-room building was moved from Independence School to St. Cecilia for a classroom around 1936. In the late 1950s, even the church basement was used as a temporary classroom. (Peggy Powers Baum.)

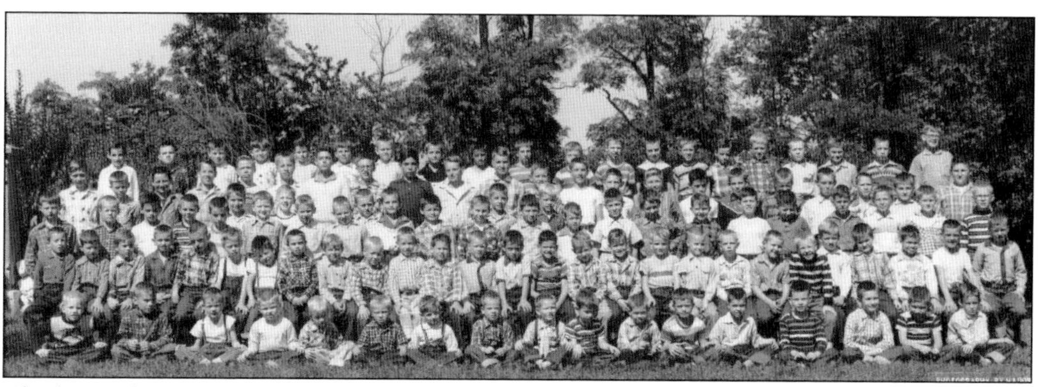

The boys of St. Cecilia School pose in this c. 1957 image. As shown by this and the previous image, the school had outgrown its space. In 1958, a new eight-room brick school was completed with seven classrooms, a library, and an office. (Peggy Powers Baum.)

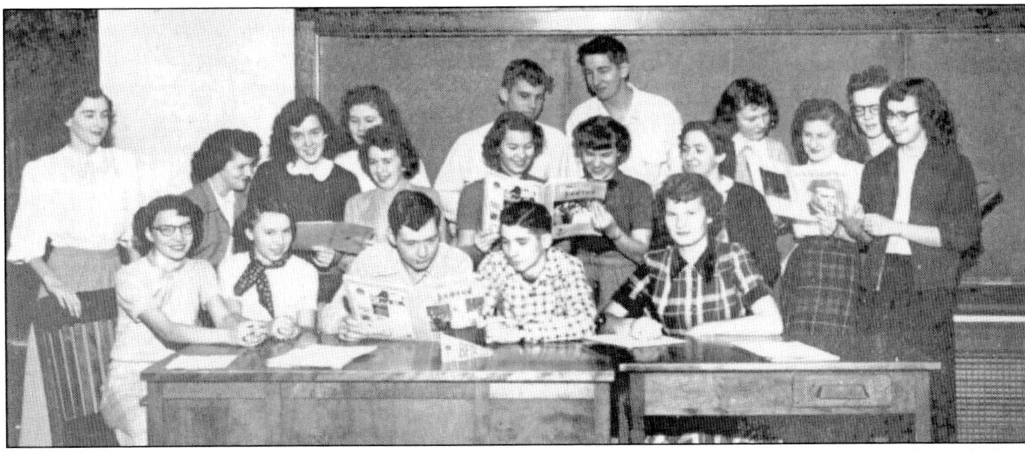

The Simon Kenton Beta Club meets during the 1950–1951 school year. They are, from left to right, (first row) Barbara Giles, Glenna Lancaster, Harold Rice, G. Wayne Bridges, and Rose Heideman; "(second row) teacher and advisor Rebecca Copher, Elsie Fisk, Mary Ellen Bruce, Katie Maus, Billie Beck, Alice Gayle Rich, Marsha Bachmann, Wilma Beck, Joan Carlisle, Betty Riddle, Alden Steinhauser, and Bert Bowling; (third row) Cliff Vaughn and Jimmy Free, who was one of four researchers to develop Gatorade. (Glenna Lancaster Bridges.)

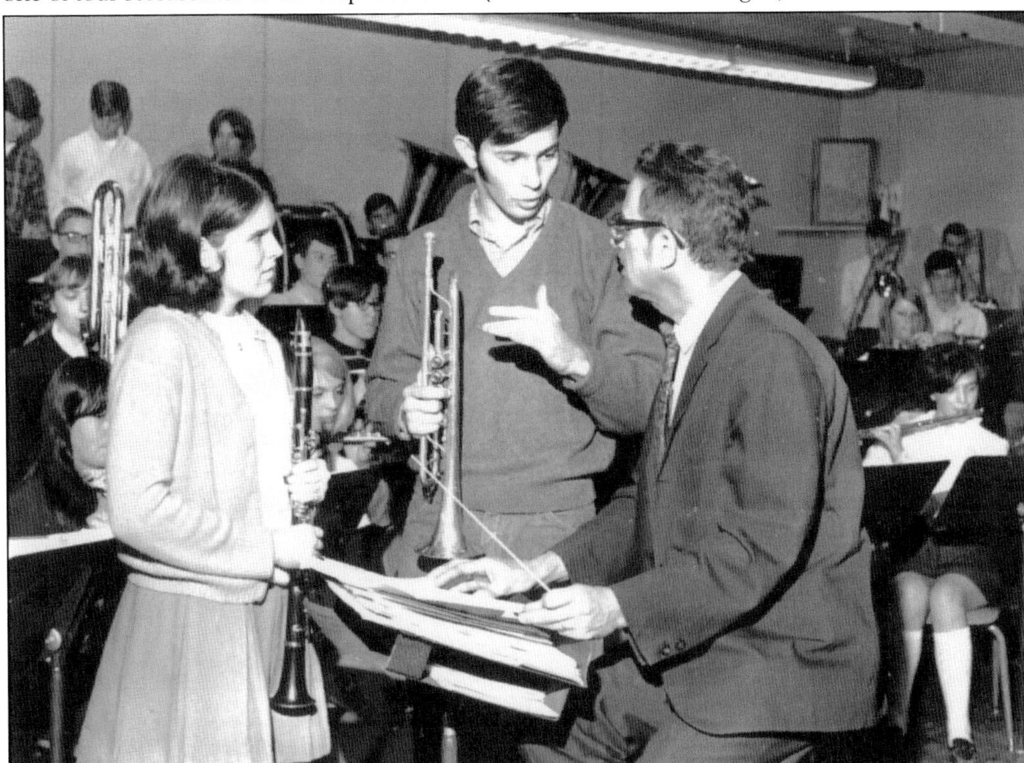

From left to right, Cathy Phillips and Mike Straw talk with Simon Kenton bandleader Robert R. Roden in December 1969. He composed "The Simon Kenton Fight Song" and led the concert band from 1948 until his retirement in the mid-1970s. His bands almost always received the highest ratings possible in concert band contests, and he published many musical compositions. (Kenton County Public Library.)

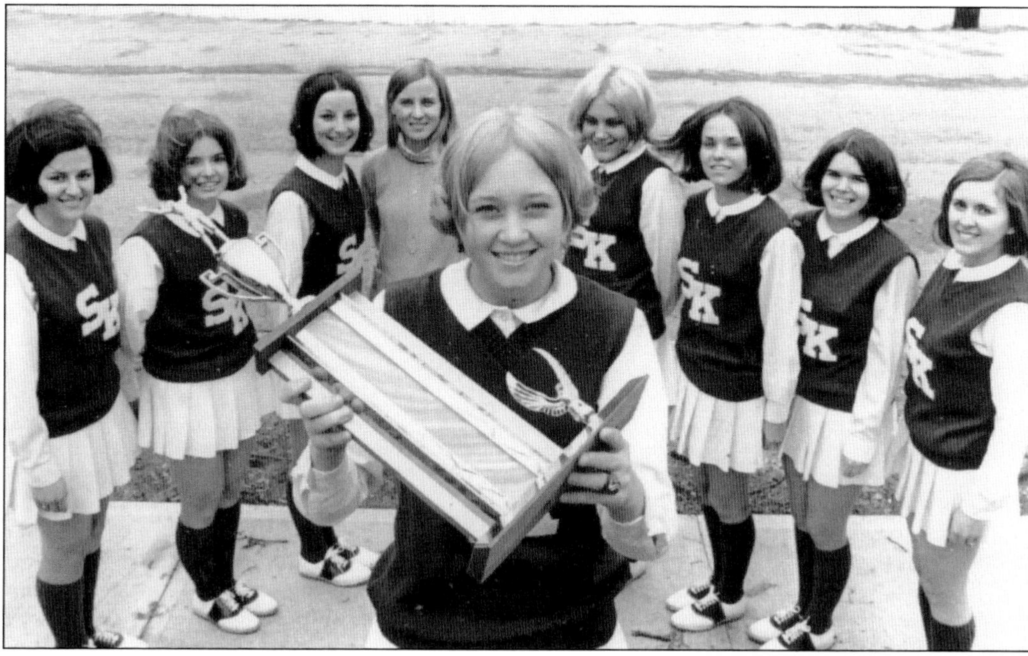

The Simon Kenton cheerleaders competing for the state title after winning the region are, from left to right, (in front with the trophy) Diane Garrett; (behind Garrett) Debbie Barnett, Barbara Harms, Bev Napier, coach Rebecca Short, Melissa Wincher, Rhonda LaFollette, Debby Coppage, and Rhonda High, shown here in March 1971. (Kenton County Public Library.)

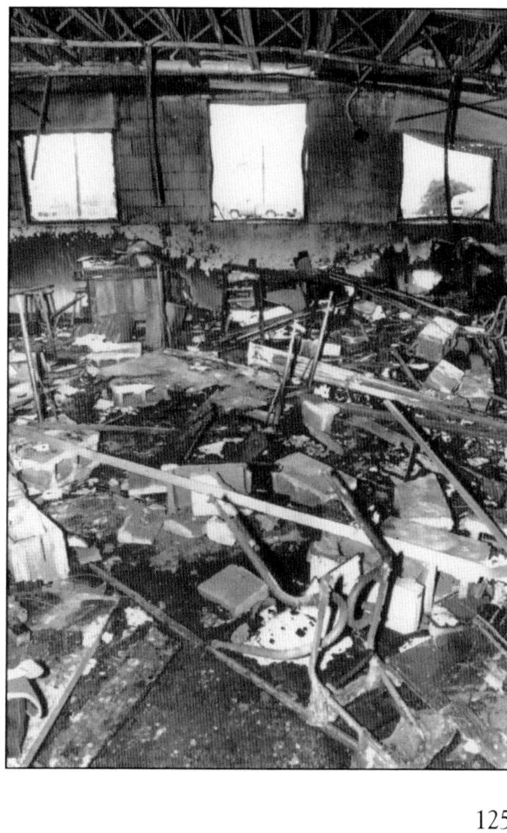

At 11:56 a.m. on October 9, 1980, a gas explosion at Simon Kenton's north boiler room blew out a wall in the art room (shown here) and practically destroyed the room. Standing in the corner by the boiler room, away from most of the other advanced art students, Robert W. Williams II was tragically killed in the blast. He was a 16-year-old junior and a very talented and promising artist. An existing plaque outside the school art room reads "In remembrance. Robert W. Williams II. 1964–1980. Donated by Simon Kenton PTA and his loving friends." His memory is still honored by a $500 annual scholarship, begun in 1982, to a talented artist. (Kenton County Public Library.)

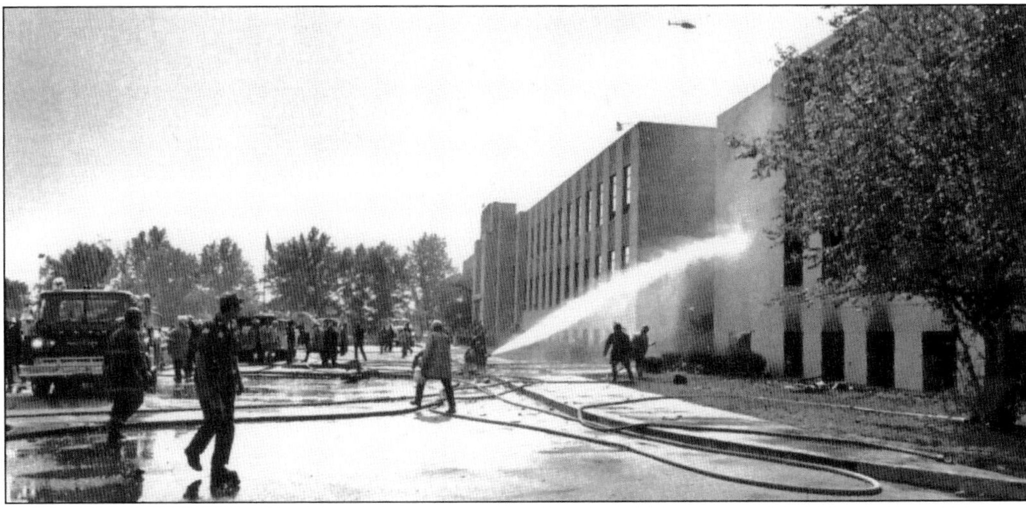

As firefighters responded to the blast, a second, stronger explosion struck at 12:20 p.m. The students had evacuated, and 37 people, mostly firefighters and utility workers, were injured. One injured firefighter had the last rites administered but fortunately recovered. The cause was determined to be an improper gas line connection placed under increased pressure for a line test. The danger continued as utility workers could not locate the shut-off valve, which was buried. Union, Light, Heat & Power Co. was fined $100,000 for these explosions. (Kenton County Public Library.)

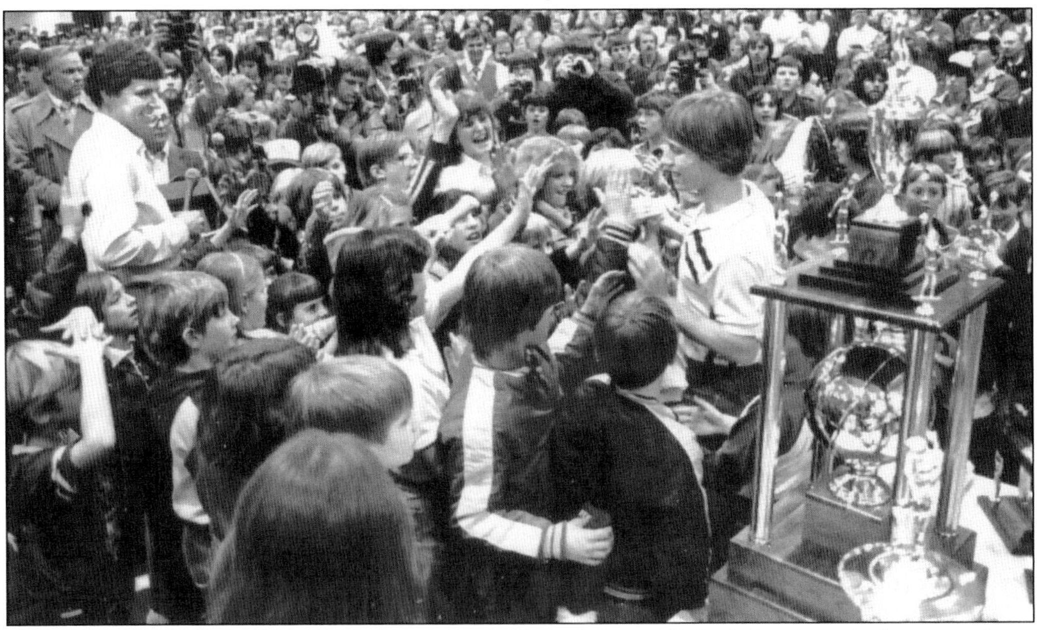

After the explosions, Simon Kenton students shared Scott High School, with Scott students attending from 7:30 a.m. to 1:10 p.m. and Simon Kenton from 1:30 p.m. to 7:10 p.m. Classes resumed at Simon Kenton on January 5, 1981. The Simon Kenton boys basketball team overcame the tragedy and inconvenience from the explosions and turned tragedy into triumph with an improbable tournament run to the first-ever state championship for a Ninth Region basketball team. Pandemonium reigns at Rupp Arena in Lexington, Kentucky, as the Pioneers win the state championship on March 21, 1981. Here coach Larry Miller introduces guard Alan Mullins to the crowd. (Kenton County Public Library.)

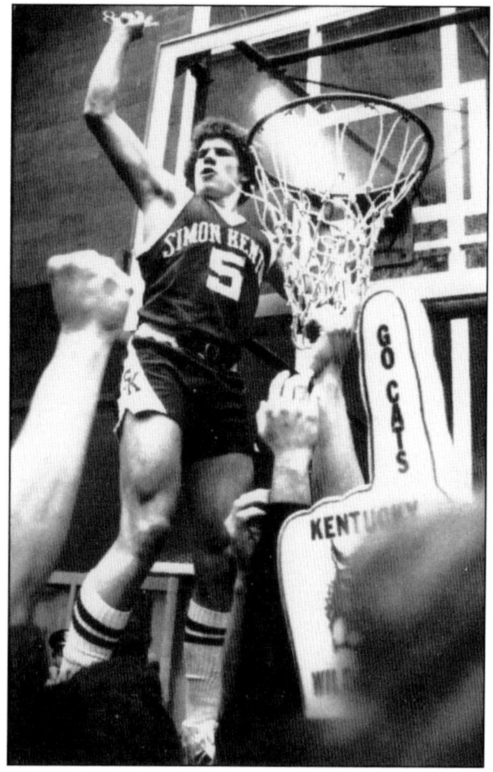

Senior guard Greg Ponzer cuts the net after the Pioneers win the state championship. Senior forward Troy McKinley averaged almost 25 points per game as he led the team to their first and still only state championship. He was named tournament MVP. McKinley went on to play basketball under a scholarship for four years under coach Joe B. Hall at the University of Kentucky. (Kenton County Public Library.)

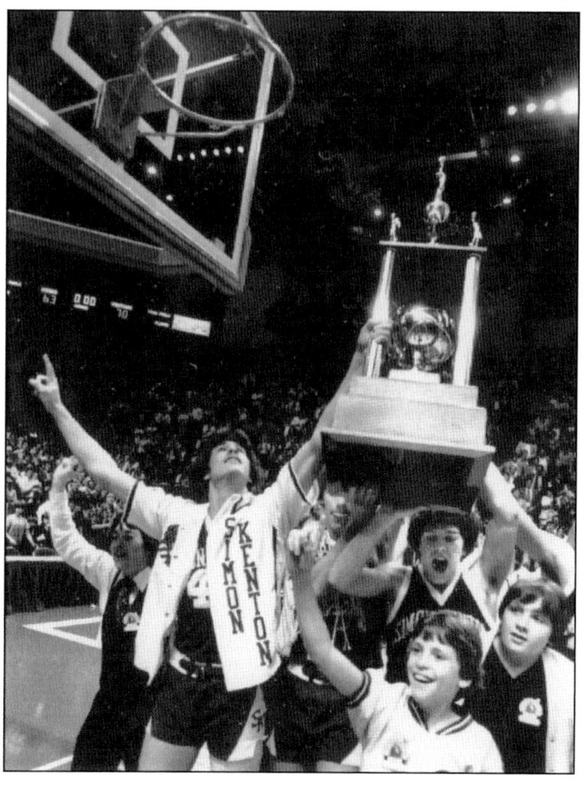

The Simon Kenton Pioneers barely won the 33rd District Tournament and then won four games in approximately 48 hours at the championship in Lexington. The first three games were won by a total of four points, and they defeated Mason County 70-63 in the title game. Here, from left to right holding the trophy, are Bill Meier, Troy McKinley, and Dave Medley. Today it stands in the school trophy case. This celebration of Independence ends, appropriately enough, in a moment of celebration and triumph. (Kenton County Public Library.)